NeuroDiversity Works Here!

Optimising organisational productivity by embracing innovation and inclusion in the workplace

Leigh O'Regan

ଞ RISE PUBLICATIONS ଛ

RISE Publications

Published in Australia by RISE Publications
© Leigh O'Regan 2020
The moral rights of the author have been asserted.
First published in 2020.

National Library of Australia Cataloguing-in-Publication entry.
    Author: O'Regan, Leigh
    Title: NeuroDiversity Works Here!- Optimising organisational productivity by embracing innovation and inclusion in the Workplace / Leigh O'Regan
    Edition: 1st edition- paperback
    ISBN: 9780648935797
    Notes: Includes bibliographical reference and glossary
    Subjects: Business; neurodiversity in the workplace; enhancing productivity; diversity and inclusion; workplace innovation practices

Final Proof-reading and editing by: Leigh O'Regan
All images © Leigh O'Regan unless otherwise stated
Printed in Australia by Lightning Source

NB: This work is published in sans serif font to accommodate the needs of the neurodiverse population and to meet the needs of the individuals whose mind works in a neurodivergent way.

Sans serif font has been used throughout. Whilst this is not publishing industry standard, without sans serif font, many would not be able to easily read the text and content of this book. The printing industry standard is currently to print in serif font. This excludes those who may be neurodivergent, have challenges around literacy and those with issues affecting their executive functioning and information processing. All of these are addressed in this book. For more information on this, check the appendices for further references and information.

I hope to change this industry standard, over time, so that more people who are neurodiverse are able to read books and magazines and enjoy the value of the written word. In the workplace and through study and education, I am fully supporting the accommodation of the needs of this large community across the globe.   **NeuroDiversity Works Here!**

For my wonderful sons, Dylan & Brad-
the sublime Lights (and highlights) of my life!

Thank you for showing me the immense value of neurodivergence and
for so fully encouraging me to express the deep joy, creativity, richness
and passion of truly Being who I am!

There is great value and resonance in Being, Doing, Feeling and
Thinking in a neurodivergent way. Through this state of being, I have
been gifted with a deep passion and a sense of creativity that has been
my life-blood and offered me my life's work.

And for that, you have only the deepest of my gratitude and love.

"According to the model that underpins the Australian leadership Index, the public regard leadership as leading for the greater good when it creates social, environmental and economic value in a way that is transparent, accountable and ethical..."

The Australian Leadership Index (ALI), Uni of Swinburne, 2020.

More than 40% of Australian businesses are not meeting their performance targets because leaders and managers are not mastering the basic fundamentals of management

University of Melbourne

More than 55% of Australian Business leaders have rated leadership as being in their essential skills top 5

Australian Institute of Management, 2019

Managers have begun thinking more deeply about leveraging the talents of all employees through greater sensitivity to individual needs

Austin & Pisano, 2017

As much as 70% in the variation of employee engagement in the workplace is as a result of the quality of leadership from their managers and team leaders

GALLUP, 2019

Contents

SECTION ONE

Introduction

Acknowledgements Page

Firstly, I would like to thank my sons. Without their input and feedback on my own 'unusual' ways of 'being' in the world and my, sometimes, unique ways of parenting, I would never have realised that I also identify with being neurodivergent.

It took me a long time to realise this. That I am neurodivergent. And, my sons have been an integral part of my personal exploration of neurodivergent living and working, travelling the world and exploring life. It has almost been a parallel journey of discovery with both of them, coming to an awareness of our individuality, and our realisation that there are many people out there who share those similar ways of responding to the world and our environmental stimulus.

We have each chosen different path ways to explore our uniqueness and individuality.

Mine has seemed more meandering than theirs, purely because it has taken many, many more years to get to this point of realisation.

However, I know that their own journeys have been no less painful, disconcerting and confusing, at times. I have watched on, as a parent, as a fellow employee in the workforce, as a teacher of other individuals who have fallen through the educational and societal gaps, as one of my own children did (without my even realising it, at the time), and also as a human being who does not like to see others struggle with issues. In those many hats, I have taken on the roles of being able to support and provide some resolutions to assist them with easing their path through life.

It is essential for our next generations, that we begin to address the issues that affect us, across all spheres of life. I spent decades, struggling, in an education system that only saw me as 'competent', because I could "do" things "okay". To the outsider's eyes, I was coping well, "able to achieve things" and "doing fine". My internal processes were very different.

This was because I was not aware that I was struggling, initially. When I did begin to realise this., I thought I was the only one being challenged. Them. When I realised that there were others out there who felt and did things similarly to me, I began to do some research.

In the midst of all of my personal research, I began studying to be an adult and vocational educator. My speciality was working with adults who had 'fallen through the cracks'. It was to become the frame for all of my future work, in training and development, adult education, working with people from vulnerable backgrounds and in my current work.

My own journey to self-realisation of my own neurodivergence has been long and convoluted. I do not wish that for anyone else. That is why I have written this book.

Our workplaces have begun to recognise other forms of diversity, but have not really taken into account the nuances of neurological differences and cognitive and sensory differences that occur within our neurodivergent employees. These employees are part of the diversity within our workforce.

They are yet to be 'heard' fully, in the workplace setting.

My book is dedicated to them.

Secondly, I am acknowledging those individuals I have met along the way, who have inspired and encouraged me. I want to thank you from the bottom of my heart!

Thank you to those who have been a part of my Adult Education and work-based learning classes- you taught me more than you could ever know about what it means to be the seen/not seen in our society.

There is another book in all of this, especially for you. Don't worry, it will come. You, too, will have your space.

To those who have crossed my path who had "issues" with their workplace, Manager, life! Thank you for sharing your many stories of being neurodivergent and living in a non-neurodiverse world, with me. You helped me see that I was not alone in feeling this myself and that there were many, many people in the same situation.

Your stories fuelled my desire to write this book, to inform managers of the great treasure-chest of worthy and valuable assets that lay inside their workforce and to address any misconceptions, misunderstanding and demystify any uncertainties that were there, for anyone involved in workplace management and supervision. This book is for you!

Thirdly, I wanted to thank a number of people who have crossed my path at just the right time. My friend, Sue McGrath, for chatting with me for endless hours about neurodiversity, being neurodivergent, workplace guidelines and implications (from an Australian perspective), including potential and real-time breaches of Office of Fair Work Ombudsman workplace guidelines. Your support and friendship have been a lifeline! Thank you.

To "NZ Jo", as you have come to be known in my household (as I know a few different Jo's and Joe's). Who would have known, when I first say down to coach you, that we would become such good friends! Thank you for the bond and the depth of friendship. It means the world to me.

I also wanted to thank Kerri, for listening for endless hours as I chatted about the ins and outs of what my book was all about, and how I wanted to structure it and my insights into what was happening for people in the workforce. You gave me a wonderful sounding board! And, for that, and your love and support, I am eternally grateful.

Thank you to Tanya Aitkins, as well, who, in the early days of me thinking about this book, talked with me about blue-sky concepts and ideas. I don't think you really knew how much that consolidated what I was thinking and enabled me to 'gel' and crystallise what I was thinking. As much as it seemed like general conversation, it was worth its weight in gold! As are you.

Thank you to Irma Zimmerman, who has regularly coached me to succeed and to show up as my true self! Without you, I would not know the full extent of who that woman is.

To Andrea Buck, hearing your creativity and encouragement in the early days of me considering what to do with all of this inner world thinking, and considering how I might express that. Thank you for your unique way of coaching me to draw all of my ideas out and place them into a structure and format that worked for the business world. Thank you for suggesting, initially, that I write down all of my ideas about neurodiversity and put my many different ideas into different articles, across a variety of different publications. Those ideas have evolved into this book.

I also wanted to thank the (Australian) Human Rights Commission representatives (I won't name them, to maintain privacy. Let's suffice to say that I needed them for a workplace issue and that issue was resolved enough for me to be satisfied that my being neurodivergent was something that I was right to address, with their support). I want to thank them for talking me through legislative guidelines and potential for breaches of the (Australian) Human Rights Act, the Anti-Discrimination Act (NSW). I also talked with Fair Work and WorkCover as well as the FairWork, in order to get further guidance on a number of issues that were impacting on me. Each was very helpful.

Finally, thank you to a number of people in the publishing industry, who have provided me with encouragement and support, in one way or another.

To Gerry Robert at *Black Card Books*. I took a lot out of your wealth of publishing experience, skills and knowledge, as I got to the middle of writing this book, your guidance provided me with jet fuel! So, thank you!

To everyone at *Commonword Literature Development Agency*, *WomensWrite* and *Crocus Books*, Manchester, UK- you started my avid interest in all things publishing (and sustained my life-long passion for writing!). And, I have only continued from there! I wanted to acknowledge you for all of the years I spent honing both my writing, editing and proof-reading skills, and for all of the wealth of knowledge and information I gained about publishing whilst in your realm.

A special thank you to Aryamati (my dear friend [VALE] Olga Kenyon), who I came to meet at *CommonWord* in Manchester. You reignited my passion for writing, through our extensive conversation about women, women's literature and the value of friendship. I will never forget those memories and our time together. Thank you for your peaceful ways, friendship and generosity.

And, to Sonya Murphy, at *Adala Publishing*, Melbourne, Australia. Wow! What a short but amazingly productive journey I have taken with you! Thank you for all of your guidance and support in the structuring, layout, design, marketing and launch of this book. I will be forever grateful for your coaching, advice and weekly check-ins.

More often than not, we have a way of being in the world that enables us to 'sense' it and feel its energy and 'pulse', 'feel into' it through feelings and emotions and gauge it and the people in it on a sensory level, much more clearly, at first than we can initially can engage with it and identify with it through spoken words.

My preference has always been written communication. I can articulate anything when I write it down. However, if you ask me to speak, I really need to know my 'stuff'. I am, of course, a teacher, tutor, educator and facilitator. I do very well at this. It is one of my key passions. And, when I know what I am talking about, inside out, I can roll it off the top of my tongue. However, when there is an emotional content to something, or whenever I am emotionally engaged in content, this is where things get a little tricky.

I know many neurodivergent individuals who have a similar preference. It is not the same for everyone. However, speaking up, speaking out, being verbally effervescent is not a common trait amongst neurodivergent people. That is not to say we can't do it. In our comfort zones, of course, we can be competent at whatever we are able to do.

My writing 'skills' have always been my lifeline. And, they have been my saving grace.

It is to everyone above and all of those who finds themselves feeling like they don't quite fit in, to their social world, to their educational space, to their friendship circle, to their community, to their workplace, that I am dedicating this book. We all have a right to be here; to be validated; to feel that we are contributing; to feel significant in our contributions; and to express our uniqueness.

The Preface

The Author

I am a business woman, consultant, trainer and facilitator, well-being and success coach. I am also a mother of two (now adult) children who are neurodivergent. I am an entrepreneur. I have qualifications in Business Studies, Leadership and Management, Adult and Vocational Education, Disability Studies, Health and Social Studies, Youth Work, Training and Assessment, Counselling, coaching and am currently completing my second degree, and have post-graduate qualifications in several areas.

But this is not all about the pieces of paper I have accumulated, nor the amount of information or book knowledge I have in my head. It is about the kind of person that I am and the way I live my life. It is about the people I have come to know. And, it is also what I have come to know about myself.

I started my own business, after completing the NEIS (New Enterprise Incentive Scheme) in Australia, in the 90s. Since then, I have completed a variety of business qualifications and undertaken many years of business start-up support in the UK, co-ordinated and managed disability support programs for the recruitment of unemployed people, provided both workplace and study for students with sensory & physical disabilities, as well as intellectual disabilities; to my ongoing work as an adult educator, teacher, facilitator and trainer in a wide range of environments, including both the UK and Australian.

Over this time, I have gained a wealth of insight, knowledge, experience and workplace wisdom (specifically in relation to neurodivergent employees and their needs and alternative considerations for employees from neurodiverse communities, including the reasons why it is so important for employers to meet these needs (they are not just whimsical or frivolous requirements).

I gained this experience and insight, working with people in a huge number of environments, including: SME start-ups and diversification; UK and Australian prison system Adult Education; TAFE and community-based education; Work-based Learning environments; working with CALD communities, marginalised and disadvantaged communities; in her roles in online learning co-ordination and management; when consulting for small business, developing bespoke training for organisations, developing European-funded training and development packages for UK-based firms, and in her roles as online content developer for SMEs in the UK. I have also taught extensively in Adult Education Centres, providing Foundation Skills, as well as Australian Level 1-Level 6 English skills, along with English as a Second or Other Language (ESOL), English language skills for business and academic use to individuals with low levels of literacy.

I spoke before about the diversity of my career experiences and the variety of roles I have undertaken and the many fields I have worked within. There have been three key fields of practice I have established myself within, over the breadth of my career:

→ Business

→ Adult Education

→ Social work, community development and human services

And, if I can, I have a hand in each of these, at all times, as I love to give back to my community, wherever I can!

In each of these spaces, I have found individuals who were not able to absorb information via mainstream systems, processes, practices and procedures. There were a number of reasons for this, but there were five key factors involved. They were:

a) Often had lower levels of literacy and numeracy than standard, due to issues around capacity to focus, not being able to "read" the words and comprehension

b) Identified as having differences in Executive Functioning (concentration levels, easily distracted, unable to focus, time management "issues"/challenges)

c) Talked about having differences in communication styles and unique communication strategies (including how people made connections with each other; social sensitivities; emotional regulation; and social anxiety)

d) They stated that they had Sensory Processing Disorders (SPDs), making it challenging to do some tasks/assessments and fulfil some obligations while in certain spaces (for instance, in certain lighting, where noise was present, when not able to have quiet space; when there was too much information offered all at once, when information was offered to them in a different way than they could 'process' that information)

e) The environment they were absorbing/learning that information in/ and/or processing and regenerating information for output, was not conducive to meeting their needs

f) Were neurodivergent (whether they were diagnosed or not; whether they were aware of it, or not)

There were clear indications that their brains were working differently, in terms of processing and absorbing information and communicating it back to others.

I realised that, often-times, my brain utilised similar ways of "doing things". I was attuned to these individuals. It was the key to my own discovery of my own neurodivergence. And, it was the powerhouse that enabled me to establish myself as solidly as I have, in my own sense of confidence in what I do and how I go about doing it (just a little secret- sometimes, I felt as though I was SO different to everyone else, that I did not 'fit' and therefore did not have a place. This included work, at times).

Why am I talking about this in the lead-in to this book?

Because these were adults, not children.

They were adults who had found it a huge "challenge" to work in a "standardised" workplace, because they didn't feel like they "fit" (either), because of all of the above reasons (or even more!). Many of them had gone on to become self-employed. They had employed others to fill in the gaps, where they had not been able to overcome the challenge that they had initially felt in their first workplaces.

What I came to see as that they were very bright, highly talented, amazing problem-solves, incredibly gifted and creative workers who could "innovate" and, as one so eloquently put it, "craft a gilded sword out of a butter knife, better than a blacksmith could!".

What he was trying to say was that he could make anything out of anything.

He had just never been given that chance, in a workplace environment.

Now, I'm not asking you, as a Manager in an organisation, to offer everyone who is neurodivergent, "a chance". What I am asking for is for you to start reading and digesting this book by considering the numbers of people you might bypass, leave out, not notice, or even dismiss (metaphorically or even literally) because they don't fit a cookie-cutter representation of what an employee looks like to you.

They might already work for you, or they may be part of the general workforce. They *may* even be someone who has repeatedly tried to get a job, but can't, because they don't fit that cookie-cutter shaped box that we, in business, and in society, like to place people inside.

I want you to think a little differently. I am hoping you already do! That is most probably why you've picked up this book and started glancing through it.

I appreciate that your business means a lot to you. Your role, the work you do, making a profit, keeping your business going... All of the many aspects relevant to business today all bear down on business owners, managers, team leaders, HR specialists, Senior Management Teams and CEOs.

I understand. Truly, I do.

I have run my own business, too. I have put in the graft. I have seen it grow and flourish and I have also watched, during challenging times, while it started to falter and crumble. So, I know what it's like to sit on the edge and not know what to do next.

I do. I've been there.

I've also sat in pretty much all of your chairs! So, I understand the complexities of your roles, may not your specific businesses, but certainly the tasks that are required of you and the pressures placed upon you.

I want you to revisit what your workforce looks like. I want you to redress any anomalies in "diversity" that may be present, after reading this book.

I want you to consider whether there is any room at all for someone, even one more person on your team, in your workforce, who could bring their uniqueness and their amazing neurodivergent self into your working space and really take your organisation to a brand, new height!

In my final words in the lead into this book, I just wanted to state that the concept for writing this book came from a personal need.

I wanted to be accepted... in the workplace.

And, I don't feel like I ever have been.

This is a challenge for many neurodivergent individuals. Because we live in a world designed from a neuro-typical perspective. We are asked to accommodate our every-day selves to 'fit in' to this neuro-typical space. Every. Single. Day.

We are asked to absorb information via emails written in fonts that are designed to bend and swirl before our eyes. We are asked to speak up in meetings, when we have social anxiety and find it so much easier to discuss complex issues with people 1-1 or even in writing. We may need time to get into the swing of our day, or required 'deep-focus' time, which may appear to be 'social ignorance' or 'special treatment' to some people.

We are required to communicate in ways that are sometimes deeply uncomfortable for us, meet work schedules that either seem too simplistic or overly complicated for one task/project. Maybe the communication from others is too obtuse, or not directive enough, or maybe instructions and directions are given, but key pieces of information are left out, meaning that we do not have all of the building blocks and then become frustrated and confused by what may seem to be a simple task to someone who does not have our neurodivergent stream. However, for us, it then becomes a little like climbing Mt Everest every time we go to do a task, until we are given clear and concise, detailed instructions.

If you looked at any of my school Reports, you would have seen a child and then a young adult who was curious, intelligent, articulate (when in company she trusted), was hard-working, energised, fun to be around, conversational about a wide range of topics, creative and able to apply some fairly high-level skills such as problem-solving, self-initiative, independent working, team-working, collaborative working, innovative practice (thinking outside the box), critical thinking and cultural and social sensitivity. All of that was true and none of that has changed.

However, if you asked me what I was experiencing, you would have 'seen' a very different individual. Although everything said above was true and valid and applicable, whenever I was not feeling comfortable in my environment, whenever I felt environmentally overwhelmed, and whenever I was 'forced' to fit into a mainstream standard that was not right for me, I internally felt like I was burning up on the inside, as though no-one was listening to my needs and as if everyone around me did fit in, and I was the only one who didn't fit.

It was both a surreal and also uncomfortable space to be in. I spent more than 35 years trying to 'fit in' at work, doing something that people who are neurodivergent may know as 'masking'. I was endlessly trying to figure out what did work in the world and then trying on a range of different coats and hats, to see if any of them fit any better than the one I was currently wearing. The big issue for me was that I felt most comfortable at home, where I could equip myself with the furniture and resources that I needed to do the work and experience my life the way I needed to, in order to feel on an even keel.

I know that many of you, as managers, team leaders, co-ordinators, HR staff and CEOs, have already started thinking along the lines of 'how can we do this better?" How can we make the workplace better for all of our staff? How can we be more inclusive? How can we shift things internally, so that our ROI in staffing means that our productivity increases, our workforce development is enhanced by the steps we take in enhancing our environment in the suggested ways, we become a more cohesive and congruent workforce, and, our profitability is maximised?

Ultimately, in relation to organisational behaviour, we are looking at the way in which people are 'treated' within the workplace. Not purely from a 'reciprocal arrangement' kind of paradigm. That is, "you do your work to my standard and I will then pay you an amount of money equal to what I determine to be your equal skillset and knowledge base".

What I am relating to here is more of an ethical consideration and one underpinned by a set of values that I hope all business owners would have.

We ALL deserve this in the workplace. This is true.

However, for one reason or another, we do not always have access to it.

In relation to *neurodivergence* and a broader neurodiverse paradigm, we have not yet started to be considered in the workplace, in a holistic, grounded, centred and well-thought out manner.

Neurodivergent individuals are, at best, squashed into a 'specialised corner', and at worst, receive limited consideration at all.

From an ethical and a moral perspective, this is not good enough. From a Corporate Social Responsibility level, it leaves an awful lot to be desired from an organisation that has signed up to be CSR-accountable, but won't apply this to their own employees. From a HR level, we'd be answerable to some stringent disability-related questions regarding accommodations and adjustments made/not made for those neurodivergent individuals who DO have a diagnosis of at least one medical condition or state of being that could be attributed to the 'way they do what they do'.

From a Human Rights perspective, Western countries have all signed up to the UN Declaration of Human Rights, which we apply in each and every one of our countries and we all have entitlements to be treated respectfully, with dignity and with self-determination, under this series of Declarations (AHRC, 2020).

I could go on, but I feel that you are getting my drift.

Whilst I am talking from a much broader place than "just the workplace", I am applying some stringent social models to refresh our understanding of what it takes to be accountable, ethical, responsible and compassionate leaders in our own businesses.

From a global level, down through national policy level, cascading further down towards business legislation, and then "landing" in the workplace environment, there is a steady stream of reasons why we need to be more attuned to the needs of neurodivergent employees!

Aside from the fact that bringing them on board is going to bring a diverse mixture to our teams! There are SO many benefits to having a neurodiverse set of employees that works here!

Right where you are!

Notes About the Book

What is this Book About?

I could state this in one line: This is a book that outlines how people in supervisory and management positions can work with their neurodiverse teams and the neurodivergent individuals in their workforce to create a more conducive and welcoming workplace for all types of individual employees.

Many of you might be saying- of course? We already do this!

That may be true. And, yes, you may be doing this in many ways. However, if you are still experiencing issues, as a business, then something STILL isn't working as well as you'd like. Correct?

I want to ask you some questions. They may have you second-guessing yourself, but I'm hoping that they'll also be flags to assist you with reading the content of this book with an open-mind and an open business-heart.

- o Is your productivity high or low? (and would you like to change it for the positive?)
- o Have you wondered why some of your employees work a little 'differently' to other employees? (and you didn't know who to ask?)

o   Would you like to increase retention levels for your employees, but they keep on leaving in droves?
o   Do your employees make complaints about lighting, noise, open-plan office space, open-desk policy? (and are you wondering why?)
o   Do your employees take a lot of sick days? (and have you tried to figure out what the key issues are, but haven't quite figured it out yet?)

Now, I have gone a little deeper and looked at employees in two camps, not to separate people and 'other', but to highlight differences in how humans are cognitively wired. That is, how their brains work.

This book is in four sections, the first, focussed on your neurodivergent employees and their responsiveness to the workplace, how they may be influenced and affected by variations in their environment and ways in which you can seek to address some of these accommodations in an inclusive and ethical manner. The second section is focussed the standard workplace and also how you can convert your workplace into a neurodiversity friendly working environment. The third section concentrates on the topic of the book, optimising productivity through inclusion, diversity and innovation. It also highlights how you can more successfully meet the needs of your neurodiverse workforce, by utilising their skills, knowledge, experience and capacity.

The final section is all about how you, as a manager, can apply an ethical framework to your management team, to enable you all to develop new and innovative practices to grow your company, develop your neurodivergent talent and optimise the strengths that you have within your human capital. Ultimately, you may even learn something new about workplace relations that you may not have known beforehand.

In a workplace context, we are well-versed in 'diversity', as a general concept. We know it from our diversity and inclusion policy, our HR manuals and our Induction Programs. We are familiar with 'diversity' as it is shared whenever we hear statements about gender, sexual orientation, religious and spiritual beliefs, age, disability (generally), and race. We have policies and practice that enable us to adhere to guidelines and standards of practice around these business elements. We have ethical guidelines and a framework of ethical principles and values that underpins what we do and why we do it.

However, we are not often drawn into the world of neurodiversity and its many variations and variants.

This book will provide you with valuable insight into the core needs of a neurodivergent employee, which will enable you to understand a little more about why someone may come and ask you for a particular accommodation or workplace adjustment. It will provide you with a range of conditions, neurological variants, injuries and illnesses that may mean that someone is, or becomes neurodivergent, whilst working for you. The book will provide real life scenarios that highlight some of the pitfalls and also highlights of adjustments made and not made, that have contributed to an improved set of working conditions. This book will also provide a handy resource to managers who are new to neurodiversity, as a concept, or in managing someone who has asked for a workplace accommodation.

This book will also act as a reference guide for anyone who wishes to know more about what it means to be neurodiverse in the workplace, from personal experience, and how that insight can be applied in a way that can enhance and improve workplace practices, to benefit all employees, and also optimise workplace productivity and overall employee performance. Finally, for any of you who are studying management or business, I hope that this easy-to-read book can highlight some areas of business practice that you may not have considered before. Ensuring that we include neurodiversity as part of our 'Diversity and Inclusion" Action Planning and future strategic planning processes will ensure that our organisations continue to grow and expand. It is vital that our neurodivergent employees are included in this process.

What You Will Learn More About in This Book?

- Definition of 'neurodiversity'?
- Definition of 'neurodivergence'?
- What are 'neuro-kin'?
- Demystifying neuro-typical, neurodiversity and neurodivergence
- The effects of neurodivergence on your employees
- Why neurodiversity is important in the workplace

- Reframing "diversity" in the workplace
- Models to develop and optimise innovation strategies in your workplace (utilising your neurodiverse employees)
- How utilising neurodiversity more effectively can increase your employee engagement and reduce HR issues such as employee on-boarding issues, retention, 'performance management' and high rates of sick leave
- Providing some strategies and tools for further building team cohesion, trust, rapport and congruent working relationships with your staff and clients
- A toolkit to address neurodivergence from an inclusiveness perspective
- How to practically re-establish your workplace environment to re-energise your employees and meet the needs of your neurodivergent employees in a more conducive manner
- Ideas for enhancing your brand reputation, as a business, by promoting *NeuroDiversity Works Here!*

Why is This Book Important?

Every employee, from the CEO down to the cleaning staff, deserve to have the correct workplace environment to enhance their own productivity, job satisfaction and desire to continue to come into work.

Each one of the elements listed above is an overall business objective of every organisation, large or small. However, not many organisations look to what is or isn't happening at grassroots level, in terms of staffing, environment and the effects of workplace environment on staff, in order to resolve these issues, I've outlined above. However, with some tweaking, you will find that this WILL work for you. And you will soon be celebrating the fact that NEURODIVERSITY works here, too!

If you'd like to know more about what we do, explore our website at: www.neurodiversityworkshere.com

I have written this book for all of those neuro-kin of mine, to ensure that their own workplace begins to work towards a standard of neurodiverse acceptance in the workplace. And, that by managers and other supervisory staff reading this book, that individuals who identify as neurodivergent find the workplace support, resources, and 'right space' to flourish and grow more fully in the workplace.

I have used my insight into the world my 'neuro-kin', those employees who are neurodivergent and part of the neurodiverse community, my adult children, my friends and colleagues, and my own lived working experience experiences, to write this book.

It is based on both extensive research, and personal experience, anecdotal conversations with others and the informally used experiences of others I have talked to in more formalised environments. All of this has been done while supporting the establishment, start-up, development and expansion of small and medium businesses all over the world. I have utilised both informal and formalised interviews with hundreds of employees, students and people who have had to move from working in an office-based environment to working for themselves, from home, to find out why it was that so many individuals who were neurodivergent experienced 'issues' at work, within the workplace, which ultimately led to them making alternative workplace choices.

In addition, I have also talked with employers and HR managers about their choices when hiring and retaining staff, especially in relation to staff who may "do things a little differently", which, up until quite recently, has been the common workplace parlance for individuals who are neurodivergent.

After sitting and pondering this for many years, I decided to take the bull by the horns and write a book that outlined what the REAL issues were, from a neurodivergent point of view, how an office-based environment or workplace could work to embrace more employee friendly and workplace efficiency oriented practices and furnishings that would enable those businesses to not only thrive, but flourish, as their employee began to feel more supported and in-tune with their workplace environment.

There has been much in the media over the past 5 years or so about organisations who, individually have championed the on-boarding of specific communities of neurodivergent employees. This has specifically been those from the Autism and ADHD communities.

This book has a broader approach to neurodiversity and neurodivergence, as the above are not the only two presentations of neurodivergence in society. Neither is neurodiversity limited to medically diagnosed conditions, which is a common misconception by many people.

It has to be stated here that the majority of business owners believe that they are 'doing everything they can' to provide for the needs of their employees. From a purely business-based perspective, this may be true. However, as you will come to acknowledge, there are many 'missing pieces' that business owners and team leaders, managers and co-ordinators can grow and develop, in order to more effectively and efficiently grow their workforce in a holistic and 360-degree manner.

It is here that this book will be of great value.

Fact, Fiction or Fantasy? (just a hint, it's not the last two)...

I'm not a medical expert, but I have done a lot of research over the past 30 years or so.

I also have lived experience of much of what I'm going to talk about, and/or I have spent a lot of time with people who do, too.

I have two children (who are now grown adults who are both working) who have experienced much of what I have referred to, here.

In addition, I have been teaching, training or facilitating workshops for individuals who fall within the parameters of neurodivergent, for over 30 years.

More often than not, when they have heard that I, too, have found challenges with various aspects of the working environment, they open up and share their stories with me.

And, so, I have not only my own personal awareness of observing, feeling, being in that space and also knowing what it's like to experience much of the following, but also many, many anecdotes and experiences retold from others who have found themselves in the same or similar positions as my own.

In addition, I have chosen to write this book from the perspective of a socio-cultural model. By that I mean that I have been looking at how someone's environment influences them and may impact on them, their ability to participate fully in the workplace and in their social environment and also on how their environment might affect their behaviour.

This is key as we often hear of all of the detrimental effects of having various conditions, health issues, injuries and other medically diagnosed (DSM5- the current medical manual that medical professions use to determine the scope, depth and breadth of a medical condition) and related "disorders.

I have purposely not gone down that route, as I believe in a strengths-based approach. However, so that you can more clearly "see" some of the underpinning rational for someone coming and asking for an adjustment or workplace accommodation, I have included both the physical, cognitive and sensory effects of having many neurodivergent states of being, just so that you are aware of wat experiences an individual may have that are different to your own, or that may make them more responsive to their environment at work.

I would not normally look at someone's behaviours or actions first, in assessing anything about them. I would look at their environment and the systems and processes they were asked to participate in, how they were asked to participate and then what happened when they did participate.

From this, I could gauge a lot more than only identifying behavioural patterns and assessing and analysing those.

This comes from my many years in multiple careers. I have spent a lot of time working with people who have metaphorically 'fallen through the (educational and therefore, often-times, employment opportunity) gaps', working with them to patch up what they missed in our educational institutions and offering them resolutions to learning that were not offered during their 12 years of formal education.

I have spent a further many years in a work-based learning and work-force development context, deciphering what was occurring in a multitude of organisations, trying to uncover common ground, common 'mistakes' that employers were making, and reassuring those who were under the pump, not feeling that they fit in, or feeling completely overwhelmed by an alienating workplace, for reasons they themselves did not understand, were soothed by the knowledge that they were not the only one.

And, finally, for those who didn't quite manage to keep their head above the water, who may not have been able to keep a job, might have had one drink too many down the pub, been unable to keep on paying their bills over and over again, or just been overwhelmed by the relentless pressure of everyday life, with it ultimately affecting their mental health and wellbeing, I have stood by them. I have spent a further number of years working with individuals who were left by the wayside by society, with rock-bottom self-esteem, zero self-worth, limited self-confidence and more belief in the faithfulness of their pets than any abilities, skills, knowledge or strengths that they themselves may have.

ALL of these individuals who have crossed my paths have, in some way, been a part of the neuro-kin I have come to call my own. And, that is why I chose to work with them.

I want them to be portrayed for the strength, courage, enormous range of skills, knowledge and experience fortitude, courage, determination, self-initiative, loyalty and positivity that they showed me, every day we were together!

And, I want you, as their managers and potential future managers, to see how, with just a reframe on an alternative way of thinking and doing, you can ultimately benefit from their place in your workforce.

Just for a short while, I am going to speak from an Australian perspective, purely because I am anchoring my experiences in the two places in which I have worked, across my career. This does not discount the global arena, nor the many other countries in which I know this book will take hold and have and influence on the way in which you choose to do business.

I currently live in Australia. Up until very recently, I was employed by a third- party organisation, in Australia. For many years, I worked in the UK, in a wide and vast range of jobs, across a plethora of fields and positions. As such, I want to anchor what I am saying in some Australian statistics. I am sure, for international readers, you will be able to extrapolate these for your own national populations and come to your own statistical 'rough estimates' just as I have done.

Why have I used 'rough estimates'? Mainly because there are no solid, concise and consistent statistical representations for exactly what I want to say. And, so I have had to cobble together many different numerical and quantitative calculations to address what it is that has had an impact on my own life and working career, as well as the lives and working careers of many others who identify as neurodivergent or part of the neurodiverse community.

I have also aimed to provide much qualitative evidence in anecdotal and case study format, so that you can see the direct impact of what happens in the working life of a neurodivergent employee.

I have done this for two reasons:

1) to bring a face to something that society often talks about in numbers and statistics and 'facts' and medical evidence; and
2) to highlight some 'features' of neurodivergence and the neurodiverse community that you may recognise in yourself or in others around you (in the hope that this gets you thinking about your own approaches to these individuals outside of the workplace).

What Did I Choose to Leave Out of This Book?

I had to leave out many things. This book is specifically aimed at managers, business owners, team leaders, co-ordinators, HR representatives and those who are interested in the dynamics of organisational culture, strategic leadership and ethical practice within organisations. It is also for new and upcoming students and Managers who wish to "do business" in a new and innovative way.

It has been written in order to provide an 'insider's viewpoint' on what a mainstream workplace looks like and how this can often-times look quite uncomfortable and out-of-place, not meeting the workplace needs of society's neurodiverse workforce and the neurodivergent employees seeking employment and/or already working for you.

My key aim was to provide you with more guidance, more ideas, more understanding of what it is like to be neurodivergent and also, why individuals who are neurodivergent have the workplace and environmental needs that they do.

Oftentimes, employers can fall into the trap of believing that individuals are being picky, or asking for specific things that aren't really necessary. This is not the case. This book will talk through why it is really important to have certain key elements in place, to make coming to work far more comfortable and enjoyable for your employees, and a much more open, communicative and free-flowing, innovative and productive workplace for you, in your managerial and supervisory positions.

Why Did I Leave This Information Out?

If you have picked up this book and are not a manager, team leader, company boss, co-ordinator of a project or team, or interested in becoming one, don't be disheartened! You may still be interested in reading this piece as it is packed with some useful information about how we might work with adults in general, in a much more diverse way.

If you, yourself, feel that you belong to the neurodiverse community, and/or identify with being neurodivergent, I have written another book for employees that provides some key tips, hints and ways of working with your managers and team leaders to get the best out of you as an employee, and also, so that you can gain some more understanding of how, why and when you might work best. It took me until I was in my 50s to figure this all out for myself. I don't want that to be the case for you!

Where Else Can You Find Out Information About This?

My plan is to publish both books within a close timeframe, so that both workplace managers, supervisors and team leaders, as well as employees who identify with being neurodivergent have the opportunity to work together to create more congruent, harmonious, aligned and power-house organisations that are streamlined and able to work towards their business objectives in a far more innovative and people-centred manner!

If this feel feels like you and your business, please read on.

Check the Appendices, in the back of this book for more areas of research that have been covered in this book. I have included a bibliography and some in-text annotations, where appropriate, to point you in the right direction for further research.

What Have I Included that Will Support This?

Statistics

There are no solid, concise and consistent statistics that state how many individuals there are, globally, or country by country, who are neurodivergent. There are statistics that relate to how many individuals may have one condition, or experience one neurological variant that would place them in the community of neuro-kin we call neurodiverse. I have been able to find statistics on how many people have a disability, in any particular country, but not how many people from that statistical group also work, and how many of those then work in an office-based environment.

I have been able to find country by country statistical break-down of employees by industry. However, these industry break-downs are not the same across the globe. Equally, I have been able to assess many of the cognitive variations and how many people (as a whole population total) may have these variations, but not how many of those people, per variation, or per grouping of variation, are working adults, across all forms of neurodivergence, nor in all of the range of neurodiverse states of being.

From a workplace perspective, it may be challenging to get a full grasp of what this means for you, as you would have to do what I have spent many hours doing, poring over global and national country-based reports to try to determine how many individuals may 'fit' into the neurodiverse community, in Australia, in the USA, in the UK, in Canada, across Europe, in Asia. These statistics are not consistently found, nor are they easily accessed in all areas. Reports, such as those from the OECD, Australian Bureau of Statistics, the Australian Institute of Health & Welfare (AIHW), the USAs National Institute for Health (NIH), Asia and the Pacific's Asia and the Pacific Employment and Social Outlook Report 2018, the UKs NIESR – Neurodiversity at Work report (2016), have all provided some answers. But, not all.

This has provided a general challenge for me to 'prove' the validity of what I have established, myself. What I have, instead decided was to narrow down my field of reference, choose a set of 'states of 'being ', separate from those that I have defined as neurodiverse, and utilised the statistics from that statistical range.

Why Have I Bothered with Statistical Information?

Firstly, I think it is important to not just pull a rabbit out of my hat!

I am not a magician. I am also not in the habit of making up information that I cannot justify.

Second, I have to be accountable to myself and the neurodivergent 'neuro-kin' in the workforce, to be as transparent and open about what I am presenting is presently quite disarming and, at times, very uncomfortable for many neurodivergent employees.

I also wanted to show you that the foundation for writing this book is based in real-time, real-issue, real-life framework of people who are neurodivergent. I wanted to show you real-life, real-time statistics for this, across the globe. However, to do it for every single country was an impossibility, unless I was choosing to do it for my PhD. And, even then, the scope of statistical evidence currently available is not conducive, the sample sizes are not the same, the population categories are not the same, the population categories are not the same.

However, I did want to give broad examples across as many countries as I could, to show a wide enough set of examples to deliver a large enough 'sample' of neurodivergent working individuals, so that you could clearly see that your own workforce, your own employees include many more than 1 or 2 individuals indicated by some articles I have read recently.

In doing this, I have given anecdotal and case study evidence, rather than statistical evidence, I have then signposted you to further areas where you can look up further statistics, if you wish to do so.

A Bibliography

I have done this to evidence that fact that this book is founded on not only my own personal experience of being neurodivergent, but also on research into the field of neurodiversity, ethical practice, organisational culture and management, business law, social inequality in the workplace, disability law, Human Rights and inequality, strategic management, innovative business management and practices, WH&S and occupational therapy, the environmental, emotional and psychological impacts of neurodivergent employees experiences in a neuro-typically designed workplace and many more areas I have been exploring and researching since I started my business studies over 25 years ago.

It was clearly not acceptable for me to just tell you what my own opinion is. Although very interesting and entertaining, it would not have held weight with many of you, standing on its own. As such, I have included references, research and other bits and pieces that will evidence what I am saying.

In saying that, I have not written this as an academic piece. It is written in everyday English, so that it can be easily read by as wide an audience as possible.

The references are included for further reading opportunities and also so you have some further reference material, whether you are a manager, whether you choose to be the one to take this to your manager and start the process of workplace 're-structuring' for further innovation and neurodiversity inclusion, or whether you want to open up a doorway for further conversation in your workplace, this book can be a point of reference for you.

If you are not the one to make the ultimate decision, maybe your senior Manager might need these references to help them make their final decision, too.

A Glossary

Finally, I have put in a glossary. It's not always easy to learn new words, or understand new concepts. I know that many of you may have come across some of the concepts I am using.

As I was told many times whilst in the process of writing this, "Not everybody will understand that terminology, Leigh". That is true. They may not, at the beginning.

However, with continuous usage and repeated inclusion into our conversations, I am hoping that we will all come to be more comfortable with all of the terms, phrases and references I have used in this book. They are a part of mine and hundreds of thousands, if not millions of neurodiverse employees across the globe.

Language and Use of Terminology

It is here that I will raise the issue of language and terminology.

It may come up many times for many people.

I will not be using any language that is offensive, that minimises, belittles, aims to harm, discriminate against, disempower or alienate anyone in any way.

However, I do need to state that some agencies, institutions, government-based services and medical establishments use terminology and references that will do this. Also, on a global level, language use in one country often conflicts with preferred terminology in another country. Finally, individual preferences for conditions, states of being and preferred languages for identity vary and differ and individuals have the right to identify in any way they so choose.

For the purposes of writing this book, I had to come to some common ground about this. Firstly, for diagnosed conditions, I went with the DSM-5 and/or ICD which are the current medical references across the global Western world, for medical and health practitioners. These are also the reference points for the documentation referred to as the United Nations Convention of Rights for Persons with Disabilities, the Australian Disabilities Act 1993 and also any references made to workplace compliance around accommodations and adjustments that I have made reference to, in an Australian context. For international compliance legislation, in the USA and UK, the DSM-5 and ICD will also have been utilised as a reference document for workplace compliance.

My personal preference has been to steer away from terminology that negates the positive, engaged, contributory and participatory experiences of neurodivergent individuals in our society, including in the workplace. As such, terminology often used in the medical and scientific field, such as 'disorder', deficit, 'lack of...' indicate a gap or limitation. The perception here is that this limitation is preventative of participation, engagement, fulfilment or achievement. It also implies that there is a focus on all that is not there, rather than a focus on all that is present and can be used, applied, and focussed or refocussed to obtain a positive outcome.

The language we use to define someone, what they do, how they do it, when they do it, why we think they do it (which may actually be very different to why they believe they do it!) and with whom they do it is very, very powerful.

It can make or break someone's belief in themselves and create a raft of ongoing issues that far exceeds that one moment in which we have interacted and engaged with them.

Across the decades, there have been many names used for various states and conditions I will be referring to in this book. Many individuals will identify differently to how I have referenced them in this book. My use of language will be for one of two reasons: a) many people prefer Identity First Language [IFL] use, today. That is, if they have a condition, diagnosis or something that affects their health, they want to refer to themselves with that as being a part of their identity. For instance, one of my friends has diabetes, she uses IFL and says she is diabetic. This is using Identity First Language. b) that is the way that something has been used in the most recent issue of diagnostic medical manuals, the DSM-V and the ICD.

Some individuals have personal language preferences, or have been known by their condition/diagnoses for a long time and prefer to continue to use that specific terminology. You may hear people referring to 'autistic', Asperger's and Autism or Autism Spectrum Condition [ASC] in the same way as I have used Autism Spectrum Disorder [ASD]. Some individuals, including myself, do not appreciate the use of the word, 'disorder' as it relates to something which belittles and negates the individual. I have only used this terminology as it is referred to in this way in the current DSM-V diagnostic manual.

I am aware that the ICD, used in the UK and Europe and other places across the world have differing parameters and terminology). Please feel free to insert whatever fits best for you and most importantly, for your neurodivergent employee/s).

Some of the language used in this book may be more appropriate for some regions than others. For instance, I know that in the USA, the term "Asperger's" is still widely used when referring to ASD. That is not the case in Australia, although some individuals do prefer to identify in that way. I will aim to use Identity First Language (IFL) rather than Person First Language (PFL), unless this is in reference to myself. I will also use medical terminology from the DSM-V, which is the most up-to-date medical reference available. I will not be referencing the World Health Organisation's International Classification of Diseases (ICD), which is primarily used in the UK. However, there will be some references to models and practices from the UK and across Europe who do refer to the ICD.

I will be working from a social or environmental neurodiversity model with a neurodiversity paradigm. That means I am not writing about neurodivergent employees to 'pathologize' them. If I offer some examples, they are real-life examples I have come into personal or professional contact with. If I offer some examples of how neurodivergent individuals may be influenced, affected or impacted by their neurodivergent variation, it is to highlight some of the challenges faced by them and also to raise areas in which further support can be offered to minimise any impact on overall productivity, individual anxiety levels and also to ensure streamlined work performance.

In addition, in reference to language about people, I will not be using language such as "problem" (unless it is relation to 'problem-solving'), 'deficit', 'disorder' (unless it is specifically referred to in the DSM-V or other research), or 'impairment', as I am writing from a strengths-based perspective.

This doesn't mean I am denying the fact that being neurodivergent can be challenging and bring its own range of daily and lifetime "issues", which are sometimes not perceived by others as 'issues' as they are rarely visible.

The 'invisibility' of many of the challenges faced by neurodivergent individuals is part of the greater 'issue' and also part of the reason they are often perceived as not requiring support or accommodations or adjustment or alternative (anything's).

You see, our society has gotten by on the things we can see. If we can see it, we can do something about it. And, we are okay about that (most of the time). When we can't "see" something, it is invisible to us, we can't 'prove' it, it is nebulous, and then is more challenging to those of us that like predictability, certainty, 'provability' and established 'facts'. If you can't "see" something, it is very hard to prove it.

It's a long and philosophical argument. But, let's say I broke my arm, or cut my finger off. Gory, I know. However, you could see the damage I'd done. I could "prove" it to you. Whereas, with neurodivergent conditions, it is often challenging to do this, even when trying to get a diagnosis from a specialist who specialises in the field of what you are trying to be diagnosed in!

So, the use of language around conditions, identity, individual expressions, actions, responses, differences and subjective experiences can become quite an operational field of stepping stones, crocodiles and the proverbial snakes and ladders!

It also does not describe the breadth and depth of lived experiences of individuals who are neurodivergent and are part of the neurodiverse community, nor the broad range of experiences and that bring them to your workplace, as part of the neurodiverse community.

Not all people who are neurodivergent would say they have a 'disability'. However, they may state that they are influenced and impacted upon by their environment in a way that affects how they engage with and respond to the world around them. And, that would include while they are at work.

Many find that when they are in an environment in which they have had some say, or a lot of say in determining the structure and layout of their environment, they are able to respond to and engage with their environment band the people in it with relative ease and skill.

In writing the book, I have used my own preferred terminology here, but am in no way negating the preferred terminology chosen or used by others.

Being a part of the neurodiverse community is not limited to those individuals. There are many more individuals who also have brains that cognitively, and in a sensory processing manner, vary from the neurological 'standardised norm'. These brains are known as neurodivergent. The individuals with these brains form a part of the larger neurodiverse community.

Statement of Intent

I have worked with a whole range of people across my career who have been disenfranchised, discriminated against, exploited, abused, excluded, disempowered, dispossessed of what is rightfully theirs, not given a 'voice', unable to advocate for themselves, and in a very vulnerable space. The majority of them have been women, although, circumstantially, not all.

With any group of people who is subjected to this kind of action and behaviour, there is overt and covert behaviour present that blames the person who has been treated poorly. This 'victim-blaming' is a form of abuse and is a larger part of our socio-cultural sway towards some of the more offensive things that human beings like to do to each other.

I am by no means stating that any of this goes on in your workplace. However, I want you to consider that no matter how much we might think we are 'doing our best' to ensure something isn't happening, there may always be that 'one thing', that 'one person', that one unseen behaviour or statement or comment about someone that is not above board, not ethical, not adhering to anti-discriminatory policy and practice, no compliant with human rights legislation.

Any time someone gets 'labelled', categorised, 'pathologized', placed in a 'box'

As a global society, the collective 'we' tends to treat women in a much less favourable way than we behave towards men. In fact, statistically, if we look at the demographics alone, the proportion of women to men who are in the workforce, is somewhere in the region of 1:3 for fulltime neurodivergent employees.

As we move through the book, you will see that some of the co-occurring conditions associated with neurodivergent conditions and states of being include anxiety disorders and states that are not always easy to determine via a medical or other clinical assessment.

Just recently, I read a newspaper article from Ireland that stated that women with neurological challenges, learning 'difficulties', auto-immune conditions and psychological illnesses were more likely to be diagnosed with "mental illnesses, including depression and anxiety, and medicated as such, than men with the same symptoms. Ultimately, no matter where we look, it appears that women are 'treated differently', blamed for requiring additional supports (Taylor, 2020) and ultimately not believed (Russo, 2018).

This is not the book for me letting you in on all of the research that defines and articulates this. Suffice to say, there is a lot of it. Further, in circumstances where there are 'invisible' indicators of a women's situation, it may prove more challenging for her to "prove" that she requires additional supports, accommodations and assistance.

In this book, I am advocating on behalf of the neurodivergent employees that are already working for you and those who may have slipped through the gaps. I am also speaking up for the many thousands of people who have not been able to work, because someone has told them that they can't, because they "weren't good enough", "couldn't do it in the 'right way", "didn't have the same kind of brain as everyone else", "didn't think like the rest of the world", and so on.

Our wider culture has belittled, blamed, judged, and sometimes violated the self-esteem and self-belief of the neurodivergent individuals who may not have made it into the workforce. The ones who have made it through your doorway have often fought very hard to get there (Megrew, 2019; Mellifont, 2019; O'Regan, 2020a; Siegel & Smyth, 2005).

It would be such a shame to let them go.

Our world and our society aren't designed for the neurodivergent mind. It just isn't.

You may believe that we 'cope well'. And, yes, sometimes we do. We may often appear to be flourishing. It is a pretence of masks and mirrors that is a set of strategies we employ to get through every day without wilting and falling into a heap. For those of us who get through the days, it exhausts us.

Maybe not every day. Maybe not every week. But, eventually, we do fall down.

I fell down after 53 years of pretending I was okay. That I could do it. That it was alright. That I was just like everyone else who went to work.

I wasn't.

But that is another story, for another day.

In this book, what I want you to seriously consider is the effect, influence and impact you, as a workplace team leader and manager can and do have on your neurodivergent employees.

Because you do. And you will. And, it will be profound.

The Environment

This, in a way, underpins the framework for my book. That which highlights the fact that if we, as individuals are placed into an environment that is not suitable for us, nor optimised to ensure that we are able to 'perform' and utilise our skills, strengths and talents, then we will be disadvantaged by our environment, rather than optimised by it.

This can happen very easily in the workplace, without us even knowing.

As managers, it is part of our responsibility in implementing our equality and diversity, inclusion and diversity policies, to ensure that these individuals are not left by the wayside, with unmet neurodiversity-related needs.

It is also an amazing opportunity to get on board and become trailblazers and pioneers for a whole swathe of our employees who may not have quite been able to articulate what was going on for them, and actually restructure and redesign our workplaces, systems and processes, procedures, protocols and practices, to make them more inclusive and more equitable for them to be able to more readily and easily able to participate in.

The purpose of this book, from a philosophical, moral and ethical perspective is to promote, protect and ensure the full and equal enjoyment of all human rights and fundamental freedoms by all persons who are neurodivergent; to promote respectful workplaces that are conducive to these employees contributing to society in a fulfilling and life-enriching manner; one in which they can work with inherent dignity, attain overall job satisfaction and develop professional competencies.

This is my personal and professional hope for all of us.

Foreword

A Word to You, the Person Reading This Book

I know that you have picked up this book for a reason. Maybe you were curious about the title. Maybe you felt an affinity with the first few pages I have written, or what you read when you first flipped through the book. Maybe you like the way I write. It's not your standard, 'dry', business style. I can appreciate that.

I don't want to bore you.

I know you are a busy person.

I know that you have a lot of things on your mind.

I know that, at least in the workplace, you have some responsibilities that include people.

I also know that you are a human being.

With your own needs and wants and desires. Someone who may or may not get those needs met all of the time.

I want you to read this book with that in mind.

And, with an open heart.

I know you picked this book up for a reason.

Maybe you believed it was going to be your average business book. In some ways it is. It contains classic information, statistics, research and new sources of knowledge for you to ponder over.

And, in many other ways, it is a call to action.

The fact that you already have it in your hands tells me that you have an open mind.

In this book, I am asking you to think along two lines of thinking: One is that not everyone in your workplace is going to do everything in exactly the same way in exactly the same timeframe, nor be able to 'deliver' against their KPIs and outputs in exactly the same way.

It is part of you taking this journey into the world of neurodivergence with me.

Some of you may choose not to go there first. That will be very sad. Why? Because, without that insight and knowledge into the 'lived experiences' of neurodivergent individuals, it will be a little challenging for you to understand why someone may feel and act and do things the way they do. If you are willing to engage with the first section of this book, you may uncover some interesting, at least, and compelling and profoundly moving information that could change the way you see and perceive your neurodivergent employees. Here are some of the things you may learn about:

a) Neurodivergent people might find the standard workplace a little more difficult to navigate
b) Neurodivergent individuals can be such an invaluable asset to your organisation
c) Neurodivergent employees deserve to be validated, acknowledged, supported, accommodated, included, nourished, nurtured and celebrated for all of their contributions and achievements to the workplace and to society

In the second part of the book, I will provide you with some practical tips and hints for creating a much more refreshing and easier to navigate space for neurodivergent employees. Some of these you may already be aware of. Others, may be very new to you.

The third part of the book explores your whole workplace culture. Why have I decided to go there? Because it is highly relevant to the way is which your neurodivergent employee/s may or may not feel as though they fit, or 'don't fit' into your workplace.

The fourth section focusses on the sub-title of the book, and looks at ways in which the intersection of inclusion, diversity, innovation and productivity can come together and become a compelling force for competitive advantage for your organisation and business strategisation and monetisation.

And, finally, we will look at the plethora of ways in which your leadership and management teams across the board can enhance their leadership and practice to ensure that the overall running of your organisation, and the management of your neurodivergent employees.

I am not expecting that you will throw yourself and your business headlong into change and recreate your workplace from scratch.

I have titled this book the way I have because I truly do believe that neurodivergent employees have so many strengths, and yet are often under-valued or under-resourced, or not even known about, making them invisible to their employers. By standing up and taking our place within the workforce, we can both take a stand for those who are not able to do so, and also forge a new pathway forward, along with our supportive managers and organisations.

I know that you will be one of these.

As you read through the five sections, I have guided you from information relating to the neurodivergent employee through the standard workplace, to ways in which you can create a more neurodiversity friendly working environment. Then, I have touched upon ways in which inclusion and neurodiversity strategies can optimise and enhance your organisation's productivity and profitability, through innovation and the application of an ethical management and leadership framework. Finally, I provide some innovative ways forward that can support your organisation to get the most out of your managers but also your neurodivergent employees. This is on an employee to manager level, at an operational a book strategic level of leadership and management.

Ultimately, by becoming more adaptable and more open to providing an enabling space for neurodivergent employees to feel comfortable, safe and accepted in your organisation.

If I take this back to you, as a person. Reading this book will also be a journey of discovery for you. Maybe you will find out something new about someone you know, someone you love and care about, or someone you work with. You might find pour something about yourself your own manager, a friend or colleague. It may even be a more important realisation than that, and this may resonate with you because you recognise a child or parent in what I am saying.

Yes, I am writing about neurodivergence in a business context. However, I am providing you with an enormous amount of personal and anecdotal insight into the neurodivergent world of life and work, throughout this book.

For many of you, this will resonate on a deep level, I have no doubt.

I know the journey to self-discovery is not always paved with large boulders and massive crevasses to find ways to traverse.

You might be wondering why I am talking about 'self-discovery' when this is a book about business.

It is true that many business books start in quite a dry and sterile manner. The last decade has brought about some humorous business expose's and some thought-provoking tomes that have led us all to think about what we do in a deeper, wiser, more considered way.

We all thought we had a very clear idea about what 'inclusivity', 'diversity', 'innovation', 'productivity', 'human capital', 'workforce development' and 'organisational culture meant'.

In the context of keeping an open mind, being flexible and opening yourself up to even more great ideas, refreshing one that you may not have thought about before. Ones that might not have yet crossed your mind. Or, if they have, might not have been presented to you in quite the way I am going to "present" them to you now.

It is for this reason that I want to sit back and take this journey with me.

This is not just a moderate paperback about something that's been rehashed again.

These are also not "new ideas". However, I have reframed them, in a way that may make more sense to you, and may, hopefully, have you making some in-house observations that you weren't previously making before, within your own organisation.

Hopefully, you will also choose to take some action, after reading this book! There are many points along the way, in which I have overtly and less blatantly (let's say "invitationally", requested that you join me while we chat about some of the features of a neurodiverse world, what it means to be neurodivergent, how being neurodivergent in a world that is not designed for neurodivergent people can sometimes be fraught with challenges, and how, with just a few slight adjustments and accommodations, our neurodiverse working population can not only exist quite comfortably amongst their working peers, but also thrive and even come to be your organisation's greatest asset!

It is with this in mind that I start this book in this way.

There are often moments of pure joy, fun, laughter, and happiness. These are the times when we are in the flow. This is when I personally know I am in the right space, the best environment for me, and when I know I can maximise my productivity. It is also when I know that I can give my best to those around me. That is really why I wrote this book. To encourage those of you who are motivated and inspired to create a 'new order' of workplace environmental design, workforce development opportunities, and space for innovation and inclusion, to come to the fore and really take action.

One of my own key skills is being able to 'flip' problems around so that they appear as a resolution point (first), and then I work backwards from there. This is what I have done with the 'issue' of neurodiversity in the workplace.

I, myself, am neurodivergent. I am finally happy to claim that part of my identity.

I wasn't always. Firstly, because I didn't realise there was anything 'going on' that made my way of thinking, processing and "doing things" any different than anyone else. Then, when I began to realise that I was rarely "doing things" the same as anyone else, I started to watch my own processes. I've always been quite self-reflective and as I watched myself "do" things, at work, and in life, I began to see some significant differences. Then, over time,

I began to see a couple of other people who sometimes did similar things in similar ways to the way I did it.

My meandering conversation is leading to the fact that one day, I too realised that I was neurodivergent. It took a long time. I'm sure I frustrated more managers than I could count. And, along the way, I also became very frustrated with a range of things, as well. Mainly how my various workplaces were not able to or chose not to make accommodations for my neurodivergence.

When I started to articulate my challenges to my employers, I also found that some were more amenable to making changes than others. Some became highly concerned that now that I had 'disclosed' my neurodiverse condition, I must not be able to do the job. On one occasion, less than 10 days after I let my manager know that I had recently realised that I had Sensory Processing Disorders and that meant 'X', in terms of why I had a particular work pattern. When I explained what was occurring from my end, and how my own condition affected me, and why I needed the adjustments, I was told that "it may be better off I look for work elsewhere."

Although this has not been the 'norm' with all of my workplaces (thankfully!), It has happened on many more than one occasion.

Through my work and through my research, I have come to see that what happened in the role above was not because of anything that I had "done". More because of the attitudes, beliefs, assumptions, misconceptions and discrimination I faced and was challenged with in my own workplaces, whenever I stepped out and decided to "disclose" my neurodivergence.

This was a huge part of the reason I write this book.

I have met so many people throughout my career, who have divulged that they, too, are neurodivergent. Some have talked to their employers and some have chosen not to do so. They have all had their valid reasons for making their decisions. For the ones that chose not to, or decided after disclosing this aspect of themselves, that they would prefer to leave the workplace, it was most often because their workplace was not conducive to them continuing as an employee. The key three reasons given have been:

environment challenges and the negative attitudes/ assumptions about their neurodivergence and or capacity to do their role.

In saying that, I have also met many individuals who have had very productive and responsive managers and bosses, who have been incredibly supportive. That also includes me. Not all of my workplaces have been detrimental to my workplace wellbeing or working life. Many have been incredibly beneficial and mutually respectful environments in which to work.

It is these workplaces and the anecdotal evidence gained from talking with friends, colleagues, acquaintances and people I have undertaken facilitated training and development opportunities for, that I have utilised the case study material for this book.

It has all been de-identified, unless it actually happened to me. Then, I have referred to it in the first person, but have not given identifying details of my workplace, managers nor colleagues. This is to protect the privacy and interests of those concerned.

My interests in writing this book is not to lambast anyone, but to raise the consciousness level of our global workforce, including our Managers, team leaders, HR force, Senior Management Teams and CEOs.

When I am writing, I am speaking from personal and lived experience. This is not something I know someone else has felt or experienced, something distant that I have studied and researched. It is my own life, lived over almost 40 years of working. It is based on navigating and negotiating with my managers, team leaders, supervisors, CEOs, HR Managers. Some of whom have been very accommodating and some who have been downright hostile and dismissive. One or two have even been abusive, discriminatory and I have had to take further action against them, as they have not seen the damage they have done, in holding firm to such outdated ideas and concepts that held them firmly in a conservative management style, where they felt that non-inclusivity and social conformity was a far better option than meeting the needs of our global working population.

My, and everyone else who is part of the neurodiverse community, otherwise known as my "Neuro-Kin" (Silberman, 2016), from here on in, are worth putting in the effort to accommodate their needs.

We deserve to have our needs met, the same as every other employee. We are able to provide you with all of our skills, knowledge and experience, and fulfill our employment obligations, just like every other employee. However, on par with everyone, we also deserve to have our needs respected and accommodated, to have adjustments made where we require them, and also not to be dismissed or belittled when we ask for an accommodation or adjustment, for whatever reason.

What Does it Mean to Say That I Am NeuroDivergent?

That means my brain is wired differently from the neurotypical brain. It means that I communicate in different ways. It means that I don't always socialise in 'standard' or necessarily 'socially acceptable' ways. It means that sometimes I need more space than others always understand. It means that I process information differently, in my brain. It means that my whole environment affects me in ways I am sometimes aware of and sometimes completely oblivious about.

It often means that I need more time to complete tasks. It does not mean that I do a "worse" job. In fact, it often means that I do a far better job, as I am always committed to the task in front of me, always focussed on the detail of my work. I can more often than not see both the big picture and the fine detail, all at once! I am a great problem solver. I can be trusted with the completion of a task. However, I may not follow the exact steps you may follow, in order to complete it, as my brain thinks in lateral ways, rather than sequential or systematic ways.

This is not always understood by my bosses. In fact, sometimes I have been severely reprimanded for not "thinking about this correctly!", in relation to a development project. It also means that some places and spaces don't always 'work' for me. I am involuntarily affected by my environment, as my own particular neuro-hardwiring means that my body and my senses respond to the environment in divergent ways. This is completely out of my control. It is involuntary. It is more often than not something I am even aware of, at the time.

I want to add that this is also the case for many, many people out there in the world. I have become more and more aware of the numbers of individuals who are in our workforce, who are challenged by their working environment, every day.

I hope that as a Senior Manager, or someone in a position of authority in your workplace environment, you, as the reader of this book, will be able to reflect on what I have said and reframe some of what goes on in your space. It only takes one small step to start the change.

I don't want you to think that I am 'radical', as I am far from that kind of personality. However, I am known for being non-conformist in my approach to most things, and that includes my work. As I have explained above, this has far more to do with my being neurodivergent than anything else. Some things, I just do the way that I do it. I always have done. I have never fully known why I do some things in a very 'different' way to some of my peers. Now that I am aware of my neurodivergence, I can see how it has played a significant role in everything I have ever done. It is part of who I am.

Recognising my neurodivergence has been the key, for me. This has, at times, really peeved some my employers! These have been the more conservative, less explorative, less curious, less open, less able to acknowledge that not everyone does everything in a cookie-cutter style, under cookie-cutter conditions in a cookie-cutter environment. Some bosses have loved my 'way', though, and they have been the ones I have been drawn to and stayed with for longer.

It is *THIS* that you are looking for! The neurodivergent employees that find you, *want* to be in your space. Want to offer you their uniqueness, their skills, their knowledge, their experience and their creative mind. They are the ones who will enable your business to thrive! These individuals are the keepers! They are the creative, curious, compassionate, committed, focussed, innovative, aligned, congruent and dynamic people who want to work for you.

Why would you want to push them away?! ...

They are business gold!

SECTION TWO

The NeuroDivergent Employee

In the Beginning...Key Definitions

To be neurodivergent is to be neurobiologically diverse, as a human being. That means that my brain works a little different from a 'standard', 'neuro-normative' brain. That is, one in which science says it works to a certain cognitive pattern, biochemical manner and in a certain neurological 'way'.

Being neurodivergent means I share the way I think, 'be' and 'do' my life with a range of others in the world, who each have our own way of 'being', 'doing' and 'thinking', which is divergent from the neuro-developmental 'normative' brain. They are also 'neurodivergent because their brain is also 'hard-wired a little differently than the neuro-developmentally normative brain. Every one of us has a brain that works slightly differently, however, there are more similarities between people whose brain works in a neurotypical way, with each other. And there are similarly, a range of neurologically based responses that occur that are similar for individuals who are neurodivergent, depending on which kind of neurodivergent condition they have.

I don't want to get too medically or scientifically technical, here. Let's just say that there is one way in which science states that neuro-normative, typically brains develop under standard circumstances, from conception to old age. And, then there is everything else. Any variation from that is either a development variation, a neuro-cognitive variation, an acquired variation, or some variant in the way that brain has been 'hard-wired' to work.

Which, ultimately means it will work a little differently.

It will have different needs, it will process things differently, it will respond differently and it will approach things differently.

People who are neurodivergent are impacted by co-occurring conditions and environments that differ from person to person. For each, there will be varying impacts and influences. For some, there will be little impact in environments where they have more control over how that environment is established and managed For others, where they have limited control over their environment and their social world and its composition, they may find it more challenging as they aim to respond, process and approach the world with their neurodivergent way of doing, being, feeling and thinking.

The diversity of human brains and the many differing ways in chich human minds work and are 'wired'. That is, the many variations and infinite variations in neuro-cognitive functioning that occur within the human species.

NeuroDivergent/NeuroDivergence

To 'be' neurodivergent means that I have a brain that functions in a divergent way. It is divergent from the scientific cognitive and structural 'standard'.

Oxford English Dictionary definition:

Differing in mental or neurological functioning from what is considered typical (or developmentally neuro-normative).

Neurotypical

This neuro-scientific or genomic 'standard' referred to above is also referred to as 'neurotypical'.

Oxford English Dictionary definition:

Neurologically typical; *specifically* exhibiting 'ordinary' thinking and behaviour.

NeuroDiverse/NeuroDiversity

Neurodiversity refers to a group of individuals who are neurodivergent. Neurodiversity relates to a group or community. From a scientific perspective, when an individual separates displays alternative neuro-cognitive functioning, they are known to be neurodivergent. So, when we talk about individuals, we would refer to them in this way.

They are not neuro-typical. Because of this, they exhibit social skills, communication skills that are unique to neurodivergent people. These individuals are highly likely to be highly influenced and affected by their environment and surrounding. This may be in a positive way. Equally, depending on the nature of their environment and how it is set up, they may also be negatively impacted by their environment.

Oxford English Dictionary definition:

A range of variation in mental or neurological functioning in a group; the state or quality of being neurodiverse.

NeuroDiversity Paradigm

Without writing a whole thesis on the paradigm itself, my main point of support of this concept is that the neurodiversity paradigm believes that although the person may have a health condition, disability, neurological variance that is divergent from the social norm, it is actually their social context and physical, emotional and social environment with "disables" them. In short, "a person is disabled not by their impairment, but by the failure of their environment to accommodate their needs (Oliver, 1996).

Overview

Have you ever wondered why some people in your workplace do some things one way, and others do them in a very different way? I don't mean how they butter their bread or peel their apples.

I'm talking about the way they work. The way they approach their tasks. The way they might go about planning, scheduling, prioritising, and apportioning their day. The way that people approach and connect with each other- or not. The many different ways in which people choose to communicate, and by which means. The way in which people share information and via which channels. The way people respond to each other, their environment and their 'world'. The way that people think in different ways. And, also, the way that some people just seem to be 'wired' a little differently.

All of these things are true for people who are neurodivergent.

That fundamentally means that their brains work differently than people whose brain follow a more 'standard' developmental 'pattern' of development.

What it means is that they respond to the world in a different way.

'Differently' in a sensory, cognitive, emotional and neurological way.

I just want to say here that I am using the term 'differently' to apply it to a state of being that is scientifically assessed to be a 'standard' scientific way in which brains develop. Medical specialists and scientists though for a long time that this was the ONLY way that brains developed. So, they thought this was 'the norm' or "normative neurodevelopment", in technical terms.

I'm only explaining it to you in this way, so you can see where the terminology I am using comes from. There reference point for 'difference' comes from the medical or scientific reference to 'neuro-normative development'. That which was once perceived as being the only way that brains developed.

Once some more research was done, scientists and medical practitioners realised that brains developed in all sorts of ways. In a very simplified explanation, this became known as 'divergent neurodevelopment'.

And, so, someone who's brain does not work in the same way as the "neuro-normative development" way, would be called "neurodivergent".

From that, a whole group of people who fit into that larger group, with all different sorts of neurodivergent ways of thinking, coined the term 'neurodiversity'.

Of course, the term 'neurodiverse', or 'neurodiversity' refers to a group or collective of people, rather than an individual. And individual would be called 'neurodivergent'.

Something else to mention here is that the term, 'neurodiversity' was initially used to refer to individuals who identified with diagnoses of Autism, ASD, Asperger's, ADHD, Tourette's Syndrome, Dyslexia and Dyspraxia.

More recently, some researchers and academics have started using the term, more broadly, to include other conditions, including those that are not present at birth, but acquired. They could include: brain injuries (Traumatic Brain injury [TBI] and Acquired Brain Injury [ABI], as well as other conditions and health diagnoses that impact on how the brain functions and is altered by those conditions. This could include depression, anxiety disorders, auto-immune conditions and so on.

I have used this broader definition of neurodiversity' to define individuals who are neurodivergent and working, to encompass and include as many people as possible.

I also want to state that you may rarely hear me talk about 'disability', during this course. Whilst I understand and appreciate that many people who are neurodivergent have a disability, not all people identify in this way. Neither are the terms interchangeable.

In addition, the focus on this training, also exploring the influence and impact of neurodivergence on employees is actually on ways in which managers and team leaders can more effectively work together with their neurodivergent employees to address neurodivergent needs and accommodate those needs to the benefit of both the employee and the organisation.

One of the key findings from my years of work as a consultant, training facilitator, business woman, manager, adult educator and someone who has worked with thousands of disenfranchised, disadvantaged, disempowered and vulnerable people is that sometimes, all it takes is a shift in the little things to make a massive positive impact that enhances their lives in an extraordinary way!

Oftentimes, in the case of someone who is neurodivergent, lives can be drastically affected by the external environment.

If someone has 'control' over their environment and their setting, say at home or in their favoured space, then they are able to manoeuvre it so that they can be comfortable, not overtly affected by it, and feel secure within it, knowing that however they need to be productive within it, they will be able to do so.

If they have little or limited 'control' over it, it is much more difficult to navigate that space and also to find ways in which to be productive within it.

This is where you, as their manager, team leader and support, come into the picture. It is also where this course can benefit both you, the neurodivergent employee and also your business.

What Do I Mean by NeuroDiversity?

I'm going to start this conversation by talking about disability, in the way it is outlined by the AIHW.

There is a reason for this, which I will explain in a minute.

According to the Australian Institute of Health and Welfare (AIHW) website, a disability is "an umbrella term for any or all of the following components, all of which may also be influenced by environmental and personal factors:

- 'impairment'—problems in body function or structure
- activity limitation— 'difficulties' in executing activities

- participation restriction—problems an individual may experience in involvement in life situations"

Although this is valid, in some situations I will be talking through and using in my case studies, it does not represent all of the anecdotal and research-based information I want to present to you.

So, the question remains, why not use "disability" instead of neurodiversity?

Firstly, because the term "disability" does not fully capture and encompass what I am talking about, in relation to the employees I am referring to in this book.

Not everyone who is neurodivergent identifies as having a disability, nor has been diagnosed under the DSM or ICD. Therefore, they wouldn't ordinarily be perceived as "having a disability". However, the semantics of "having a disability", identifying as having a disability" or being diagnosed with a disability are not wat this book is about. It is about what happens when one of your employees does things in a different way, at work, or responds to a workplace instruction in a different way than other employees, or communicates in a different manner, or approaches their work tasks in a different manner due to a neurological or cognitive difference.

Following on from this, some individuals have chosen not to get a diagnosis for their own reasons. In other cases, such as myself, in the past. I have many, many signs and indications, and even had surgery. However, I did not realise that the every-day challenges I faced in the workplace were an inherent part of my neurodivergence. I just thought that everyone went through those trials and tribulations at work and soldiered on.

For the past four and a half decades, I did not even realise there was a name for some of my states and conditions! I just was who I was and tried to work with what I had and deal with whatever arose in the workplace, whenever I faced a challenge.

Also, not everyone who has a disability is neurodivergent. So, I have chosen not to use those terms interchangeably, as they don't fit that way, in this context.

Secondly, although some communities within the broader neurodiversity realm have taken 'neurodiversity' on-board to refer to themselves, more specifically, technically the term means as it reads: 'neurological diversity'. That is, neurological variation, across a broad spectrum of neurological possibilities. So, it may be inclusive of individual or specific groups, like those with ADHD or individuals on the Autism Spectrum (or, in using Identity First language [IFL] some now prefer to be identified as 'Autistic".

Why are Some People NeuroDivergent?

There are many reasons why someone may be neurodivergent, many of which will be discussed and addressed in this book. The term 'neurodiversity' has been used by various researchers to refer to differing groups of neurodivergent individuals. For some, it refers to those who have a diagnosis that includes: (all of the different variations of) Autism Spectrum Conditions and ASD, ADHD, Dyslexia, OCD, Tourette's Syndrome and Dyspraxia. Others have broadened their umbrella to include Social Anxiety Disorder, General Anxiety Disorder, depression and depressive disorders, and autoimmune conditions, which can change the way our brains are wired.

Others again include a much broader range of health conditions, neuro-cognitive variances, neurological conditions and cognitive and neurodevelopmental disorders. I have used as broad a set of examples as possible, as our workplaces include as broad a range of individuals as is possible, and from my perspective, we need to be inclusive of all neurodivergent conditions that require or hard-wire our brains in a manner that creates a divergence from the 'standard normative' (this is scientific terminology) brain. Some examples of these are: health conditions, such as diabetes, migraines, Traumatic Brain Injury (TBI), auto-immune conditions, and so on. Other reasons may be due to a variance in a person's genome.

Many people believe that only genetic differences create neurodivergence and therefore neurodiversity. However, this would assume that everyone who is neurodivergent is born that way and only those who are born that way can have an entitlement to claim their neuro-cognitive difference.

Personally, and professionally, I know that many individuals have acquired their neurodivergence along the way, having received an injury to their brain, become ill with a disease or illness that has shifted the way in which their brain focusses, absorbs information, or their senses take on board information. All of these scenarios would also lead to neurodiversity (AIHW, 1999; AIHW2007).

It is for this reason that I have broadened the scope of this book to include everyone above and not just the individuals who have a variance in their genome. In doing this, I am not discounting nor dismissing their relevance and importance in the greater neurodiversity community and their contributions to it.

There is a particular thought process or mindset in society that follows a more social model than that which is a standard scientific or medical model of seeing neurodiversity as something 'different'. It is the neurodiversity paradigm. The word paradigm just means 'mindset'.

The concept that there is one type of brain that works in one particular way is now outdated. Both medical professionals and scientists realise that our minds biologically and cognitively work in diverse ways. What this means in every-day terms is that as individuals, everyone processes things in slightly different ways.

However, from a neurodiversity point of view, and in terms of processing information, there is a 'normative' group of people, who process things in what has come to be known as a 'standard', or 'neurotypical', neurodevelopmental way of information processing, communication expression and approaching social connectivity. And, there is now a recognised healthy alternative range of neuro-cognitive processing, social expression and ways of communicatively expressing ourselves. It is in this range that individuals who are neurodiverse and identify themselves as neurodivergent would be found.

As a society, we have established our realm as one in which only those who are in the neuro-normative range would be. So, individuals and communities who do not have brains and minds that are wired in that way can find it challenging to 'fit in' to the environment created for them. Let me put it this way- if someone, an architect- decided that their town was to be built entirely of concrete, because that's what they liked. It was their preference (read, 'neuro-type', or the way their brain liked it to be, and the way they preferred their environment to be), then everyone in town would have to accept that the town was made of concrete. Some people would be perfectly fine with that.

Other people might find that a little grating, but still be able to find ways to 'cope' with that environment. They may at times also have to get out of there and find an alternative environment that was much more comfortable to be in. And, others, again, would not be able to tolerate it at all. They may not be able to live there. They may find it very stifling and it may adversely affect their ability to participate in their community, take part in activities and daily tasks, and also their ability to be able to communicate effectively. They may also find that they had adverse reactions to the concrete, because it caused some interesting responses in their body and mind. This might put further pressure on their body, their mind, their biological system and their mental health and wellbeing.

If we use this analogy as a workplace environment, with the concrete township representing the workplace and the individuals in the town representing the employees, you can see that the environment and its structure and composition could have an adverse effect on the individuals in it, socially, emotionally, psychologically, physically, in terms of mental health and wellbeing and also in relation to communication, and social wellbeing and community participation. These social dynamics form our relationship to others and underpin our relationships to others. They also underpin the dynamics of social inequalities in our society, and in a smaller part, in our workplaces.

One way we can work to overcome this inequity is to enable a space that embraces creative potential for all neurodiversity and enables all of our workforce to grow and flourish.

This is the aim of me writing this book.

In it, I hope to encourage you, as leaders and managers, to promote the strengths and value of our neurodiverse workforce and embrace its innovative and creative abundance, so that our organisations can also grow and flourish accordingly.

What Happens When a Neurodivergent Person is Influenced by Their Environment?

The way someone is affected or influenced is more often than not due to their environment, how it influences their senses, which are usually heightened and/or super-stimulated. This is very common for people who are neurodivergent. It is due to differences in the way they absorb and process information from their world, through their sense and also in a cognitive manner.

None of these are voluntary mechanisms, so it is out of the control of the individual. How long it takes to absorb information, how long it takes to process information, the adjustments required for them to be able to process information effectively and the environmental stimulus or "calming" that they require is all out of their control. This is all due to their brain's 'hard-wiring'.

In line with this, and the fact that our general Western society has been developed and established to provide for the needs of the neurotypical population, neurodivergent people may have developed a range of skills and strategies that enable them to more effectively cope with the pressures placed upon them by all of the extra stimulus of a neurotypical environment.

Who Might Be Neurodivergent in My Workplace?

Firstly, if you work in an office-based environment, I have statistically demonstrated how between 30% and 50% of your workforce may identify some characteristics or traits that are neurodivergent. These could be anything from not being able to concentrate on a task for a long period of time, to having low level literacy skills, to being hyper-focussed on a task and unable to be drawn out of it (without getting very grizzly). Others may be not liking 'change', needing quiet space (as opposed to an open plan office), being unable to initiate tasks, having issues with prioritising and planning, not being able to keep desks "tidy", being ultra-sensitive to lighting and noise. Each of these are forms of sensory and executive functioning issues that could indicate neurodivergence.

It is always better to leave it to the employee to bring this to your attention, however, as a manager, having this awareness can provide you with some awareness that can enable you to externally manage a complex seating arrangement, for instance and re-seat someone who appear to be 'struggling' with sitting at the outer end of a row of desks, as it is always the space where people congregate for a conversation. They may actually be hyper-sensitive to noise and distraction and unable to start their work, and also concentrate, due to people around their desk space all of the time. Moving them to the other end of the line of desks could resolve their anxiety about lack of task initiation and your anxiety about them under-performing. It could also provide you with some insight into what may be happening, so that you could start a sensitive conversation.

Here are some results from some research I conducted that indicate what the highest numbers of neurodivergent states and conditions are that affect employees in the workplace, below, in a pie chart format:

Baseline Neurodivergent Examples
(with population percentages)

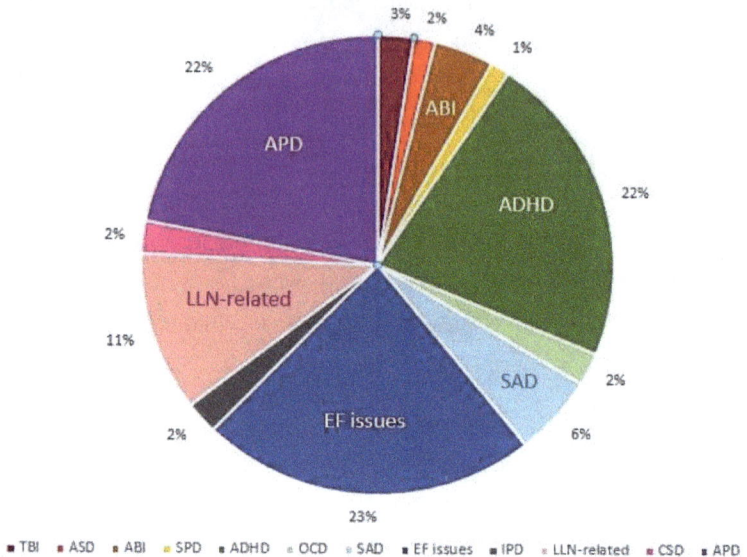

These are examples of some of the more familiar neurodivergent populations that may be present in your workforce:

- o Attention Deficit Hyperactivity Disorder [ADHD]
- o Sensory Processing Disorder (SPD)
- o Traumatic Brain Injury (TBI)
- o Acquired Brain Injury (ABI)
- o Obsessive Compulsive Disorder (OCD)
- o Social Anxiety Disorder (SAD
- o Executive Function (EF) issues
- o Information Processing Disorders (IPD)
- o Language Literacy and Leaning (LLN) related issues, including dyslexia, dyspraxia, dyscalculia
- o Auditory Processing Disorder (APD/CAPD)
- o Communication and Social issues (CSD)
- o Autism Spectrum (ASD/ASC/Asperger's)

For other industries, there may be up to 70% of your workforce may be neurodivergent. This is due to the fact that many people who have some challenges with executive function (which affects planning, sequencing, task focus, concentration levels, reading and writing skills), more often than not are drawn to more trade-based, hands-on industries. They tend to be what are called 'kinaesthetic learners' and that means they absorb and process information by 'doing', as opposed to reading it, or listening to it, or by looking at someone demonstrating it to them. They literally have to get in there and do it themselves! You may be one of those people yourself!

These individuals are also far less likely to move into an office-based environment. However, if their speciality or niche is found within an office-based environment, then they will be drawn to work there.

There are many factors involved in why this may be the case. From an adult education perspective, much of it is in relation to lower levels of literacy achievement, a preference for hands-on, skill based (therefore trade-related employment) and a preference for jobs in which these neurodivergent individuals can expend their physical energy in a practical manner, i.e. by working at their trade (ABS, 2006).

If we go back to our 30-50% of our office-based human capital, we can see how this will have some impact and influence on their ability to effectively participate in the workplace. This won't always be a negative impact, but it will have some influence on how your neurodivergent employees respond to their working environment, to their colleagues, to the information they are asked to absorb and process, how they may go about taking on board that information, how long that may take them to do, what they may require to do that, and also how they communicate that back with others (Chowdry, Shulz, Milner & Van De Voort, 2014).

Also, not everyone will be the same and so, not everyone will have the same need for changes to their working environment, or need to "do things differently".

Many neurodivergent people in the workplace try very hard to do things in the 'standard' manner that is established in their workplace. For some, they keep this up this for a long time. However, for these employees, as their brain processes information differently, both in terms of cognition and also in relation to their sensory experience of the world, trying to absorb information from their world and the workplace and process it in uniformly 'standardised way' can be very exhausting and emotionally and psychologically quite damaging.

Over time, this can develop into serious workplace 'burnout', 'overwhelm' and even be associated with the development of life-threatening and chronic health conditions, such as auto-immune diseases (Mellifont, 2019; Russo, 2019; Vibert, 2018). This 'masking' and pretence, or pretending to be able to 'fit' into a workplace environment is one of the key issues that neurodivergent individuals face with their workplaces. As they 'struggle' against an ever-increasing tide of neuro-normative environmental, cognitive and sensory stimulus that does not compute well with their own system.

For someone else to be dismissive of this, negate it through their use of language, behaviours, actions (or omission of actions) or other by other means, is unjust and unfair, at the minimal end of injustice and discrimination, oppression and social injustice at the other end of the scale.

In the workplace, none of us want to be a part of someone's 'undoing'.

However, sometimes, in our not being aware, not having received enough information, not being attuned to someone's needs, not having enough background about a situation, or not fully realising what our own responsibilities and accountabilities are... we can sometimes slip up.

Ultimately, this is why neurodivergent individuals require some adjustments to be made in the workplace. To accommodate for their nuanced differences they have in processing, communicating, and absorption of information.

So, it is pretty safe to say that with an average of approximately 30-50% of your employees being neurodivergent at any given time, you may need to consider some ways in which you may need to think a little differently about the way you approach a number of internal structures, systems and processes within your organisation, as well as how you may have standardised processes within your organisation. It is also interesting to note how many times I have and will continue to mention the workplace environment (Swain, French, Barnes & Thomas, 2004; Winkler, 2009).

Our surrounding influence so much of how we feel, how 'comfortable we are, how 'well' we work towards whatever it is we want to achieve. Our environment also influences our frame of mind and our ability to apply ourselves at our optimum level of potential.

This may be surprising, I know!

Much of the research that has been conducted, to date, has focussed on one or two specific groups within the neurodiverse population, and this has provided somewhat of a skewed perspective on:

a) How many neurodivergent individuals there actually are in the workforce, generally
b) How many of them are influenced, or impacted by their workplace environment?
c) The diversity of ways in which someone can be influenced by, and impacted upon, by their working environment
d) Some of the sensory processing, executive functioning, language and literacy processing, bio-chemical and neural pathway for this being the case (indicating that these "needs" are actually out of the voluntary control of the individual)
e) How many people do not even enter, or stay in the workforce, due to issues around not being able to have their neurodivergent needs accommodated for, nor addressed, adequately

I do believe that the research that has been conducted is valuable and most definitely has its place. I also believe that any work that is done in this area is at the forefront of a new wave of social and societal re-fabrication, placing us in a position of remodelling how, and in what ways, we choose to take our workplaces, and our society's, forward.

This is new ground being broken. And you are pioneers in this new development. As a manager reading this book, you are at the forefront of a new and exciting phase in business remodelling!

I know this will be surprising to many of you, but as you read on, you will see what I mean about the expanse of neurodivergence already present in your working teams. You will also see the many ways in which we, as a working society, have come to accommodate the needs of the 'standardised' populations and subjugated the needs of the much larger, diverse populations.

I am only talking about one population here- that of the neurodivergent population who work for your organisation.

It may only require a simple adjustment, for many, such as a different kind of light globe or a change of desk or positioning.

We'll go into this in more depth later in the book.

Secondly, as a note to employers, your staff may, or may not be aware of their condition, illness, injury, state of health, condition and/or disorder. It may, or may not be diagnosed. They may or may not have support. And, they may or may not feel 'comfortable' disclosing this to you, bearing in mind that they may have had some negative prior experiences with past employers who may not have been as open and non-judgemental as you are.

Finally, as stated before, you may find yourself aligning with some of what is said here, which could mean that you, yourself, are neurodivergent.

And that is perfectly wonderful!

It is possible that you, or someone very close to you, may have experiences some form of discomfort or dis-ease, being in the "standard" workplace environment. Maybe it is why you chose to branch out and go into business for yourself! Because you were not happy working for someone else, in their space, in their "world", in their environment.

These are all 'clues.'

But, please, don't let me go off on a tangent.

It IS something to think about, though...

Statistics

Australia has a working population of just over 12.8 million people. Of those, approximately 3.5 million work in an office-based environment (ABS, 2019). That is roughly 27% of the Australian working population are employed, in some capacity, within an office-based environment.

If we look at the overall statistics for some communities of neurodivergent people (in Australia- I appreciate I am being Australian-centric here, however, just bear with me for the moment, whilst I make my point with a 'control'/known population), we can see that for some neurodiverse communities, there are more people working in the general working population than for other communities.

Based on the Australian Bureau of Statistics (ABS, 2006), roughly half of the Australian population is working (12.8 million out of 25.8 million people). According to the ABS, (2006) approximately 27% of that population is working in an office-based environment (3.4million people or so). I have not included every single office-based job role here, but have tried to loosely interpret these statistics in a way the assumes that the industries I have specifically chosen to represent office-based industries (see Appendix for full details) are completely representative of an office-based environment, whilst those I have not chosen are a mixed office-based/other working environment.

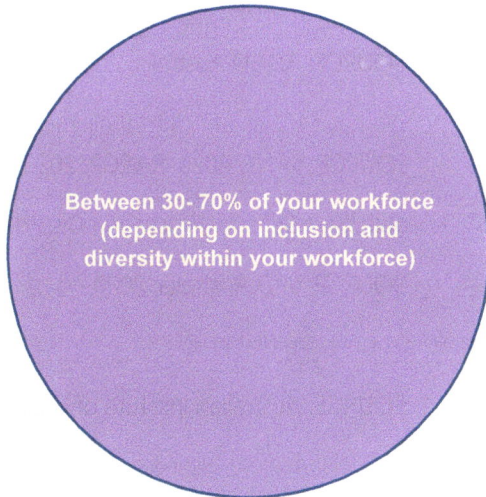

Between 30- 70% of your workforce (depending on inclusion and diversity within your workforce)

What Does a Neurodivergent Workforce Look Like?

What the information above means is that there will be far more than 27% of Australians working in an office-based environment, overall. I have only chosen occupations in which the majority of employees work in the office for the majority of their working day and working week.

If we use the same statistical analysis to determine how many neurodivergent individuals might be working in your organisation, we come up with some fairly rough) statistics. However, it will give you an indication of how many people may be working for you.

NB. For your reference, this is also how I came up with my percentage of individuals who may be neurodivergent in our own population!

A sample of Australian population statistics

→1/70 people are on the Autism Spectrum

SOURCE: Autism Spectrum Australia, 2020

→1/20 people have ADHD

SOURCE: ADHD Australia, 2020

→1/5 people have issues affecting their mental health and wellbeing
SOURCE: SANE, 2020; RACGP, 2020

→1/20 people have Sensory Processing Disorders

SOURCE: SPD Australia, 2020

→1/50 people have diabetes

SOURCE: Australian Institute of Health & Welfare, 2020

→1/20 have Social Anxiety Disorder

SOURCE: Beyond Blue, 2020

→ Approximately 700,000 people in Australia have a diagnosed brain injury (including ABI and TBI); 1/45 people have an ABI

SOURCE: Brain Injury Australia, 2014

→1/20 people have health issues that affect the way they process information/they require support in the workplace, in order to fulfill their workplace obligations

SOURCE: AIHW, 2007; NIESR, 2016

In addition, I have compiled a set of statistics that represent the industry- based groups I have chosen for our office-based occupations. I have given my rationale, above. The chosen industries are outlined in the Appendices.

I wanted to visibly demonstrate this to you, in way that was transparent and also in order to dispel the notion that neurodivergence is only represented by less than 1% of the working population. I hope you can see from my preliminary findings that this is not the case.

Statistics on individual neurodivergent conditions and variations are few and far between. Those that have been collectively sourced and compiled are even rarer. In fact, that is part of the reason I decided to compile this table. I literally couldn't find a concise "list" of reference material for me to look at. I'm hoping this will be useful to someone else, at some point in the future.

Source material and statistics from other countries, within the same exact parameters and the same set of qualitative or quantitative reference points is near on impossible. However, it IS within a reasonable bandwidth to assume that what I am using to represent the Australian population could be extrapolated across most Western countries. Of course, there are some discrepancies, which I won't be drawn into, as this is not the focus of my book. I am purely using these statistics as a visible optic for you to determine how effective an innovation and inclusion program that specifically focusses on your neurodivergent employees may be for your organisations.

You May Be Thinking- Why is There Such a Big List?

As I stated earlier, neurodiversity is a term that references a group of people who are neurodivergent. Being neurodivergent can arise from many scenarios. One is a variation in your genetic material. It can also be acquired by an injury or by an illness or other health condition that alters or impacts upon the Central Nervous System's neurotransmitters.

Changes to our neurotransmitter receptors or transmission can have an effect of our mental health and wellbeing, emotional regulation and many other bodily functions, such as sleep hygiene and appetite. Changes to our hormone and/or endocrine system can also affect the way our body responds to our environment and also how it perceives our world, on a sensory and cognitive level. This often happens with conditions such as diabetes, or auto-immune conditions such as thyroiditis or ME or Lupus. Neurodivergence can be due to an injury or illness of the brain's structure or neural pathways, the brain's cognitive ability and/or our Central Nervous System. Neurodivergence can also be acquired through other illnesses, injury, or health conditions (Barkley, 2012; Brain Injury Australia, 2014; Grant, 2017; Menon, Schwab, Wright & Maas, 2010; NAS, 2017; Rodden, 2020; STAR Institute, 2020, Synapse, 2013; The British Dyslexia Association, 2020).

In this book, I've used this broader scope to frame, refence and talk about neurodivergent individuals and employees, to encompass a broader number of individuals than is currently outlined in many research papers and books that relate to 'neurodiversity and neurodivergence'. This is because I have come to see that the small number of states of being currently talked about, although completely validated as neurodivergent, are not the only ones represented in the mix. Therefore, as I am promoting inclusivity and diversity in business practice, I need to follow my own lead.

I am also embracing, highlighting and emphasising the broad range of individuals that can be a part of your neurodivergent workforce. This is specifically to emphasise how many may need you, as their employer to consider that they ways in which your organisation has structured its environment may be out of date, not efficiently 'styled or designed to suit the needs of your employees, in order to optimise their capabilities and ultimately enhance your organisational productivity.

What I'm saying her is if we start to look at the actual needs of our human capital, the people who work for us, we can more fully assess where we are going wrong (or right!), and address that in-situ.

By adopting adaptive systems and strategies to more effectively manage our workforce, we may be able to not only address our current organisational needs, but also enter into a new business phase where it is not only survival of the fittest, but more of an environmentally adaptive model that embeds flexibility, adaptability, collaboration and innovation into the current system.

Although this book is not an academic reference, I am aware that there is limited research undertaken in this area. As I have been undertaking some of it along the way, I would like to include it as a reference point, even if it does not meet the academic criteria for peer-reviewed empirical work, at this stage. I know that it is a useful benchmark and starting point.

I did not want to write this book as an academic 'tome', but something that can be utilised as a reference book, as a working guide, and also something that is easy to read, insightful and hard to put down!

This Table shown on the next page is not meant to be a comprehensive guide, but merely a representation of how many neurodivergent employees may exist in our workplaces.

(For those of you into emojis, or needing a visual here, this is where you'll see my cheeky, winky-face!).

Neurodivergent state	Percentage of Australian population	Percentage in working population	Percentage of population working in office-based jobs *
Autism Spectrum Disorder (ASD)	1/70 (368,400)	50% (184,200)	27% (49,734)
Attention Deficit Hyperactivity Disorder (ADHD)	1/20 (5 million)	50% (2.5m)	27% (675,000)
Sensory Processing Disorders (SPD)	1/20 (5 million)	30% (155,040)	27% (41,860)
Auditory Processing Disorders (APD)	1/20 (5 million)	50% (2.5m)	27% (675,000)
Traumatic Brain Injury (TBI)	1/45 (500,000)	40% (206,400)	36% (73,300)
Acquired Brain Injury (ABI)	700,000	50% (350,000) BIA	36% (126,000)
OCD	2% (516,000)	50% (258,000)	27% (69,660)
Social Anxiety	5% (1.3m)	50% (650,000)	27% (175,500)
Generalised Anxiety Disorders	3% (774,000)	50% (387,000)	27% (105,000)
Depressive disorders & mental health disorders	25% (Beyond Blue) (6.45m)	50% (3.225m)	27% (870,000)
Cancer	Approx. 145,000 per 25m, per annum	30% (43,500)	27% (11,800)
Diabetes	1/50 (516,000)	50% (258,000)	27% (69,600)
Immune System Disorders (estimated)	1/100 (258,000)	30% (77, 400)	27% (20,900)
Hashimoto's Disease	2% (USA statistics) (516,000)	50% (258,000)	27% (69,660)
Issues affecting neurotransmitter levels; hormones and endorphins (estimated, based on AIHW figures)	Between 14 and 20% per year Average 15% (3.9m)	50% (1.95m)	27% (525,000)
Other gut disorders (estimated)	2% (estimated) (516,000)	30% (154,800)	27% (42,000)
Post-Traumatic Stress Disorder (PTSD)	6% (1.55m)	50% (770,000)	27% (209, 000)

Executive Dysfunction	1/20 (conservative estimate) (5m)	50% (2.6m)	27% (702,000)
Communication and social differences	1/50 (conservative estimate) (516,000)	50% (258,000)	27% (69,660)
Information processing disorders	1/50 (conservative estimate) (516,000)	50% (258,000)	27% (69,660)
Issues affecting literacy and numeracy	1/10 (conservative estimate) (2.58m)	50% (1.3m)	27% (348,000)
TOTALS	4,998,339 (5m) ESTIMATED (known total population, based on cumulative totals. Representative of office-based industries)		

NB: Not all neurodivergent states have been listed here. Therefore, we can assume that these numbers are even higher than I have estimated. I have also not included all of the office-based industries. Those included can be referenced in the appendices. This will also impact on numbers and will increase figures substantially.

+This is empirical data taken from specialist websites that are relevant to each area of neurodivergence. For instance, for each health condition, I checked facts and statistics with the peak or national body for that issue. As an example, for diabetes, I looked at the Australian Diabetes website. For more generic issues, such as LLN (Language, Literacy and Numeracy, I looked at Australian Bureau of Statistics research for recent years). These sources have been listed in the bibliography.

++ The final total is a cumulative total. For statistical purposes, this number has been used to represent employed neurodivergent individuals who are working in office-based occupations, for two reasons: (a) I have not included all office-based industries as some are mixed between office and manufacturing, warehousing, education, hospitality and human and health services, as well as 'other'. This could account for a further one-third to half of all neurodivergent individuals; (b) to account for neurodivergent individuals who are not represented by statistics. Although this only provides "rough" estimates, it does begin to assess national neurodivergent populations, workforce neurodiversity and diversity by neurodivergent state/condition and/or diagnosis (however the neurodivergent individual has identified).

*This is the extended list from the Baseline Neurodivergent examples shown on page 52. This series includes other conditions that have an influence, affect or impact on neurochemistry or bio-pathology in a way that changes the way the brain functions on a permanent basis.

#This is based in empirical research; it is not just my personal opinion. Whilst this book is not aimed at uncovering more empirical data, I found it necessary to develop some raw data in this manner, to support my premise that there were many more neurodivergent employees in the workforce than many people originally may have deemed to be 'true' and the numbers that have already been calculated in other research. I decided to delve a little deeper and use my interrogative skills to uncover more evidence to support my theory of a broader neurodivergent workforce population.

** Where possible, these figures have been taken directly from evidence-based sources. These sources are listed in the appendix at the back of the book.

*** Where it was not possible to source an exact figure, an estimation has been made, based on broad research, or for example, Executive Dysfunction, in association with another divergent state of being, where the two states are directly linked and therefore must be directly statistically associated.

**** This list is not exclusive and does not account for the fact that someone who is neurodivergent may have more than one condition, state of being, illness, health issue or injury that creates their neurodivergence.

Over the coming pages, I will represent this table in a more visual, graphical format. I have done this for a number of reasons. Firstly, going back to our original conversation about the terminology I have used, why I have included and excluded certain words, and also why I am now including certain groups of people, within my use of the term "neurodiversity", and also due to the fact that most people respond much better to visual information than written information, I have compiled the information into various formats, as such.

Re: the broader inclusion of individuals- various researchers have included differing ranges of conditions, diagnoses and states within their scope. As the term is indicated as an umbrella term, I will also use it as such in this book.

There are many individuals believe that the term neurodiversity only relates to those who are within a certain group of conditions and diagnoses that are determined by the DSM-5. You may or may not have heard of the DSM-5. It is a medical manual used by medical practitioners to ascertain what is "wrong" with us, whenever we go to the GP, specialist, psychologist, or psychiatrist.

There have been previous versions, numbered 1, 2, 3 and 4, prior to DSM-V. DSM stands for Diagnostic Statistical Manual. The most current version is version V (5). Thus, DSM-V.

For those who follow a medical way of thinking, or who like to refer to a medical or diagnosed approach to neurodiversity, they will be thinking of it as a range of conditions such as ASD (Autism Spectrum Disorder/Condition or even Asperger's (depending which part of the world you are in), Tourette's, Dyspraxia, Dyslexia, Dyscalculia and ADHD/ADD.

As I have mentioned before, I have looked at neurodiversity from multiple angles. Yes, partially from a diagnostic angle, purely to offer a range of influences and impacts that certain conditions can have on a neurodivergent employee, and the neurological or neurochemical reasons for this. However, for the majority of this book, I have looked at neurodiversity as a whole and a more personal experience and its influence on neurodivergent individuals, from an environmental perspective, to provide evidence of how the divergent ways in which a brain works can impact on the outcomes sought and gained from an employee.

You may read some of this information.

It may confuse you.

The best way to get "un-confused" (I like to play with words) is to keep reading about it, from as many different angles as you can.

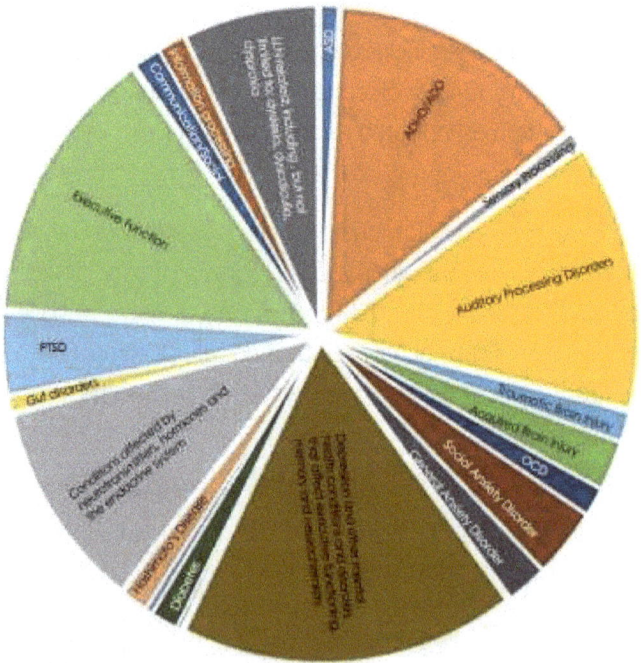

▪ ASD	▪ ADHD	◂ SPD	◂ APD	▪ TBI	▪ ABI
▪ OCD	▪ SAD	▪ GAD	▪ DD/MHD	▪ Cancers	▪ Diabetes
▪ ISD	▪ HD	▪ NT/H/E issues	▪ Gut disorders	▪ PTSD	◂ EF issues
▪ CSD	▪ IPD	▪ LLN-related	▪ Other		

I have created a graph to show the proportion of your office-based working population from each of the categories shown. Although these are Australian statistics; they can be extrapolated to represent any other Western country to get estimated figures, as current numbers for Australia compared to USA and UK only vary by a maximum of approximately 10%. For research purposes, this may not prove beneficial, however, for extrapolation purposes, it will provide an indication of numbers.

Whilst this is a relatively new and emerging field of empirical research, re: the targeted impact of innovative resources, management of neurodivergent employees and engagement with broader and more diverse range of management strategies. For this reason, I have collated and articulated my own research in this way.

Later, I will graphically highlight the influence of neuro-biological differences for neurodivergent employees who experience differences in executive function, sensory functioning, communication differences and social challenges, including social anxiety disorders.

LET'S DIG DEEPER

Potential Neurodivergent Influences
Executive Functioning

"Executive function skills enable us to plan, focus attention, remember instructions, and manage multiple tasks. For instance, up to 90 percent of people with ADHD/ADD struggle with executive dysfunction, which impairs goal-directed behaviour".

(SOURCE: 'What is executive function disorder?' J. Rodden in *ADDitude* magazine, 2020)

Executive functioning is highlighted in many other conditions that affect the way in which people's brains operate. Here are some of the ways in which someone may be influenced by executive function:

- time blindness, or an inability to plan for and keep in mind future events

- difficulty stringing together actions to meet long-term goals
- trouble organizing materials and setting schedules
- trouble controlling emotions or impulses
- difficulty analysing or processing information

There are some key areas in which this is emphasised, in relation to how someone might be impacted by executive dysfunction, in the workplace:

1. **Self-Awareness**: being able to gain the spotlight; commanding attention from others; and also, self-directed task management and contributions

2. **Self-Management**: inhibiting yourself, especially in the face of general 'impulsivity' or lack of self-regulation

3. **Utilising Your Non-Verbal Working Memory**: being able to contain things in your mind; having thoughts, feelings and memory patterns that guide behaviours towards others and self; sustaining working memory of general behaviour towards others and in relation to 'social norms'

4. **Utilising Your Verbal Working Memory**: retaining internal speech and using these to guide work and structures and systems that support work

5. **Emotional Regulation** using words and images along to articulate how you might think and/or feel; utilising self-awareness to shift how you feel about things. If you aren't able to think through your responses, you may not be able to articulate or communicate properly and this may mean you are responding from and emotional base only (in the short-term).

6. **Self-Motivation**: intrinsic motivation; being able to start, maintain and complete tasks and projects when no outside consequences or rewards exist

7. **Self-Initiative**: getting started on projects and tasks; maintaining pace to be able to deliver KPIs; displaying autonomy

8. **Problem Solving**: being creative, bringing innovations and new ways of thinking to the table; finding new approaches and solutions to old issues; utilising big picture thinking in places where fine detail thinking was previously used.

9. **Planning and Completion:** Establishing routines; being able to schedule and diarise effectively to accomplish milestones and goals; setting task lists and checklists; creating GANTT charts to guide progress within larger projects.

Any of the above could also mean that someone with issues that influence their executive function may feel 'overwhelmed' of given all of their tasks all at once. Whereas, given one section or one task package at a time, they would easily be able to complete their work, in 'smaller' packages. A little bit like 'chunking' information, for those of you who are familiar with this concept. There is no difference in task-loading or in completion of KPIs, only in how the task is initially conveyed to the employee.

This could mean that they require smaller task loads, still making up the larger task package, but designated so that they do not become overwhelmed with the larger task they are given. They may also not respond to a 'set' of instructions, given all at once. They may respond better if they are given one or two instructions at a time. This is not about them being "difficult" or "unruly", it is in relation to the fact that their brain most likely will not function well if they are overloaded with things to do, all at once. They will then look like they are giving up, when in fact, they are just feeling completely cognitively overwhelmed and unable to say anything about it.

Social Connections

Everyone needs social connection of some kind. As humans, we are hard-wired for connection. When you are neurodiverse, often there are challenges with starting or maintaining relationships, even workplace connections. There may also be alternative ways that people choose to deal with conflict, which may seem out of the ordinary or unusual to others. This is part of their process and needs to be accommodated, so that they are able to fully function in the workplace.

If someone isn't able to experience ongoing workplace relationships, they may face significant challenges. An example of this may be someone who does not easily socialise in a group but is quite happy to socialise 1-1 or in a small group. This is quite a challenge when many contemporary office spaces are only equipped for meeting up in open-plan kitchens and /or in large spaces. This can be quite overwhelming for someone with a condition that influences their ability to make and maintain social connections.

Communication Representations

For some individuals who are neurodivergent, whilst they can communicate readily when they are in a calm and regulated emotional state, feeling emotionally connected to the people around them and comfortable in their environment, if there are any discrepancies, or if there is any incongruence in their environment (e.g. if there is too much noise in the background while they are communicating or listening to someone else), they may involuntarily withdraw from communication, until there is a more optimum time available.

Many neurodivergent (ND) Individuals also require things to be explicitly outlined for them. They may find it challenging to 'read between the lines' or assume what someone is intending or conveying. For people who are not ND, this can appear to be 'petty' or 'trivial', however, for an ND person, it is vital for them to be able to gather all of the information required, in order to make a full assessment of a situation, or required task, is that they can complete it.

Let me give you an example. If you are the Team Leader for the Training Team. And, you decide to call the team together and ask the trainers to "pull together all of your ideas around training sales staff". They ask if there is a timeline, and you say, "No longer than a day or two". All of your trainers may bring you a list of different topics that could be covered and ask you which one you'd prefer they look at in depth. If you say, "I don't mind, you choose", your non-ND trainers might just choose one and move on to another piece of work. Your ND trainers might choose to cover all of them, or just one of them, but under different topic areas.

Non-NeuroDivergent trainers may have only chosen one training topic, which is what you asked for, but weren't explicit about. It took them roughly 1.5 hours to pull together a draft of the training pack for you. Your ND staff member has taken 2 days and is still working on this task. You are either curious as to why (what is taking him so long?!), or you are getting frustrated with him, as this is the fifth time this has happened and now you are thinking of putting him on a Performance Management Plan, because he just isn't following your instructions, right?! Oh! And, his time management is ALL out of kilter!" I think he might have to go.

Okay.

In their 2016, 'Diversity at Work' Report (NIESR, p. 28), Bewley & George, from the UKs National Institute of Economic and Social found similarities in some neurodivergent employees perspectives on their non-capacity to meet neuro-typical workplace standards, including the feeling and often reality that neurodivergent employees "either felt that they were more vulnerable to disciplinary action because of their neurological condition, or reported that they had been subject to disciplinary action or performance review in their current or past job . This was often because managers were (often) unaware of their condition or its impact". This only serves to highlight both anecdotal case study references and also personal and lived experiences of neurodivergent employees I have spoken to in writing this book.

So, what is likely going on in your ND staff members head is:

A) I am focussing (this is something that many ND individuals do very, very well, and often it takes many hours out of their day, if they become completely absorbed in what they are doing)

B) I want to do a great job, because I haven't been pleasing my Team leader lately, so I am going to focus on a couple of different alternatives and come up with a few different alternatives we can run with, right off the bat!

C) My Team Leader didn't say how many he wanted doing, so I'm going to choose a few and run with that, it won't take me long. He also didn't give us a timeline, so I should be okay with a day or two to complete it (If I do a great job, he won't mind if I take a little bit of extra time)

Do you see where I'm heading with this? You weren't explicit with time or topics or number of topics to choose. The person who needed that is running on assumptions. You yourself are also making some MASSIVE assumptions about them because they aren't fitting into your own NT or mainstream thinking bundle of employees, and so, there are a lot of miscommunications occurring. Most of them are not really anyone's fault. However, it is the ND employee who will ultimately pay the price, if you, as his Team Leader, decide to take him down the Performance Management route or even sack him.

There is no need. For any of it. All he needed was explicit information. He thought he was doing what you wanted. He was really trying hard to please you, and actually, in the end, did 3 times PLUS the work that anyone else on your team did. However, you have a sour taste in your mouth and believe that he has poor time management and doesn't follow instructions. None of which is true.

Emotions and Emotional Regulation

Emotional regulation can be influenced by neurotransmitters, hormones, nutrition, brain injury, neuro-developmental and neuro-cognitive variations in the way the brain absorbs and processes information. If someone is not regulated on this level, it can significantly affect and also enhance their ability to be effective, efficient and productive in the workplace. There is far too much to go into, on this level. However, auto-immune conditions like Diabetes, issues with their thyroid, having ADHD, having issues affecting your sensory processing or executive functioning can all play out on emotional regulation.

Sometimes, there may be strengths around empathy or compassion, for a neurodivergent employee, where they are able to 'tune in' to someone and 'get a feel for someone' very easily. This is a common occurrence for many neurodivergent individuals who can often 'sense' someone's overall character just by being in a room with them.

In addition, many neurodivergent individuals may have differences around the way they perceive and interpret facial expressions and other people's emotional states. Also, quite a few ND people I know have a condition called Alexithymia, where they need more time to process situations where there is a heightened or emotionally laden content. Say, where something that may have caused excitement or anxiety or anger may have occurred. When neurodivergent individuals who are also 'alexithymic' do not respond in neuro-typical ways, they can be misinterpreted as 'not caring' or being 'unresponsive'. This is not the case. It is purely a matter of a time lag on identification and processing of emotions.

A last thing I want to state here is that anxiety can play a huge part in many conditions that are connected to being neurodivergent. Diagnoses such as Social Anxiety Disorder, General Anxiety Disorder [GAD], Rejection Sensitive Dysphoria [RSD]; and even aspects of Obsessive-Compulsive Disorder [OCD], Attention Deficit Disorder [ADD], and Attention Deficit Hyperactivity Disorder [ADHD] are influenced by anxiety.

Any aspect of the workplace or environment that may heighten exposure to, or exacerbation of anxiety above a 'standard' daily exposure to anxiety and stress is likely to cause a not-so-positive impact on your neurodivergent employee, with a negative result.

Exploring ways of minimising heightened anxiety and assisting your employee in developing and implementing strategies that regulate their emotional state and reduce or minimise anxiety is a great way to create a harmonious environment not only for your neurodivergent employees, but for all of your workforce!

Cognitive Challenges

The way my mind works is very different to the way your mind works. We all have minds that work to process information in different ways. Some people do it in a more 'standardised' way than others. Neither is 'bad', it is just different. Cognitive function works like this to, in relation to the effects of cognitive functioning and the environment. For instance, if I am in my office, in a space I have designed, which faces out of a south-westerly aspect, so that I can get my writing done during the morning, without the glare of sunlight streaming into my world, I like that much more than not having natural light, or having very bright, full-sun light streaming in. If I had the latter two options, I probably would not be able to concentrate very well, would most likely get a migraine and would find that I had other issues impacting on my capacity to work as effectively and efficiently as I could. My cognitive ability hasn't changed, no matter which room you put me in. However, due to my environment, my cognitive ability has altered, even if slightly, to impact on my workplace function.

Environmental and Spatial Requirements

I know that many of you will be very certain that you have designed an office space that works for everyone. Or, one that works for the needs of the business. What would you say if I told you that what works for everyone doesn't always work for individuals who are neurodivergent? And, if what you have already established as a 'great' working space doesn't, then," work for everyone", will it then achieve your business aims and objectives?

It may, in part. It may not. At the end of the day, what it will do is create a scenario where some of your employees feel quite at home and ready to roll, every time they arrive at work, and others will be very reluctant to get started, because the environment is not suitable or conducive to them doing their best work. Ultimately, the only person that is truly going to impact on is you! And, the business.

Later on, we will explore ways in which you can optimise your office space, enhance your workforce ability to participate and create a great space in which to work! One where people will be itching to come and be!

Many neurodivergent individuals find it disconcerting when people walk behind them, or stand behind them. They may also be easily 'startled' or put off their paces by people seemingly coming out of nowhere to ask them a question (for example, coming up from behind them, or quietly). They may have a reflexive response that may seem out of the ordinary or overly sensitive. However, it occurs because they are completely unaware that someone else is in their realm. This is especially the case if they have been concentrating on something. This could pose an issue if their desk is in a thoroughfare, or near an exit doorway, as it would cause an ongoing distraction that would be very uncomfortable for them.

If you want to get the best out of your employees, ensuring that they are feeling calm, centred and grounded when they are at their desk is the best way forward. The chemical effects on the brain, for someone who is affected by sensory processing disorders (as just explained) can be quite uncomfortable, even to the point of those moments in time feeling like physical pain. This is because chemicals are released into the brain that the body reads as 'pain'.

Information Processing (time/duration/method differentiation)

Now, this is a tricky one. There are some tasks and processes that have a timeline and deadline attached to them because they are pivotal to the ongoing mechanisms of business systems, structures and procedures. I completely understand why you might want to have these things completed within a certain amount of time. They might be in relation to logistics, distribution, planning, scheduling, maintenance and so on. Very important work to get done within a required amount of time. It would be remiss of me to sit here and say that you need to be allowing more time for ND individuals to complete those tasks, as they are time-oriented, time-specific and have a specific end point.

However, for ND individuals, what it is important to note is that, we have a brain that functions entirely differently than yours does. So, assuming that we are able to do everything you can:

A) In the same way you can
B) in the same timeframe you can
C) with the same outcomes and conclusion, you come to

... is not fair (we cognitively wired completely differently than our neuro-typical kin are), unrealistic (we sometimes need extra time to achieve the same outcomes and objectives, with no less quality or effectiveness), not equitable (some of our conditions fall under the disability act, NDIS, and other support systems that allow for additional accommodations and adjustments in the workplace and in society, for individuals who require extra support in place), sits outside of the ethics of human rights practices (Would you really want to be that mean to someone who is more than likely trying their damnedest to please you and achieve their highest output?)

I'm not trying to guilt trip you. I want to highlight the often-misplaced misconception that Managers have about individuals that appear to be 'not achieving', 'failing', ', not pulling their weight', when in fact they are actually neurodivergent and in the wrong working space, type of office, job role, or company.

I'd rather yours be the right company for them, than have you continuously losing employees, having a high ratio of sick leave accumulating for one or more staff members, and have an undermotivated, underwhelmed workforce.

Other Ways in Which Being NeuroDivergent May Influence Someone

The way our brains interpret space and location can be impacted by having a neurodivergent brain. For those of you who are interested, the front part of our brain includes the section that helps us coordinate voluntary movements, including walking and running. What does this have to do with your workplace environment? Well, if you have an office-space that is too crowded, or where the office furniture is not effectively separated and delineated, then individuals with neural variances that affect their motor skills may require some adjustments to where their desk is located or how far-away they sit from other desks. They may even need clear signposting to other sections of the building, as they may also have other parts of their skill-set affected.

Some individuals may appear to have challenges in forming and maintaining social relationships and/or in communicating "effectively" with their peers and colleagues. This is potentially due to the fact that they do not conform to the ways in which many of us were "taught", as children, to respond to social cues, in a reciprocal manner. Neurodiverse people are full of love, caring and compassion. Many people believe that they 'lack' dimensions of empathy, understanding and the ability to socially engage with others. If you have someone like this in your realm, it is problematic to fall under the spell of this way of thinking, as it then pre-determines behavioural patterns for your employees. Many neurodivergent individuals do find it challenging responding to pre-established 'social cues and social patterns of behaviours that non-neurodivergent or neurotypical individuals find relatively easy to 'follow'.

So, in relation to understanding and reacting to the feelings of others, for instance, you may notice that someone in your work teams is not joining in on "kitchen conversations" that occur every mid-morning break time. They also spend their lunchtime separate to everyone else.

It would be wrong to assume that they did not have social skills, or that they could not effectively communicate with their peers. It is more likely that their comfort zone is in talking 1-1 with individuals in their peer groups, and potentially in taking information absorbed within a larger group setting away with them, processing it, and then bringing it back to a later group catch-up, for conversation and further discussion, once they have fully considered and absorbed the information.

So, something as simple as a social conversation can appear to be a minefield for someone with neurodivergence, if they are not feeling comfortable within their environment.

The Retention, Recall and Formation of Memory

In relation to how each of our brains retains and form memories, just about every section of our brain takes on a function. Research has indicated that the front part of the brain (the frontal lobe) does play a vital role in forming long-term memories, though.

I can see your own brain considering the implications of this, in relation to the workplace.

Without the capacity to absorb information, accumulate that information in the correct part of the brain, and then store it effectively and efficiently (so that it can also be retrieved, at will) our brains could become ineffective, in a workplace context.

Some individuals with complex neurological variances are still able to utilise this process effectively. They just do it in a more lateral way than other people.

What does that mean for the workplace?

Sometimes, the way in which someone absorbs information, processes it, and also goes about retrieving it again may look complex, 'complicated', 'convoluted', even non-rational. And, I don't mean that in a derogatory sense, as I know that I may have appeared this way to others, in the past, and I am merely using their feedback here. You may have sensed this happening in your workplaces, too and not been able to rationalise what was occurring for your employee.

Although it looks as though the wheels may have fallen off, we do have solid strategies for continuing on with our day-to-day work.

It's just that our work processes don't "look the same", from the outside.

Our memory is in two basic parts (without complicating things too much). There is our Short-Term Memory [STM] and our Long-Term Memory. If we leave the LTM for now and just look at the STM, we can see why this part of our memory might affect how someone 'works' and the way that they go about their work, if they are neurodivergent.

Firstly, the part of our brain that deals with STM is located in the frontal Cortex, which is at the front of our heads. It is the bit that also deals with our central executive functions, like planning, scheduling, organising, complex reasoning, critical thinking, information processing and 'manipulation, problem-solving, prioritising, concentrating and focussing. In addition, it has a few other components. These are a kind of sketchpad- a visual-spatial sketchpad, in fact- which provides a 'sense' of the world via am imagery and sensory mode. This is often used to navigate through the world.

Another part of this cognitive system is a phonological 'loop', This can be speech perception or it can be, in which we receive information via 'chunks' of words (phonemes that our brain them tries to interpret and make sense of. These can be spoken words we hear others speak, via an auditory process; or, it can occur via speech production and the storage of verbal information. The final component is an episodic buffer zone, which basically captures snapshot moments (short-term memories) which are fleeting. They are then sent to our long-term memory, if significant enough for 'keeping'.

One of the things that can often have an impact on someone who is neurodivergent is that they can be challenged by initiating a task. Differences in the way a neurodivergent STM works is the reason for this.

In a very fundamental way, the visual sketchpad section of the STM is unable to 'visualise' the end product. This is an essential function of a neuro-normative brain's functionality.

However, in a neurodivergent brain, things work a little differently. For our brain, there is no ability to foresee the 'end product'. So, we have no point of reference of what "the end" might look like. If we have a blank slate, that is fine. However, if you, as our manager, want something specific, then you had better have given us specific instructions, or we will come up with something we have designed to meet our creative flair!

Because our brain is literally unable to conceive of what the "end product" looks like, not only can it not create or develop it, we cannot initiate the start of that process, either.

So, whenever we look like we are 'sitting around doing nothing', it is usually because we are trying to figure out what the end result looks like, and get a reference point in our mind's eye, so that we can get started. It is not because we do not want to do the work, or are lazy (as some mean-spirited people have been known to say to some people close to me).

Comparing, Classifying and Categorising Objects

There are times, in our working day or week, when we will have to utilise this skill of comparing, classifying and categorising objects. The brain's frontal lobe helps categorize and classify objects, in addition to distinguishing one item from another.

This is how we organise, prioritise and plan. These skills assist us with our executive functioning and higher order skills, as well. So, if I have difficulties in this area, then I may find that I am challenged further up the scale. Also, the challenge we have in this area could scupper anything else we need to do, further up the trail. For instance, If I can't put my daily tasks into a list of 'Order of importance" and then assess into Urgent, Non-urgent, and have to get done, but not urgent, by comparing, classifying, categorising them, then you (as my boss) are going to think that I am pretty crap at my job.

Remembering that this 'skill' is out of my control, if it is a neurological variation to my cognitive ability, it would be completely unfair of you to 'blame me' for not being able to achieve this.

However, so many managers do find this fault in their employees.

As an adult educator, it becomes pretty apparent when somebody is trying to learn something, as well! And, in the early stages of learning a new skill, process or task.

Reward-seeking, Reward Aversion Responses and Motivation

According to neuro-scientific research, most of our brain's dopamine-sensitive neurons are in the frontal lobe. Dopamine is a brain chemical that helps support feelings of reward and motivation. It is also commonly known as the 'happy hormone' by those who seek to replace it on a regular basis. You may know the feeling of a Dopamine release following a food 'high' (think chocolate, sweet foods, carbohydrates etc). Some people get this kind of high from exercise, being outdoors, doing creative things, taking part in their hobbies, etc. Dopamine is released when are pleasure receptors are activated. Without going into the technical details here, many of us seek to release Dopamine in some way, to stimulate our body's natural high. There is another hormone released.by the body, called Serotonin, which often goes along with Dopamine and another neurotransmitter called GABA, to stabilise our moods and keep our emotions regulated. It also works in conjunction with Melatonin to assist us in regulating our sleep hygiene and regulating our sleep patterns.

Why am I talking about hormones and chemical release in a book about the workplace and neurodiversity? Well, remember, this book is in relation to our workforce and in part, aims to explain why some of our employees think a little differently than other employees. Some of the factors we will cover will be in relation to environmental elements of the workplace, which you may have some control over, and other factors will be internal, and you will have limited control over why someone thinks the way they do, or communicates the way they do, or reaches out to another the way they do. However, you will be able to assist them in finding alternative methods, structures, and accommodations in the workplace that can make their working day much, much easier, and allow them to flow through their days without the previous challenges they may have faced due to their neurodivergent mind operating in a neuro-normative workplace (Old, school, unhelpful past employers who wouldn't be accommodating or listen to their employees perspective and try to find an alternative solution. You definitely don't want to be one of them!) (Stewart, 2013).

Self-regulation and Self-Management

For individuals who are neurodivergent, there is a heightened importance placed on establishing regular patterns and day-to-day routines that assist in regulating states of being, emotions and also psychological mindset. I could write a book on this!

Basically, we all need routine to some degree. This is heightened when someone is neurodivergent. The reason for this is that ND brains more often than not process the information in their world via a pathway of symbols, patterns and pre-established pathways. So, for instance, in the office, first thing in the morning, Joanna may have to check her emails before she 'starts' her day. If she is called away to an early morning, unexpected meeting, this may throw her whole day's 'pattern' out of kilter and place her into a tailspin. This is not because of anything other than her normal routine has been changed and she is unable to self-regulate against that routine, establishing a baseline for the day. It is the same as some people needing a gym visit prior to work, or having to walk to work via the river, otherwise they are not set up for their day and things don't flow as well as they might.

Due to the neural pathways that require this following of established routines and patterns, if someone doesn't follow them, and their other micro-processes to get their tasks completed, you will find that they may appear, or literally become, disorganised, seem discombobulated, and even appear distressed by the fact that they have not been able to participate in their established working day patterns.

Using Micro-processes

Micro-processes are a more refined way of pattern-making in our day-to-day routines. Not all of your neurodivergent employees will need to do this. However, if you see this in an employee, it is usually a sign that this is a vital part of their working "self" and it is also part of their own self-adjustment to a workplace environment. Micro-processes could come about in the form of breaking down what may appear to be a simple task to someone else, into a series of even smaller manageable chunks, so that your neurodivergent employee can achieve it with more ease and confidence. It could also have to do with complex muscle memory.

I'm going to use the following analogy, as it is a little like those of us who can touch type. We don't have to look at the key board as we know exactly where the keys are on the keyboard, as we've completed the task of typing so many times before. The micro-processes equate to the steps we take prior to actually engaging in the typing, so that our muscle memory can just take over. Our 'muscle memory' is also part of the outcome for establishing and following our micro-processes.

Back to our analogy about touch-typing, usually, we have also established a set of parameters for preparing to type. And, we need a certain level of requirements to do this. i.e. the keyboard has to be at a certain height, as does the computer screen. The keyboard must also be at a certain angle. Our wrists must be placed in a certain position on the desk/arm-rest. Then, we can start typing, utilising our muscle memory. If each micro-part of that task is not completed, then we won't be able to achieve our objective.

This is the same with micro-processes and the reason they are so important for many neurodivergent individuals.

The big key to this is when someone who is ND is interrupted whilst in the middle of their micro-processes, or when we are asked not to engage in our micro-processes. This is very disarming and can lead to emotional and psychological distress for your employee.

It is not what you want to happen, as a manager. And, it may be unexpected. You may not realise what has just happened, either.

This can be incredibly uncomfortable for your ND employee and also for you. It also means that the two of you need to talk about how you can offer further support to your employee, as it is a key indicator that your employee is not feeling as supported in the workplace as they need to be, in order to fulfill their workplace obligations.

Managing Focus and Attention

Let's talk about the brain again! When the frontal lobe (that's the part at the front of our head, just behind our forehead) is 'in charge', it helps us maintain attention, keep pace with the conversation, plan, schedule, concentrate on details, take on board complex instructions and many other things. And, it assists us with keeping on top of our tasks, including multi-tasking. If it cannot properly manage attention, then conditions, such as attention deficit disorder (ADHD), may develop. People with other health conditions can also have their frontal lobe capacity impaired, and some hormonal fluctuations can impair the capacity of this section of the brain to function correctly.

Some people may find that certain times of the day are better for multi-tasking than others, depending on when they are more chemically balanced. For instance, I have a friend who has Type 1 Diabetes. She is, in her own words, "fine" at work for approximately 2 hours upon arrival. So, from 8.30am until 10.30am, she is able to concentrate, focus on any given task at hand, and able to put her head down and complete what is in front of her. Her "worst time of day" is in the afternoon, from 2-4.30pm. This is also the time when her manager likes to pop her head around the door and place 'urgent' projects on my friend's desk. Her boss always wants these projects completed asap. It is a regular occurrence.

My friend has to take insulin several times a day, including just after her lunch. This impacts on her ability to concentrate for a couple of hours. She has no other way around this situation, as her Diabetes is a life-threatening condition requiring her to take the medication at a certain period throughout the day. This medication also impacts on her workplace rhythms.

My friend is quite distressed about the fact that her manager is starting to doubt her work performance, and says she is "not performing to standard". My friend is now on a warning from her manager, who has stated that if my friend does not improve her performance, she will be on a workplace Performance Management Plan. My friend has tried to talk with her manager and even stated that the situation is due to her Diabetes and blood sugar levels. Her boss has stated that she has Diabetes too, and that my friend needs to manage her health a little better, with her GP.

All of the above is true, in some context. However, for a more rigid workplace or manager, my friend is "not performing as expected/to standard" as she is being constrained by a set of expectations that require her to fit inside a box that has been established for employees who do not need accommodations for health conditions or the effects of hormonal or chemical changes caused by medications. Her manager is not enabling her to excel, fulfill her capacity as a worker, not work within the rhythm and flow of her own day. This in itself has thrown my friend and her successful working pattern (established over 11 years working for the same company, prior to this new manager coming in) into disarray.

Whilst I am not working form a medical model, I am stating that allowing your neurodivergent workforce to work to their strengths, throughout the day, within a particular rhythm and flow that is suitable to each staff member, depending on how their body and mind ebbs and flows with the day is far more equitable and fair than forcing everyone to have all of their email communication completed within 30 minutes in the morning, and not allowing any conversation until the mid-morning break, as it disrupts the flow of work within the office.

I have seen many managers undertake these kinds of rigid, inflexible and, at times, I would say pedantic, decisions in the workplace, without considering the impact on the individual and overall workforce. While it may work in the short-term, in relation to process driven, systematic workflow, or a specific task, it does not work for our neurodiverse working communities.

Sensory Seeking Employees and Sensory Aversion Employees

I know we have already explored this in relation to motivation. This is a more generalised view on sensory seeking. And sensory aversion.

By and large, neurodivergent individuals will have a preference for, or an aversion to, sensory stimulus, when trying to concentrate and focus on getting a task done. For some, they may appreciate stimulus when not having to focus on something that requires in-depth mental focus, but can be accomplished with 'muscle memory'. A little like turning up the music when you are doing the dishes or other kinds of household DIY or chores that we all have to get done, at some point. For others, no amount of external stimulus is going to be okay, no matter what kind of task they are completing. Whether it is something at home, research, or a workplace project.

So, for Frida, who loves to put her noise-cancelling headphones on to block out all external stimulus, and listen to classical music throughout her working day, audio stimulation is vital for the completion of tasks. She is a sensory seeker. However, she also needs to have a say in what kinds of external stimulus she has around her. She cannot concentrate with other external noise around her and found it very challenging to work in an open plan office, because of the constant interruptions from work colleagues, the conversations around her and the many phone calls happening all around her, all of which posed a n issue to her auditory processing disorder. When her manager gave her approval to have noise-cancelling headphones, her productivity went up in leaps and bounds, as did her job satisfaction.

Joe, on the other hand, cannot concentrate on completing his reports unless he is in a workspace completely devoid of noise and other distractions. If he is interrupted, he needs to go back to the beginning of his research and start again. He has sensory aversion. Joe can complete all of his customer service-based work in an open plan office, as he is a sales rep. however, when it comes to writing reports, he needs to undergo a series of microprocesses and finds it very challenging being in an open-plan space.

Neuronal Sensitivities

There are many ways in which neurodivergent individuals are unique in their own right. One of these is their 'differences' in neuronal sensitivity that arise as neurodivergence in and of itself is created due to an excess of neuronal pathways in the brain. This leads to heightened opportunities for neuronal connection and also for sensory input. In effect, this means that someone who is neurodivergent is responding to their world in a primarily sensory manner, rather than through their cognition. This, at times, can 'overload' or 'overwhelm' the sensory system and provide an overtly intense experience for the individual.

Without getting too technical or too scientific in explaining why, this hyper-sensitivity in the overall mind-body system can heighten emotional responses to the world, dampen cognitive responses through the 'shutdown of the pre-frontal cortex (preventing any executive functioning form occurring during sensory 'overwhelm' or intensive sensory or heightened emotional experiences. In research being conducted in the USA, studies have found that this sensitivity is indicated in an overconnectivity in some parts of the brain and also in lesser than usual connections in other parts of the brain (Kana & Maximo, 2019). They believe this may lead to differences in neuronal sensitivity to the external environment, patterns and styles of communication, heightened sensory processing functions.

These are involuntary experiences caused at a neuronal level and therefore out of the voluntary control of the individual. As the neuronal overwhelm is at a sensory level, translating these experiences into words is a 'learned skill' that not everyone acquires. It also takes quite a lot of self-awareness and self-reflection to be able to navigate through the nuances of sensation, senses, feelings and then be able to translate that into words and then articulate that to the outside world.

If the neurodivergent individual is able to do this, that is fine. However, the majority of individuals are unaware of their internal processes and it can take many years, if not a lifetime to understand oneself. Often-times, this is a challenge, at the best of times.

I have added this particular section here so that you can begin to get an understanding about why some of what is happening for your neurodivergent employee may not be visible to you. More often than not, it is an internal, and often involuntary process that is occurring.

You may see the outcome, the actions, the non-actions, the behaviours and the responses... the truly understand what is occurring, though, it is really important to understand what is happening and also why it is happening.

Sensory Sensitivities

For those neurodivergent employees with sensory sensitivities, at times, they may have a need to take some time out, away from the rest of their colleagues and be in quiet space, or be in the quiet zone, away from excess or excessive sensory stimulation.

There are many influences that this may have on your employee, which will be dependent on the individual and their condition. For some., it may be important to note that during these times when someone is feeling highly stimulated on this level, it often means that they are not able to easily or voluntarily able to communicate verbally. Some people may have situational inability to speak or communicate at all. Others may need to go to a different space and "process" before they are able to 'resolve' or articulate what they are thinking and/or feeling and be able to articulate this to others.

This is a feature that is present in many conditions and which is not readily discussed, that affects many individuals. Many people have adapted to their needs by developing their own workplace strategies that assist them in dealing with their sensory sensitivities. They may try to 'cover it up' in front of others, by saying that they are 'shy' or have 'anxiety', or address by offering to take meeting notes or complete other tasks that do not require them to speak during times when they may normally need to be more aware of their sensory sensitivities. Other people may require some support or accommodation in having something along the lines of a 'fidget' mechanism or accessory, which helps alleviate some of the internal stressors associated with this aspect of sensitivity in the system.

It is important to be mindful that it is not your role to suggest things. Only to be aware that these things may be occurring for your employee. Many individuals have not been able to effectively identify what is happening for a number of reasons. One of them may be that your employee may not be aware that they are neurodivergent, or be in the early stages of recognising this.

Let's have another look at the graph from earlier in the book.

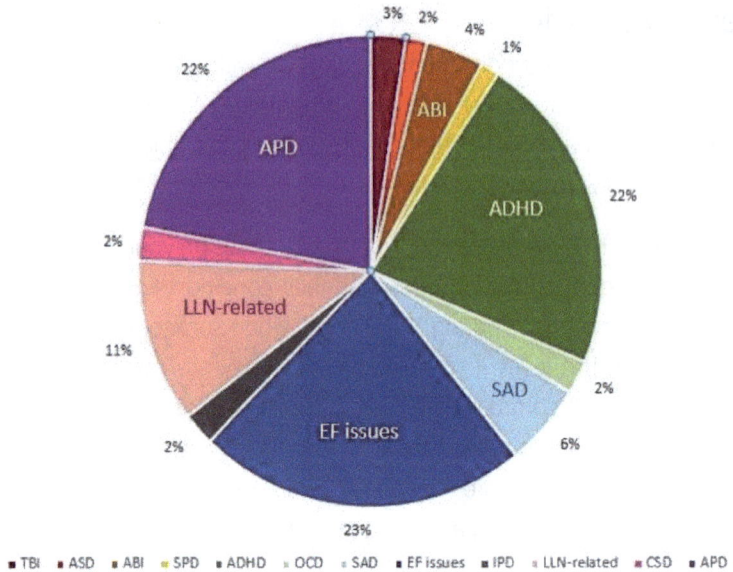

GRAPH- Executive Function /SPD/Communication/Social/Spatial needs

What drew my attention when I created this graph (which, you'll be interested to know, I only decided to do about half way through writing this book, as everything else was in tabular format) were three things:

1.   The impact that issues affecting language and literacy have on neurodivergence (shown on the pie graph as 'LLN'). For example: reading; writing conceptualising and being able to talk to, but not being able to" write things down on paper" not being able to articulate as effectively as communicate in other ways.

2.   The significance of Executive Function issues for people with neurodivergence. For example: planning; highly fluctuating concentration levels; not being able to recall from memory; differences in information processing times and duration/length; time management; the importance of visual cues; need for spatial (environmental), sensory and cognitive 'calming' mechanisms; significance of hyper-focus vs limited focus (or 'brain fog'); decision-making (especially in the moment); need to move about the office/not

stay still; needs for 'quiet' space; connection to neuro-ception (stress, anxiety, need for additional stimulus, survival responses, need for self-soothing strategies, individual , issues around 'safety' and feeling 'safe' in the workplace (raising a whole range of other issues for WH&S); individual appearing 'fragmented' if circumstance or issue not resolved

3. The effect of the audible world on a neurodivergent individual (seen here as 'APD'). Examples here include: a significant requirement for quiet space, otherwise they may not be capable of processing information, or relying on their senses and cognition to maintain their workload. In real-life terms., sounds, noise and general day-to-day open-space hustle and bustle may negatively impact on these employees' capacity to produce meaningful work whilst in an environment that is not conducive to them doing so.

From a management perspective, this is definitely something to keep in mind, as your employees may be coming to you with direct requests for accommodations relating to these environmental concerns, and/or their neurodivergent state or condition. It is important that you are able to acknowledge their need, but also that you can consolidate that within a real-time, statistical piece of evidence that asserts that these needs are firstly a human right, and secondly an integral workplace need so that your employee can fulfil their workplace obligations. Thirdly, by accommodating their needs, you benefit even more, as they will be able to produce at a better, faster, higher level, once they have their fundamental needs met.

General Influence of the Neurodivergent Brain on Someone's Working Capacity

In the 'right' environment, one where someone feels attuned to their environment, has their needs addressed, or is able to meet their own needs, and is feeling comfortable, safe, secure and cognitively, emotionally and environmentally 'regulated', there could be none.

In the 'wrong' environment, possibly surrounded by the 'wrong' kind of people (certainly not supportive and encouraging ones), and not in a place where one or more of those factors listed above were addressed, nurtured and facilitated.

I'm sure you've heard that saying:

"The fish tried for many years to learn to climb the tree until it realised that it was a fish, not a squirrel. Then it learnt to swim. And, it was free."

Our expectations of others, even in the workplace, are that everyone can climb a tree, because everyone has always done it. And, if they haven't been able to do it, we ask them to leave. Is that really fair and equitable for individuals who have a neurological difference, where their capacity, like the fish, is not for tree-climbing, but for swimming?

Why would we want to 'force' someone to do something that they weren't environmentally attuned for? Why would we put someone into an environment in which they would not 'fit' nor feel 'right' nor 'comfortable'. A literal, 'fish out of water'.

If we are being ethically adaptable and also implementing a more flexible mindset in relation to our business development model, wouldn't it be a better fit for our business to create at the very least a 'zone' where our 'fish' could swim? That would make more sense, right?

I'm not equating all of our neurodivergent employees to fish, either. Some of them may be birds, and be quite happy to come and spend some time in tat tree. Just not all of their working day. Others may be Giraffes, and more liable to use the tree for sustenance and nutrition, rather than as a structure that supported their work tasks. Others, again, may not even take a second glance at the tree, preferring to roam about in the fields and plains, being more self-determinant and autonomous. They are far more self-sufficient and don't need the tree as a space to support communication or sharing of business related 'stuff'. Are you seeing where I'm heading with this?

If we utilise the analogy of keeping a pet, we could not keep a puppy in a bird cage. It would just not be right! It is not the right environment and eventually the puppy would 'suffer' from your expectation that it could adapt to a maladaptive environment that was not suitable for her needs. Instead, you could use a 'cage for sleeping arrangement, and let the puppy out for the remainder of the day. Or, just not have a cage at all. I guess it depends on what kind of pet-owner you are, and what kind of puppy you have.

At the end of the day, a puppy requires certain things, certain space, certain comforts, certain environmental features that would allow it to thrive and grow and achieve its full potential. When it is thriving, you, as it's human, would then be able to get the most out of spending time with your pet, as she would be in optimum health and wellbeing, in a safe and comfortable and conducive environment that met her needs, and also you would be aware and acknowledge that she may have other needs in the future that you would be willing to accommodate, as her needs changed and shifted.

NB. I want to make clear that I am using the pet + environment analogy purely to discuss space and environmental impacts on different kinds of sentient beings, in the same way that different individuals may be impacted upon by their environment, even in the workplace. I want to emphasise that I am not equating people to animals.

SECTION THREE:

The Standard Working Environment vs the NeuroDivergent-friendly Office Environment

An Overview

As a Westernised Society...

In our Western societies, we repeatedly uphold those who utilise neoliberal ideologies that promote profitability and human capital as a 'tool' to achieve competitive advantage. In other parts of the world, business is operated in different ways, and supported via different mechanisms.

We favour globalised practices that enable us 'free-speech', global trade provisions and open markets. We want democratic societies that are based on a capitalist economy which provides economic advancement relief for business, such as tax relief and business support systems in time of crisis, such as the Australian JobKeeper system, during COVID-19 pandemic and the other economic response mechanisms put into place in the US and UK to mitigate economic crisis during the GFC and recent pandemic crisis. And, we want political and legal dispensation when we are required to enforce measures that are for the 'good of all', but not so pleasant for the every 'body'.

From a neurodivergent perspective, it is interesting how the world is designed to *not* meet the needs of lots of people. For instance, in our current society, we love to promote and celebrate people who have qualifications to "prove" that they can do what they have the experience and knowledge and skills to do. Remembering that I have a 4 year degree in adult and vocational education, so I am completely on board with need to evidence learning and progress in some manner, I want you to consider how someone who may have one or more of the complexities we've just discussed could move through an educational system that requires sitting down to concentrate for many hours, processing written information and only being assessed via an exam or some kind of assessment, be it cumulative or summative (that is, at the end of learning, or in stages, along the way).

This form of status and recognition is a form of 'elitism' and a power-based system that is attributed to a have or have not system. It's formed around merit and the ability to gain a piece of paper that says you can do something important. If you are able to produce and prove you can do/achieve   something,   then   you   can   have   the   'prize' (salary/job/award/recognition) at the end. If you cannot 'compete' with everyone else, on the same "playing field", usually paying a lot of money to do so, then you cannot 'win'.

If you cannot keep up, you cannot win. If you cannot compete, you cannot win. If you cannot achieve at the same level, you cannot win.

It is a ludicrous system that disadvantages and disempowers so many people. Those who are neurodiverse are just one collective.

If we are talking about diversity and inclusion, which we are, and this is where we are also talking about how to utilise our neurodivergent employees (who we now know think, feel, respond to the world and approach the world **differently** to our neurotypical staff) to enhance and even create a space for our productivity to flourish, then we are going to have to think of an alternative way to be able to work more effectively with this group. It is as simple as that!

You cannot expect someone who is responding in a different way to their environment, sensing, feeling and thinking about it and all of the stimulus, inputs and nuances that arise from it, in a completely different way, to then at the coal-face, 'do' things in exactly the same way as your other staff.

Of course, the outcomes can be the same. The benchmarks can be the same. However, the processes, systems and methods to achieve the outcomes need alternatives, potential accommodations and adjustments. The individuals need some accommodations. The procedures need some tweaking. And the attitudes, beliefs, assumptions, and biases of their peers, colleagues, managers and support people need to be optimised, so that they are supported as well as is possible, to achieve their full potential.

We just aren't very good at doing this, in the workplace.

Mainly because we haven't been taught how.

But also, because we haven't been shown the importance of the WHY...

Why is it so important for things to be done differently?

Why is it essential that someone who can't get a start on a project be supported to do so?

Why should I give someone a desk space in a quiet corner, when all of my other staff sit in an open plan office?

It is understanding WHY, on a macro level, and the rationale, from a policy level, down to and organisational level, to a workforce development level, into the office space level, into the workplace culture level and finally, to the interpersonal and personal level, that it will finally start to make some sense.

This full ecological perspective is the only real way forward.

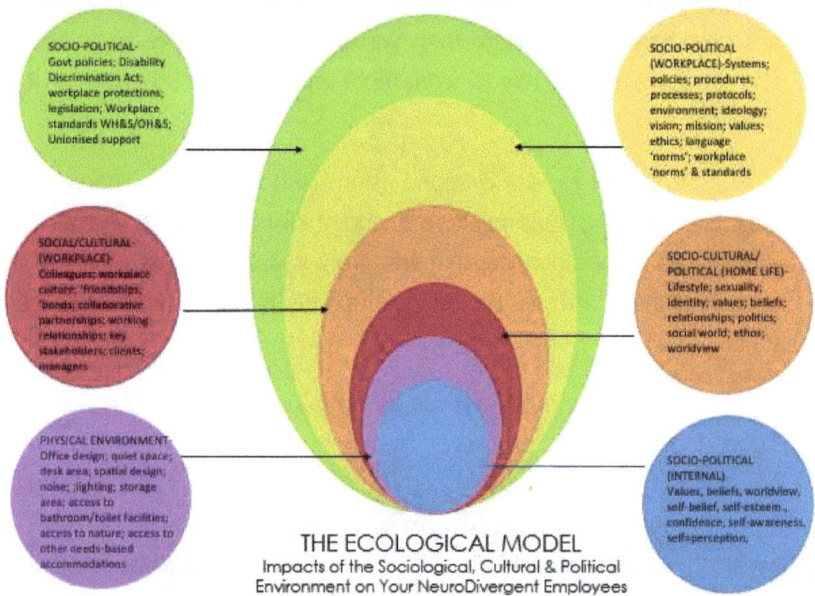

SOCIO-POLITICAL-
Govt policies; Disability
Discrimination Act;
workplace protections;
legislation; Workplace
standards WH&S/OH&S;
Unionised support

SOCIO-POLITICAL
(WORKPLACE)-Systems;
policies; procedures;
processes; protocols;
environment; ideology;
vision; mission; values;
ethics; language
'norms'; workplace
'norms' & standards

SOCIAL/CULTURAL-
(WORKPLACE)-
Colleagues; workplace
culture; 'friendships;
'bonds; collaborative
partnerships; working
relationships; key
stakeholders; clients;
managers

SOCIO-CULTURAL/
POLITICAL (HOME LIFE)-
Lifestyle; sexuality;
identity; values; beliefs;
relationships; politics;
social world; ethos;
worldview

PHYSICAL ENVIRONMENT-
Office design; quiet space;
desk area; spatial design;
noise; lighting; storage
area; access to
bathroom/toilet facilities;
access to nature; access to
other needs-based
accommodations

SOCIO-POLITICAL
(INTERNAL)
Values, beliefs, worldview,
self-belief, self-esteem,
confidence; self-awareness,
self-perception;

THE ECOLOGICAL MODEL
Impacts of the Sociological, Cultural & Political
Environment on Your NeuroDivergent Employees

The image of the Ecological Model shown above is only indicative of the many influencing factors that can impact on your neurodivergent employees, at each of those levels. We are primarily exploring the physical environment and some of the cultural workplace factors that may influence the implementation of management and leadership strategies.

It is a thought-provoking piece of background information to keep in place, when you are considering what may be happening 'behind-the-scenes' when you are considering where to next.

From a Workplace Perspective...

We have assumed that our spatial design infrastructure works well for 100% of the population, and we have perpetually replicated it in one of two ways: (a) in an Open Plan office design; which happens to be the most common office design globally, as we speak. It is also mirrored in the way we design our school rooms, our university and college spaces and also our homes.

Our only other alternative is: (b) to design something which has corridors and separate rooms. Which, whilst providing ample private space, does not invite collaborative working space, nor engender social mode working. And, we are bound to end up meeting less than the majority's needs, if we stick to one of two formats.

Also, during COVID times, with home-based working being a prominent feature of some more high-risk areas, some interesting phenomena has come to light: multiple people in an at-home working space has proven to be quite a 'tricky' situation. In my own home, more than two people, working at other ends of the house has been quite 'heady' and noisy. Even with doors shut at both ends, this has been an outstandingly frustrating situation!

So, how DO we sort out a situation that is going to work?

First, let's look at what the common, every-day garden variety of office space looks and feels like. Then, we will move into some unknown, or partially known territory, and explore some alternative that might be a better fit for you and your neurodivergent employees.

The 'Standard' Workplace Office
Who Makes Up Our General Desk-based Workforce?

Generally, this is a mixture of administrators and administration staff, developers, managerial and leadership, procurement staff, finance officers, research officers, training and development staff, banking and insurance staff, phone/desk-based customer service staff, call-centre staff, HR/HRM/HRD, and so on

From the list below, I have chosen Arts & Recreation, Education and Training, Public Administration and Safety, Administration and Support Services, Professional, Scientific and Technical Services, Rental, Hiring and Real Estate, Financial and Insurance, and finally, Information Media and Telecommunications as a reference point.

I have chosen these specifically as they are predominantly office-based. I appreciate that there are office-based workers in all of the other industries. I have chosen those above because they are predominantly office-based.

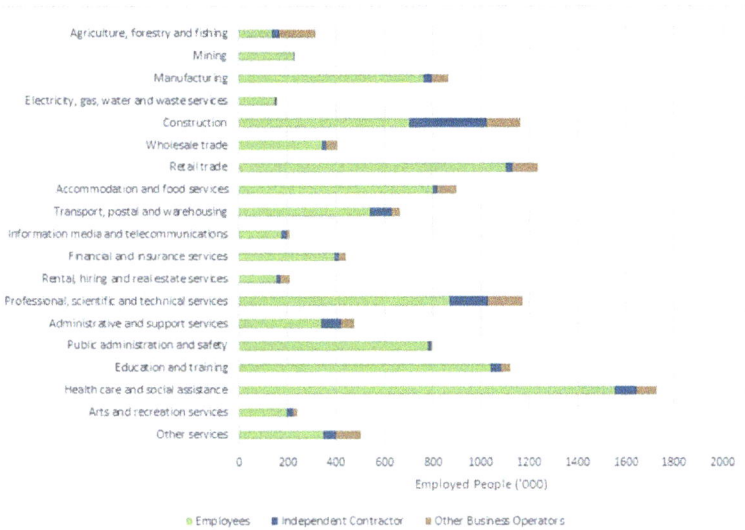

Agriculture, forestry and fishing		
Mining		
Manufacturing		
Electricity, gas, water and waste services		
Construction		
Wholesale trade		
Retail trade		
Accommodation and food services		
Transport, postal and warehousing		
Information media and telecommunications		
Financial and insurance services		
Rental, hiring and real estate services		
Professional, scientific and technical services		
Administrative and support services		
Public administration and safety		
Education and training		
Health care and social assistance		
Arts and recreation services		
Other services		

Employed People ('000): 0, 200, 400, 600, 800, 1000, 1200, 1400, 1600, 1800, 2000

Legend: Employees ■ Independent Contractor ■ Other Business Operators

SOURCE: ABS -6333.0 (2016)

NB: Figures are for Australia, only.

What Does the Working Environment Usually Look Like?

It's invariably noisy, loud, bright and busy! Whether we work in an office, in a factory, on the job, or on a worksite, our workplace is influenced by a number of key factors that are universal. These are:

- Workplace norms
- Cultural norms (organisational and also socio-cultural)
- Societal norms (national and universal societal norms)
- Legislative and WH&S/OH&S norms (state/county-wide and national/Federal laws and legislation; standards and regulations)

For instance, a 'workplace norm' at a recent workplace of mine was that everyone came and clocked on, signed in, and then went out of the office to the local coffee shop and got a coffee/tea/morning tea. This was because we usually worked through our morning tea break and had a late lunch, so our Senior Manager recognised the need to facilitate some flexibility around meeting our needs. Another fairly standard workplace norm I have noticed in the workplace is that of chatting or mingling in the tea/coffee/kitchen zone, when people are having a mini-break from work.

A 'cultural norm' that may be apparent is that of chipping in to buy a group birthday present for someone. Another may be that you go out for a drink and a chat after work, or have a meal on a regular basis, at a pub, restaurant or café, for lunch. A further norm may be that it is okay to complete development work at home, once a week, as long as it is approved with the Manager, prior to you doing it.

A 'societal norm' may be that everyone goes to work for a standard working week, from approximately 8.30am until 5pm Monday to Friday, unless they work shift work, work on-site or are in an industry where these are not the standard working hours, such as retail, hospitality or the medical field.

Finally, a legislative or WH&S norm may be that everyone has to report an accident or injury in the workplace when it occurs, in order to prevent further accidents, and to ensure effective WH&S strategies are implemented, recorded, reported and able to be improved upon. Another one might be that we need to be respectful to each other in the workplace and not exhibit any behaviours that indicate that we are bullying, harassing, intimidating or threatening another employee, or even our employer.

As employee of our organisations, we are all made aware of this, during our induction, and are asked to comply with working to the rules and guidelines of our workplace, including following policies and practices, standard systems and procedures.

This seems fairly self-explanatory to most and easy to comprehend and follow.

Or is it?

We all start work as bright, sensible, ready to work individuals, with a full capacity to get the job done. Right?

We've spent the past at least 11 years in the easy to manage school system, learning everything we can about reading and writing and numbers and how to surf the Internet and play online gaming hits and are now able to go forth and follow the instructions of our new boss.

How am I going here?

Of course, he, she or they will be easily, effectively, willingly and charismatically able to put into the correct language and context, everything we need to know to make our working life so much easier. Right?

Everything will fall into place and we will just breeze through our working life.

Simple.

Or, not.

What generally happens is that we feel completely overwhelmed by all of the documentation and paperwork we are asked to, first:

READ.

Secondly, ABSORB.

And, third, INTEGRATE.

All within the first few weeks. Usually within the first 1-2 weeks.

Finally, we are then asked to take all of our very cleverly designated "transferrable skills" and put them into practice in ways in which we never thought we'd ever be asked to do THAT particular thing! ... Creating even further confusion and a little bit of fear (that we never truly admit to anyone, because we might get the sack, on day three.

By Day 14, we "should really be getting the hang of it", and are asked to come to all sorts of meetings and events, and show our competence at tasks we didn't even remember putting on our resume, let alone saying we were GOOD at!

By Day 28, we are deemed to be 'fully competent' in what we have been employed to do, and at this point, are often asked to step up into higher roles, and even do tasks we've never done before.

FEAR away with you!! This is the land of the warrior!... You can do it!

Yes. *Of course* you can!

Given the right kind of environment, support, workplace ambience, team you have working with, for and about you.

And, if you don't, or are left at your desk for that couple of weeks, to "soak it all up" then you may find yourself in neurodivergent hellish waters!

The induction process can be very off-putting for many neurodivergent employees, for a whole raft of reasons, which you may be picking up on some points as we go along.

What Expectations Do We Generically Have in the Workplace?

I know that I want my employees to fulfill the expectation that I have set out for them, in their job description, right?

I also want them to be able to be productive and collaborative members of the "team".

I need them to be able to turn up on time every day, and to let me know if they can't and why that is.

I would like it if they stuck to the deadlines that I have established, so that we can all get on with things and meet our stakeholder commitments and service/distribution/project milestones.

Oh! And, I would love it if they could produce a little extra and show me how much they have to offer the organisations!

How does that sound, as a basic list?

I also have some other basic requirements, as a manager, as I'm sure you do. Because I work in an office-based environment, one of them is that my employees can communicate with me, in some way. The other is that they can take on board what I 'say' and provide me with what I am asking for, in a workplace context.

Many managers have an assumption that we can all read. That we all read everything that is sent/given to us. And, that we have the time, space and sensory/cognitive processing 'tools and environment to do this.

Another expectation that we have is that we all communicate with each other regularly, in exactly the same ways and confidently. This assumption that we all communicate in the same or similar ways is not correct, in relation to neurodivergent individuals.

A further assumption is that there are only limited ways of communicating. There is an unspoken assumption that we must all conform to a specific type of communicating, in order to 'process' information, and knowledge, in the workplace. As I have outlined in many examples so far, this is not the case with the majority of the neurodiverse community and may be a dangerous assumption to make with your neurodivergent employees.

This is a final expectation placed upon us in the workplace, that 'work' must be carried out in a standardised manner, in order for it to look 'productive' and efficient and streamlined. Of course, systems and processes have often been established in a standardised manner, to ensure streamlined processing and efficiency. I understand this, particularly from an IT perspective, as this has been my passion, across the years.

However, from a neurodivergent needs in the workplace level of consideration, this is also a 'dangerous state of play', as it places you in a potentially precarious situation, if you are adamant that there is no other way of doing things (than the standard model, system, process or procedure).

It is vital that you consider this in your business, as adaptability and flexibility of mindset, attitude, ability to make accommodations and be more 'fluid' will all hold you in good stead for other models of practice, such as innovation and leadership models, which we will talk about later. Any rigidity in this area will only flow on to those other areas and will potentially scupper your organisation's ability to address higher order needs to diversify, which has been a key challenge for organisations during the COVID-19 pandemic, and also to enable further innovation and creativity to be able to flow throughout the organisation.

As stated earlier, your neurodivergent employees, when fully supported, can be energised and utilised to propel your business forward in a way that injects your organisation with rocket fuel!

Common Mistakes and Organisation Makes When Thinking About Diversity and Inclusion

Organizations make two common mistakes in recruiting a diverse workforce that cause them to fall behind their competition and even lose market share.

1. "Company photo diversity"

The organization only considers the visible dimensions of diversity primarily race, and gender. The company photo looks good, but everyone thinks the same. Differences that include sexual orientation, geographic background, thinking and communication style, work function, ability and disability, religion, and work style are not valued and are even discouraged. This is a very narrow definition of diversity and offers little or no value to the organization in terms of new ideas, creativity and innovation.

We have just been discussing some of the elements and impacts of neurodiversity and also how these may impact on an individual if their working environment is not established in a way that is conducive to their neurotype.

How someone looks, is not the only way that 'diversity' can be represented in your organisation.

2. "Diversity by Numbers"

Again, diversity is defined by what you can see. Demographics reflect the outside community but it is only at the lower levels. (Production, and unskilled labour) There is limited, or no diversity, as you move up into management. When questioned about diversity in their organization, they point to all the numbers. Every year they have good "numbers", but the people are constantly changing. Employees leave and get jobs where there is a value of diversity at all levels and they are encouraged to move up in the ranks.

For instance, very few people who have ADHD are Senior Managers of an organisation (unless they are also owners of that same organisation). Furthermore, very few women who are neurodivergent, ever achieve a level of seniority in an organisation, unless it is their business (cited in Krzeminska, Austin, Bruyère & Hedley, 2019).

What Atmosphere Does This Create at Work?

A standard workplace provides for standard procedures, standard models of practice, standard practices and standardised and streamlined processes. Much of this is very warranted and positive.

However, in this contemporary and global business landscape, much of this standardised landscape is also becoming 'old school', ineffective, especially in the face of the unexpected (read- pandemic, or other out-of-the-blue events that may affect the global and national markets) and therefore, uninformed and unresourceful.

Flexibility in the system and the ability to 'go with the flow' and adapt to change are ley to being able to survive in the new global market.

Whilst the first part of this book has primarily been about the inclusion and utilisation of your neurodivergent workforce, the second section is about how you can utilise the skills of your neurodivergent human capital to place your organisation on a growth trajectory!

Let's Not Do it the Old-School Way

One of the areas that contemporary workplaces currently focus on is replicating the institutional model. That is (ref: images of school, work, house, society), that we establish a hierarchal structure in which we place the Manager at the top, or in the leadership position, and we then cascade everyone else down from that. The whole environment becomes and then stays a competitive space that is repetitively and continually replicated, more often than not, to the detriment of everyone. But, particularly to the more vulnerable employers, who are, in this case study, those who are neurodiverse (up to 14% of the population) and those with lower than is deemed workplace suitable levels of literacy, numeracy and critical thinking skills (43%+) (ABS, 2006).

Another thing that many managers forget is that, for people who can read, but still have challenges around reading (i.e. Those with low levels of literacy), more often than not, they will not be reading their emails, looking at written documents, referring to research that is online, or in large reports, and so on. This is not because they don't want to do so, it is part of their neurodiverse condition. For instance, they may have dyslexia, which is part of the reason they have not been able to acquire literacy skills as readily as someone else. They may have differences with their executive functioning, which mean that reading written pieces is not their preferred way of absorbing information. In fact, this is not about 'preference' at all. It is not a choice between whether someone wants to absorb information via books or movies. This is actually a factor in the way their brain is hard-wired. So, for some people, it is near on impossible to 'read' everything that is handed to them. If you are the kind of manager that enjoys writing extended emails to your staff, or providing intricate, detailed reports for them to read, then your neurodiverse staff members may not be able to take in the information you are presenting, in this way.

Similarly, I was just having a chat with a friend of mine in the publishing industry. We were chatting about some of the elements of my book, as it goes into pre-publication. She asked me what font I had chosen. I said, not even giving it a second thought, "Oh, definitely sans serif, as otherwise my neuro-kin (neurodivergent individuals) may not be able to read it". She was astonished and asked me why that is the case. I told her that fonts with "tail ends" on them make it much more challenging for people with Dyslexia, Dyspraxia, brain injury (TBI/ABI), those with migraines, people with ADHD/ADD and those with Autism. She said that was a huge surprise, as using a serif font (one with "tails" on) was the industry standard in the publishing and printing. This means that all books, by industry preference, are published in serif font. All magazines. All newspapers. All of everything that is in standard print (not bespoke printing) is published in serif font.

I hear you asking, "Okay, so how does this impact on my employees?". Well, imagine that you are sitting at a desk, completing your work and someone send you something to read. You have to read it by COB. It is a 16-page report on the state of your business finances and how you could encourage further productivity and growth within the business.

Seems like a normal day, right?

Except, the writing looks like this:

Wavy   Rivers   Ripple

SOURCE: White Rose Centre in Sheffield, UK

(I've blurred out the content) Are you having trouble reading it, in relation to how it is formatted?

Imagine trying to read a whole page like this? Or a book?

For someone with this condition, they may or may not know that you have a visual disturbance, Dyslexia, a learning challenge, or something called Irlen's Syndrome. They may never have had an assessment. However, that does not mean that you are not affected by the ways in which Dyslexia impacts on your ability to read. The issue is made even more uncomfortable by the fact that this document is entirely printed in Times New Roman. That is your Business Analyst's favourite font. That may also be your CEO's favourite font and your business branding standard. It is certainly the publishing industry's favourite font. Online publications are another matter, as online print tends to be in sans serif fonts which are much kinder on the neurodevelopmentally divergent mind.

In relation to reading something that appears to look like the 'wavy' font on the previous page, or alternatively the 'ripple' font. It is time for you to make a brief overview of your interpretation has come. You have not been able to make heads nor tails of the information in the report, as it is basically a muddle to you.

Does that mean you are not a capable and efficient employee? No. Does that mean you are not able to interpret that information? No. Does that mean, if you were given that information in an accessible way, you would be able to easily determine what was happening within the organisation and make some valid and timely recommendations? Of course!

However, you have a less than sympathetic manager who does not understand why you cannot interpret this report. It's your job, right?!

he wants to know what is happening. This is the third time you have been unable to report back to Senior Management on productivity. She is beginning to think they hired the wrong person for the role.

However, the Finance Manager notices what is going on. He comes over to ask you whether you would like him to read through it for you, so that you can "think about it together". As soon as he begins to get into the depth of the report, it becomes obvious what the answer is. Just hearing the information (instead of reading it) was the key for you. You took the information in straight away. The Finance Manager also prompted you with some financial forecasts bar charts and graphs. These visuals were just the extra prompt you needed.

So, what happened here was multi-faceted. Firstly, you have dyslexia and don't know it. Having Dyslexia means that some tasks are more challenging than others. However, that does not mean that you can't do them at all. It just means that you need to find an alternative way to do them, that works for you. Sometimes this will be about the environment (quiet space to read through written material); sometimes it will be about the resources provided (you were given written material to read, which really didn't work for you, especially as they were printed in Times New Roman. What worked so much better was hearing what had been written, verbally, and then backed up with visuals).

Some people know this as 'preferred learning style'. As an adult educator of almost 25 years, I know that the ways in which our brain absorbs information and processes it are not a chosen option. This happens involuntarily. People may be aware of their over-riding learning style, but it is a much more complex and complicated, nuanced framework that can make or break someone who is trying to learn something new, build on their previous knowledge and skills base, or process information that has just been given to them. This is particularly so when the information they have just received does not 'match' with the way their bran needs to process that information, as shown above.

So, remember to think about whether you are using serif font (with tails) or sans serif font (without tails). Font without tails is statistically easier to read, more able to be comprehended (more quickly), able to be read by a wider range of people (some people with learning challenges, Dyslexia, ADHD, brain injuries and Autism find that they can read Sans Serif but cannot read Serif fonts at all!... Even if it is exactly the same piece of writing (BDA, 2017).

Some other things to think about, in reference to font is, the swirlier the writing the 'twirlier' the mind! That is my own terminology for what happens inside my own mind when it gets convoluted or discombobulated! By that I mean, if you write something in handwriting or script, your neurodiverse employees may find it much more challenging to read and/or may not be able to read it at all. You may find that many people with issues that have affected their learning may be much more drawn to writing in all capital letters or all standard script (not handwriting). They may do this their whole life. I have family members that do this and were unaware that this was part of their neurodiversity until quite recently.

However, it did hold them back in the workplace, and they were unable to acquire a job in an office and could only find work in a factory. This was because their administration skills were not deemed to be 'up to scratch' and so they were stereotyped and neatly boxed into the 'too-hard basket' and told they could only ever 'work with their hands'. This is a story that many people who have a kinaesthetic (hands-on) learning style are told. On top of this, my family member has undiagnosed Dyslexia and ADHD. How do I know this? Many, many years teaching English skills to people with low levels of literacy.

When people are given the right 'tools' resources and environment to thrive, they will and they do.

My family member now reads prolifically (but only 'certain books'- those that are printed in Sans Serif font!). He writes in capital letters. He is challenged by paperwork, but does the basics. He is a kinaesthetic and auditory learner. He would rather listen to information than read it. He loves listening to Radio National and other radio talk shows on the radio, "because it is far less taxing on his brain", he says. He "always wanted someone to believe in him, but they all thought he was 'dumb'". He is not. He is a highly intelligent man. However, he was not given an opportunity to excel, in quite the ways he wanted to do so.

If I was his boss, I would have asked him what he needed. His needs would have been:

> Someone to explain things to him clearly and precisely, not leaving out any details
> Music or background information as a prompt or reminder of what he was asked to do
> Basic written instructions, in full detail
> A quiet space to work in
> An alternative to paperwork
> Demonstrations of new tasks (until he is able to pick them up himself)
> The ability to practice new tasks until he is proficient
> Praise and encouragement

Reframing What are Often Considered 'Bad Workplace Habits'

In this context, it's not so much 'bad habits', but routines, or standards that won't work for someone who is neurodivergent, and therefore, won't work for everyone.

Everyone suffers when the workplace is filled with routines that don't work, or with standards that don't make sense. These workplace 'bad habits' can make for an environment that is unfriendly, sometimes unreasonable, hard to navigate, unproductive, and even unsafe.

One core 'bad habit' that managers often have about their employees is that they know exactly what the office protocols are. For instance, it's the last Friday of the month, everyone else knows that this is when you put your timesheet in. It your last chance. Your neurodivergent employee has been told they must have it in by the 30th, at the latest. Today is only the 27th of the month. Monday is the 30th. So, she thinks it will be okay to put her timesheet in on Monday. It is electronic anyway, so it shouldn't matter too much.

However, she does not know that the office HR protocol is the 30th of the month or the last Friday of the month, which ever one falls first. For this reason, she misses out on her pay cycle.

She has done what she was asked to do. No-one gave her the extra information. Now she is having to face the consequences of not following unstated office protocols.

Her Manager believes this is because she is neurodivergent. It isn't. The HR Manager is aware that many people 'forget' to put their first timesheet in, due to this common mistake, so she has written it in the staff handbook for everyone to read.

However, it is only 2 weeks into the new staff member's employment and she hasn't been able to get through the whole Staff Handbook, yet.

Bad, workplace habit. And, potentially, something that may cause issues for both Managers and the employee, if assumptions continue to be made about access to information, retrieval of information from multiple places and so on. If there is no clearly defined approach to processes, employees may not be able to ascertain what is required and what the expectations are of them.

This is usually to do with communication expectations and communication streams, for neurodivergent employees, it is important to be very clear about what is required, when it is required, how it is required, and how often it is required.

HOW CAN WE DO IT DIFFERENTLY & SUPPORT OUR NEURODIVERGENT EMPLOYEES?

The Rejuvenated Workplace!

What Does it Look Like?

Neurodivergent employees only want a working space that is conducive to them being able to effectively and productively contribute to their working day and that enables them to achieve their workplace obligations.

We want to give back! We want to be productive! We want to be creative! And, most of all, we want to utilise our skills and knowledge and experience and experience to do all that we can to:

a) not get bored
b) be creative and innovative
c) stay occupied
d) be positively stimulated
e) make a contribution that has meaning and purpose
f) do meaningful work

g) be enabled in a way that doesn't overtly challenge us and make our brains and bodies work harder than they have to

h) drain our bodies, brains and very Souls!

Okay. That was dramatic.

I am trying to make a point though.

Imagine if every day, when you went out to work, you had to put on a wet blanket. Then, when you got to work, you had to dampen that blanket a little more. Then, before you sat down, you had to put on some headphones with amplified sizzling sounds that distracted you from concentrating on anything you had to focus on throughout the day. The, imagine that you had to sit in a room that was lit by 1000watt Halogen light bulbs every 10cms (I am emphasising this for a reason, please bear with me). The, imagine that you were sat in the entrance space of Central Station Sydney, at peak hour, with everybody walking directly past your desk.

Now, imagine that your manager came up to you and gave you a very important project that required your utmost concentration. It had to be completed in 2 hours.

Imagine you only had thick crayons and butcher's paper to complete a presentation to the Board of Directors. At your desk. In the middle of Central Station. Being completely distracted and unable to concentrate. At peak hour. With Halogen Lights glaring down on you. With sizzle sounds distracting you for hours. And, a soggy wet blanket over your shoulders.

Is it comfortable?

No.

Is fair to expect you to complete your tasks while under duress?

No.

Is it right that you are asked to be 'productive while in a state of stress, distress, anxiety and unable to concentrate?

No.

THIS is what we ask of our neurodivergent employees every day, whenever their workspace and the overall workplace environment and workplace culture is not conducive to them working 'well' within it.

It is near on impossible!

And, it is not only unfair but also unjust.

So, how could be deconstruct the work space to create a more 'sound', harmonious and beneficial space to work in?

We will have a look at the space feels in a moment.

Before that, lets recap on some cutting-edge ideas.

Firstly, utilising more residential style furnishings and office design can make your workplace more appealing and flexible, incorporating innovative design, a positive workplace culture, higher levels of productivity and positively impacting on staff retention and profitability.

Introducing 'nap pods' for staff who require break time' during working hours, such as those with auto0immune conditions, or who are feeding babies,; mobile work spaces to accommodate both focussed work and also collaborative work; private space that can be regularly used and booked for long periods of time, for individuals who require extensive concentration time; are all factors that can make the working environment more palatable and comfortable for the neurodivergent employee (Liu, 2020; O'Regan, 2020b).

What Does it Feel Like?

A 'feeling', in this context, is about the atmosphere, the sense you get when you walk into the office. How a space resonates. Does it feel alive? Energised? Calm? Serene? Dynamic? "Busy"? Productive?

The next thing to consider is how we might reframe the attitudes, misguided beliefs, unconscious biases, perceptions, assumptions of our other employees.

Even we, as managers, team leaders and business owners may have these.

We are working under the assumption that everyone is a human being.

This book is framed around human rights, social justice and supporting everyone in our workplaces to be able to excel and achieve to their full capacity and capabilities.

Just as with any other 'category' of diversity, neurodiversity is an area that is often misunderstood. People will and do make judgements about people who are neurodivergent.

It is sad, but the statistics tell us that more than 60% of all adults in Australia who identify on the Autism Spectrum are not in full-time employment. Research completed by agencies in other countries, such as the UK indicate that this is often due to the fact that potential employees cannot get across the threshold of organisations. i.e. their on-boarding systems., processes and procedures are designed to exclude neurodivergent people. In addition, if they do find employment, either the workplace is not well-suited to their working style or patterns, or they have found that their peers' attitudes and assumptions about them can be harsh, at best and discriminatory, at worst (NEISR, 2018).

This is a very unfortunate indication that other colleagues' attitudes, beliefs, unconscious biases and behaviours towards neurodivergent employees can make or break someone's workplace experience.

By ensuring that your workplace is one in which there is understanding, sharing of experiences, an acknowledgement that difference and diversity of all kinds are welcomed and celebrated, you are creating and open space for neurodiversity to flourish in your workplace.

Taking it one step further, creating innovative practices and ensuring that your employees do cultural practices training that is more than a 1 hour 'organisational culture' or 'diversity and inclusion' introduction, but includes an intensive on neurodiversity and what it means to not only tolerate difference, but also accept, celebrate and even applaud, highlight, emphasise and illuminate the strengths and benefits of difference and diversity in systems, processes, methods, innovation, thinking styles and applications, so that the whole organisation gets on board and becomes one large powerhouse of innovation!

There really is no point in just being tokenistic about how you explore and apply your awareness and knowledge about diversity and inclusion.

When you are looking at ways to utilise your neurodivergent workforce, they can truly become your organisational engine room! It would be such a shame to allow other employees attitudes, beliefs, unconscious bias and limiting beliefs about your neurodivergent employees' capabilities, capacity, knowledge, skills, expertise, specialist skills, experience and creativity to hold them, your organisation or your profitability back.

Even a simple solution such as implementing workplace mentoring and coaching programs could provide peer to peer support that will enable new or incoming neurodivergent employees a 'safe' stable and secure space to be able to be and talk about any issues arising with someone who has been there and done that, earlier in their time with the organisation (O'Regan, 2003; O'Regan2006).

This is why addressing your workplace culture is so important!

How Do Your NeuroDivergent (Future) Employees Find You?

The first step is always going to be, let more neurodivergent people through the door.

If they have the skills, knowledge and capacity to "do the job", why is it that more than half of the adult neurodivergent population is not working full-time? According to the NIESR Report (2016), many have said that part of the reason is due to previous "bad experiences" in the workplace, or a belief, based on others perceptions of them as 'bad workers' that has challenged their own perceptions of themselves. Others have clearly stated that they have not been able to pass through the recruitment and induction process, as it has been geared towards their more neuro-typical colleagues, and as such, they have been 'rejected' in the process.

Organisations such as SAP, in the UK, and the Department of Health and Human services, Victoria, Australia, have found that amending their recruitment procedures and having a non-interviewing process has eased some of the tensions created by a usually high-anxiety, low neurodivergent-retention process, such as the apply-interview-face-to-face assessment-on-boarding process normally undertaken by an organisation.

Other organisations have taken a more flexible approach to recruitment and on-boarding, and utilised a more free-flowing, elongated and non-intrusive recruitment process, that enables the key team leaders to assess and recruit staff via a week or fortnight long 'placement' process, where the future employee can be observed in-situ, can work with colleagues and complete tasks, all while taking part in the workplace. At the end of this period, the on-boarding arrangement is progressed, if the organisation is satisfied with the employee's progress throughout the week. This reduces anxiety, 'normalises' activities and tasks, and enables key senior members of staff to observe and evaluate performance without the added pressure of a face-to-face interview and obstacles that may arise for individuals who have a range of neurological variances.

Recruiting a NeuroDiverse Workforce

To be a successful business in today's culture you need to create an environment of inclusion where people feel valued and integrated into a company's mission, vision and business strategy at all levels. When employees' skills and knowledge are recognized, appreciated and utilized they are more engaged in contributing to an organizations' success. They are more willing to go the 'extra mile' and share ideas and innovation. The visible and invisible dimensions of diversity that they bring are used as resources for success and growth. In order to create an inclusive work environment, you need a diverse workforce. This includes individuals who are neurodivergent, from all different types of neurodiversity.

Australia's *Department of Human Services* (DHS) has recruited neurodivergent staff via alternative recruitment pathways and this is working successfully. It is inspiring to read the organisation's neurodiverse testing teams are 30% more productive than the others. Inspired by the successes at DHS, the Australian Defence Department is now working to develop a neurodiversity program in cybersecurity, utilising the specialised skills of their neurodivergent staff to combat inline security issues (Austin & Pisano, 2017).

Induction

One area we haven't fully covered yet is that of 'induction'. Many HR departments these days have decided that the online, 2hour, short-version course is the preferred option for induction sequences. I have no problem with that, for the most part. However, there is a danger of believing that a one-size-fits-all approach is the simplest and easiest method of accommodating all needs. Which can be a little bit like that old saying of putting the cart before the horse.

You see, for someone who is neurodivergent and asked to sit through a week or two of desk-based, screen-oriented, two-hour long training videos, one after another. And, then read policy documents, one after another, either in a paper-based format, or online, it can be a very demotivating, let alone overwhelming experience. It can also trigger migraines, executive function issues and all sorts of things we've been discussing over the last few sections of the book.

Some organisations have taken an innovative approach to induction training and started to include video-game-like, interactive training which is inclusive and allows the employees to engage with the training, learning new things and also have the ability to go back and try out different answers. This is a much more fun and conducive way of (a) learning, and also(b) inviting your new neurodivergent employees into your organisation in a fun and friendly manner.

Adding Value to the Workplace

As we have already discussed, people who are neurodivergent have many skills, talents, perspectives, knowledge and capabilities that can be highly beneficial in many work environments. Their skill-sets and knowledge may even provide your organisation with just the competitive advantage you've been looking for!

Although you may have to re-evaluate and review some of your recruitment and on-boarding processes, hiring neurodivergent employees can be highly rewarding. The cultural benefits to your organisation can include:

-Neurodiverse employees helping your business build effectiveness and diversify, encourage broader levels of cultural diversity and understanding of different ways of thinking and doing work!

-Diversity of all kinds

-Contributions to R&D, creativity within the organisation, input into innovation processes, and competitive advantage, as they share their unique and diverse perspectives and points of view with the team and the whole workforce

- An untapped pool of potential, skillsets and talent to help fill the skills gap and supply more specialised knowledge and skills to in-demand skills-based and specialised knowledge business streams

-A heterogenous way of thinking that can only enhance your innovation systems and processes

- A strong set of creative thinking skills, problem-solving and spatial reasoning capabilities, that enable them to resolve issues with a level of adeptness and lateral thinking that is unique.

GETTING IT RIGHT ONCE THEY'RE ON-BOARD

Questions to Ask Your Management Team (and Staff) When Developing or Redesigning Workspace

What is Workspace to You?
It may be a combination of the following:
- Physical space
- Creating an atmosphere
- The whole physical environment includes: lighting, windows, open plan, closed in offices, access to libraries/resources/references, seating, tables, desks, storage...
- Colour
- Design
- Furniture
- Comfort
- "Squidginess" (for those who love soft lighting, cushions and a more tactile experience)
- Lighting, desk-lamps, back-lighting, computer filters...
- Noise, music, soothing sounds, meditation opportunities, Theta waves
- Use of natural light
- Personal space
- Personal storage
- Desk space
- Collaborative space
- Quiet space
- Meeting space
- The Hierarchy of Status within the office (that is, where does the Senior Manager/Manager sit in relation to everyone else?)
- Chairs

- Footstools
- Paintings/posters on the walls
- Access to facilities
- Proximity to nature

They are just some of the things I could think of. Workspace for you and your organisation may be so much more!

The key is, that without a place to feel comfortable, physically and emotionally safe, when we are at work, we will not become and sustain our productivity, if we are not able to access our basic workplace needs, our safety needs and our emotional needs.

Restructuring the Environment for Optimum Productivity

OFFICE ITEM	MINIMUM COMFORT ZONES	OPTIMUM COMFORT ZONE
Desk	Standard height desk with adjustable computer height rest/arm	Fully adjustable; able to work at 'desk' of choice/from home or other flexible location/flexible working locations/work-from-home policy in place
Chair	Adjustable height and neck rest; ability for employee to have leg rest and cushion for back support	Fully adjustable; back rest adjustable; padded chair and back-rest; arm-rests; ability for employee to have leg rest and cushion for back support
Lighting (fluorescent)	Every second light off' filtered; *Lumens* checked (WorkSafe/WorkCover checked and verified)	Fully filtered; no fluorescent lighting at all; leave the lighting off when not required
Lighting (non-fluorescent)	Utilise 'warm' lighting, not 'cold' lighting globes	Utilise lamps and backlit computer screens with filters over screens to reduce EMS emissions

Noise (talking)	No on-going 'chatting' near desks in open plan offices	Designated 'chat zones'
Noise (phone calls)	Partitions to block noise and maintain privacy	Maximum number of desks per room or separate offices
Noise (photocopier/ equipment)	At the beginning or end of office; in the kitchen; in the store room	In its own room, separate to all desks and office space
Placement/ Positioning	End of row; against a wall, near a window; out of walkway area; next to the quiet zone; away from noisy equipment	Own office/space; back against the wall; in the quiet zone; away from noisy equipment; position staff at the quiet end of the office, away from all noise.
*The Quiet Zone	Quiet zone (to be booked)	Dedicated quiet room
	This is incredibly important for neurodiverse employees who need space and an environment to be able to concentrate and/or focus on their work. It is also vital for those individuals who are highly sensitive to sound and distractions, generally.	
**Extra Working Space (for stretching out and taking over the table/desk/room)	This could be a booked space or a dedicated space. This is at the discretion of your business. For individuals with neurodivergent ways of thinking, if you require them to think outside the box, be creative, think laterally, utilise their non-sequential, non-systematic, innovative thought-processes, sometimes (maybe a lot of the time) they may need to utilise extra space to stretch out and "think".	
***Special Considerations	Distractions and interruptions minimised by set timelines and break patterns i.e. Zone A = quiet zone, no interruptions for people working there Zone B= chats available and collaborative work zone.	
Equipment	Some offices have other equipment in them that is noisy, like printers, shredders, even IT hub rooms can be "noisy" to someone who has highly sensitive Sensory Processing Disorders (SPD) or is wearing hearing aids that are digitally attuned to pick up even the most minute of sounds. etc.	

Sensory Needs	These are outlined in other categories and vary depending on the individual. It could involve extra time to complete some elements of their workload, or time expansion for specific tasks.
Open Plan Constraints	Open plan offices are notorious for being 'loved' by managers. This is especially the case for neurodiverse employees, who will find an open plan office a working nightmare, if they are sensory-heightened, have executive planning issues that are influenced by high levels of distraction, noise and interruptions. And, individuals who are more sensitive to changes in their immediate environment, which may challenge their ability to concentrate or focus, will also not be comfortable with an open plan space, day-to-day.
Other	It may be that your ND employees can work collaboratively for parts of their projects, or tap into each other as resources, such as having a mentor or support person. There may be a need to have noise-cancelling head-phones, or parts of the day where specific music is played to stimulate the brain. Or, other parts of the day where your employee can engage in deep-focus work in complete silence. Your employee may need to develop a series of 'micro-processes' that work for them, in enabling them to complete their work more efficiently, in a timely way, or in a more structured or organised manner. You may want a communication flow-chart established, so that you and your employee are both aware of communication requirements, noting when and how you would like it to occur, when it is optimum, compulsory and when it is okay to have communication be ad-hoc. This will assist with planning and sequencing tasks as well as checking in with milestone achievement etc.

TABLE: Adaptations for the Office-based Environment

Personally, in relation to stretching space, this has been a bug-bear for some of my own employers, in the past. They haven't quite understood why I have needed to 'get creative' when I develop and design training, presentations, write conference workshops, prepare for teaching and learning opportunities, co-ordinate training events, write articles and so on. I know some of you will be appalled at this, but my desk is often perceived as "a mess"! To me, it is an ensemble of creativity and innovation in action. If someone moves something on my desk while I am in the middle of 'creating', it will often mess up my thought flow and also the way in which the project was heading.

This may make no sense to you, as a manager, to someone who has a "high level" of tidiness as their key objective for their end-of-the-day desk. It has great meaning for me, as my desk is an external representation of the internal working of my mind. Wherever I have left something on my desk is where it is positioned in my mind, and so, when I come back to it next, I can "find it" again, as I know where I have "left it" in my mind.

It doesn't work this way for everyone who is neurodivergent, but we all have similar things that will make us feel uncomfortable and will also have us feeling less challenged and stressed.

For instance, in relation to the stretching space I mentioned above, I love it when my workplaces have a zone where I have a large desk I can book out for a couple of hours, where I can shut a blind, so that I won't get distracted, where it is large enough that I can invite others, if I need to do so, and where I can concentrate, as it is a quiet zone, away from noisy office areas. I also think quite vividly, and in colour. I love to put my thoughts down on paper, in symbols, on large pieces of paper! That's my thing. It doesn't 'suit' every boss I've ever had. In fact, some have called me "childish", "too animated", "not cognitive enough" (HOK, 2020; Liu, 2020).

At the end of the day, it's the way I have to get my big, innovative, development thoughts out. If you're are my boss and you want me to develop training (cos that what I really get a kick out of doing!) then this is how I will do it. If it really gets in your face, I will do it at home. But, that's not really fair to me, is it? Making me take my work home, because 'my way' of working doesn't meet with your neuro-typical standards? That is a form of discrimination. It is discriminating against me because I do this because I have a TBI. And, most probably, because I have Sensory Processing Disorders and Executive Functioning stuff going on, too. It's an interesting mix! But I have figured out a way to do great work, in my own way.

Mapping Your NeuroDivergent Staff Member's Journey Through Your Newly Improved Office

Firstly, let me say that the newmodel of workplace may look very different when we return to our workplaces. We may have more flexible working arrangements, more adaptable workspaces and more equitable, recognition of employee needs in the workplace. This is not assured though.

I would like to invite you to consider how your workplace might be redesigned to look or feel a little different, more inviting, more accommodating, more inclusive, more welcoming and more energised by the diversity of your whole workforce team! As well as the innovative and collaborative nature of your neurodiverse employees.

We have been talking about how neurodiverse people might be influenced and challenged by their neurodiversity. We have talked about their strengths and gifts and what they can bring to the workplace that might offer you, as their boss or Manager, something a little different to your standard employee. We have chatted about how individual employees with neurodiverse needs might require something slightly different from you and your organisation that you may not have been asked to provide or accommodate before. I hope that you can see that this is not unusual in our social world, so why would it be any different in our workplaces?

I want you to consider your employees as a part of the unique infrastructure of your business. Without the 'right' employees, your business will not function correctly. We all know that, right? Have you ever thought about how utilising laser focus to specifically focus on an area that requires development, co-ordination or management and (implementing) a person who has hose specific skills (not just skills sets, but, now that you are aware that our neurodiverse communities can apply themselves in certain ways that enable them to, for instance, utilise their numerical skills, their lateral thinking skills, collaborate in more creative and innovative ways and utilise their laser focus to develop, design, investigate, analyse and evaluate your business, you may find some very unique positions and roles for them.

In fact, I was just reading about a unique program being run by the State government, utilising the talents of Autistic people (I am purposefully using Identity First Language (IFL), as it is a growing preference within the ASD/Autism community) to deliver business objectives and outcomes. This is a real positive for our Australian community, that has been replicated in both the UK, for instance, with GOOGLE UK taking on board a whole team of individuals with ASD/ASC/Autism to fulfill a specific role and utilise their unique skill sets. And, in the Silicon Valley, with many IT companies utilising the benefits of the same neuro-kin to roll-out IT projects across the country and globally.

It is very exciting times indeed!

And, by supporting your workforce in this way, they can become one of your most valuable assets!

It all starts with their environment and the atmosphere that they work within.

Whole this is true for every employee, the neuro-cognitive sensitivity of our neurodivergent employees is heightened and therefore more attuned to any nuances that may occur. This puts them in a more highly responsive space.

What does this mean in real, every-day terms?

If something is a little 'off", they'll have a more challenging time adjusting to it. And, the more time they spent trying to adjust to something that is creating a challenge to them, the less time they will be able to focus on getting the work done for you.

So, it is in your best interests to ensure that they are as comfortable as is in your power (I'm not asking you to go overboard here), however, you yourself know that if you were asked to hunker down and get your work done in a cold, drafty hallway, with people walking past your feet every two minutes, and lour music blaring in your ear, it would be a little uncomfortable. This is how it feels every day for someone who is neurodiverse. Just in different ways. Many of which we have chatted through in some of our real-life case studies, as we've been moving through this book.

What I want to do now is look at the 'status quo' compared to minimum 'comfort zones' and options for 'optimum comfort zones' for your neurodiverse workforce. If you could only manage minimum level comfort zones, and that still requires a step up from where you are right now, good on you for giving it a go! I'm sure the neuro-kin around you will appreciate your efforts.

Remember that the more you are able to accommodate the needs of our neurodiverse workforce, the more they will be able to settle into their work, feel 'comfortable (on a sensory, cognitive and psychological level... hopefully leading to all round health and wellbeing in the workplace for everyone concerned).

If we can get your BUSINESS to this point, THIS is where you will start to see *an increase in the following:*

→ROI

→Productivity

→Innovation

→Profitability

→Staff job satisfaction

→Staff retention

→Development of innovative practice

→Increased internal leadership modelling

→" High conforming" employees (those that do what they're asked and a little more, if they know it will lead to something even more beneficial for their organisation, project, team, selves)

And, a decrease in:

→ Staff sick leave

→ Performance Management Plans

→ Disruptive management practices

→ " Low-conforming" employees (those that just do the minimum and then leave for the day)   (Mellifont, 2019)

So, what does it take?

Thinking "Outside-the-Box"

This is not just about "thinking outside the box". It is more about a way of thinking that is unique to the individual. Neurodiversity may be a part of the individual's experience due to a difference in the way they think, an injury, a different way of learning of learning, unique learning style and/or condition related to a Sensory Processing 'Disorder'. People who don't have inherent neurodiversity can also think diversely, creatively, or innovatively, it then becomes a matter of preference or choice rather than an involuntary cognitive process.

Becoming an avid enthusiast of 'thinking outside the box' has been my life's mission! I love to do it and it also brings me a great deal of personal and professional pleasure, as it stimulates my creativity and expression. In a business sense, thinking outside the box, in reference to neurodiversity can enable a manager and/or an organisation to become more innovative with their resources, people, teams and ideas and implement new ways of doing things with greater ease and flexibility.

SECTION FOUR:
Redefining Your Workforce and Workplace Culture

Inclusion, Neurodiversity, NeuroDivergent Employees and My Organisation- Why Is It So Important?

The crux of the matter is that neurodiversity is another facet of diversity. We are well versed, or getting better at, representing our organisational diversity by promoting inclusion via supporting the inclusion and diversity of multicultural internal communities, including Culturally and Linguistically Diverse (CALD) community, through our LGBTIQA+ programs, showing our Rainbow Flag, by promoting and celebrating our Indigenous and First Nations Peoples, within our organisations. We can champion women in leadership roles. And, we have been working hard on parenting policies that have secured Parental Leave for both parents, post-childbirth, and Adoption Leave.

As you can see from everything we've talked about so far, the neurodivergent employee can have a positive and impactful influence on both their personal work-stream as well as collaborative workstreams; ultimately tapping into whole-organisation workflow, productivity and profitability.

However, in relation to neurodiversity and neurodivergence, although these variants are well-represented in society, they are not as well represented, nor accommodated in our workplaces, schools and other institutions.

There are many reasons for this, some political, some sociological and some socio-cultural. There is not time nor space to cover them all here. Suffice to say that there are systemic and structural inequalities for people who are part of the broader neurodiverse population and these are 'played out' in our other social 'norms' and institutions.

So, by that I mean that the world 'we' create is modelled on what 'we' think is 'right' based on what we are told/shown is 'right' by the people around us. They could be our family and loved ones, at an early age. Our peers and work environment, as we enter adulthood, and may eventually be influenced by economic and political nuances and preferences that underpin our beliefs, values, attitudes towards what happens in the world we live in and our opinions, assumptions, judgements and interpretations of it.

If we are told that there is only 'one way of doing something', then that is what we will believe (at least for an initial period of time). If we are told that everyone thinks the same way, then we will think this too, unless we delve deeper and do some research, or get to know someone who doesn't 'think the same way' as we do.

I am simplifying things dramatically here, to get my point across.

In essence, I am stating that we often believe we have 'done everything we can' do accommodate someone' or their needs, or their 'degree/form/variant of 'diversity', when more often than not, we haven't even scratched the surface.

And, as Managers, and in our people leadership, this is where we are coming undone.

At best, we are following the lead of someone else and modelling what others are doing, in order to 'fit in', conform, 'do better', 'try their way' or 'create something new'.

We do this all the time in business!

I have been talking a lot about neurodivergence, your employees and inclusivity. I have put inclusivity and innovation in the title of this book. Not through any mistake on my part, but because I want to know that you are a part of this process of innovation and creating a fully unique and inclusive program, working environment and sanctuary, not only for your neurodivergent employees, but for everyone in your realm.

Innovation starts with you. And, with our willingness to take on a new mindset, a new frame of reference, and a new(er) business model that provides a more cohesive way forward, that energises everyone inside of it, ad that empowers your workforce.

In this context, it is time to step up and become a pioneer and champion the neurodivergent employees you have, and support them in achieving their optimum potential, within your organisation, so that they can give you the very best of themselves.

That way, you will be able to start the process of pivoting, re-engaging, restructuring (if that is where you are heading), diversifying and innovation, that I am proposing for you, here.

What Does NeuroDivergence Look Like in Real-Time?

Firstly, there is no "look" as far as a person is concerned. There are some ways in which we can see how neurodivergence may impact on individual employees, in the many ways in which they need to alter or adjust their work practices, so that they can fulfil their work tasks in any given day. That is what I mean here, in the context of 'what does it "look" like.

There are as many examples I could give, as the ways in which someone's environment impacts on them. They are wide and varied.

We have already been talking about some of them in the anecdotes and case studies, above. All of these 'stories' are based on real-life examples. However, for privacy, I have changed names and not given any identifying details.

I wanted to make these representative examples as true to life as possible. They have come from real-life people living in 7 Western countries, including Australia. Their stories span more than 40 years. The majority of them have been representative of the past 20 years.

I know that workplaces have made a lot of changes in this time, in relation to diversity and inclusion, in relation to disability support and also in relation to accommodations and adjustments for employees who have asked for them.

It is impressive, but we are not quite there yet!

This book hoped that you will take the time to consider even further, what can be done.

Let's just take one set of examples: sensory sensitivities. These are involuntary and can vary from day to day, even hour to hour, in some cases. They can be influenced by: cognitive differences, blood sugars, hormones, blood-based chemistry, brain functionality, the time of day, positioning in the office and so on. Some real-time examples are: light sensitivity to light, sound or other stimulus; functioning more creatively or uniquely to other staff; needing 'time-out' to process sensory and cognitive information; and assimilate/regulate their emotions; having different needs for 'space', requiring more time to get their head around a concept or idea, needing a quiet space to reflect/tend to their personal needs.

For instance, in one workplace where I stayed for a long time, I often spent an afternoon a week on the floor, with scissors, craft glue, magazines, a reem of printer paper and coloured pens. I was a trainer and also case manager at the time. I worked for a large, well-known charity, spending time with families at high risk (incarceration, child protection intervention, drug and alcohol use, issues affecting their mental health and wellbeing, and those experiencing Domestic and Family Violence). My co-worker did the same role as I did, she also spent a portion of her week "creating things". She 'did' her creativity at her desk. I spent my creative time on the floor. Why? Because it is the only way I can get into a creative headspace.

Don't ask me why. I guess my desk was, cognitively, my space for computer-based work.

If I was forced to be creative at my desk, I would do it. However, the outcome would not be as fluid, colourful, expressive, innovative or dynamic. I know, because this very same situation has happened elsewhere, in many different other job roles.

Another of my Manager's got around this obstacle by stating that Friday was Freedom Friday and we could work from anywhere- outside of the office, in the cafeteria, out on the lawn outside of the office, or using the meeting room (with lovely round meeting table) for our own creative output. The only limitation was that we book the meeting room in two-hour slots, across the day. That was perfect for me, as I could effectively o the same thing, be creative, innovative, quirky, colourful and inventive, just sitting at a large, white, round table.

So, as you can see, it doesn't take a whole lot of money, or extra resources, to generate something extra or a little 'special' for your team, that will start to meet the needs of your neurodiverse employees.

Another example is one where an ND individual may have sensory processing disorders. Sensory Processing Disorders cover a wide range of impacts on the individual. I won't be able to cover all of them in this set of examples. There is, however, an explanation of each of the personal impacts and potential workplace accommodations are scattered throughout this book, for you to reference. There is also a QR Code for you to scan and utilise in your business, which links to my website. It outlines more fully the way in which different neurotypes and their needs can appear to those who don't share those traits. It can also be an invaluable tool to highlight some of the ways in which your staff may show their diversity to you and your organisational managers, indicating that there are further diversity needs to be met.

So, back to Sensory Processing Disorders. SPDs refers to the way the nervous system absorbs and responds to messages received from the senses and turns them into external responses. People who are neurodivergent have brains that do not respond to these sensory signals in standardised ways. More often than not, they appear in the following ways:

- Emotionally reactive to situations or events that seem overwhelming
- Have challenges identifying why they reacted the way they did
- Trouble sitting still for extended periods of time
- Disorganization
- 'Problems' socializing
- Challenges tolerating lights, smells, or sounds
- Uncomfortable with physical touch or close proximity
- Poor posture or sitting position
- Poor attention and focus
- Limited decision making and problem-solving skills
- Overwhelmed by crowds
- Fear of heights, elevators, escalators, and/or stairs

SOURCE: Adapted from SPD STAR

In real time, from the outside, this may look like someone who is confused, is picky about where they sit and/or who they sit with, a person who likes to spend time alone, someone who often spends time in darker, quieter spaces (so, not in highly social, highly noisy, highly populated areas and/or not in amongst the crowd.

Another example is anxiety, otherwise known as Generalised Anxiety Disorder (GAD), anxiety, and is also connected to a range of other diagnosed conditions. You may see someone who looks unsettled, they may be distracted, they may not want to 'get down to it' and start their set of daily tasks, they may actually be feeling highly anxious, uncertain, not sure of what to do first, unable to start tasks and other variations. What may actually be happening is a variation on an anxiety condition.

I am not diagnosing, here. I don't have the capacity, nor the qualifications to do that. Nor am I a doctor, or have a medical qualification.

However, I have qualifications that enable me to work with individuals who have disabilities and to provide high-end care, support and medication for people with a variety of health conditions, disabilities, drug and alcohol issues, life experiences affecting their mental health and wellbeing and their overall health. I have also got lived experience of some of these conditions. If I don't, my children, family members, friends, or others in my realm have done so. I have only used real life examples in this book, so none of it is made up.

Having an anxiety condition can be very overwhelming, at times, cause a state of internal panic and also be quite isolating, as it often feels as though the world is closing in on you (and no one else around you understand what is happening). Anxiety disorders are often characterised by periods of intense fear with physical symptoms that may include chest pain, heart palpitations, shortness of breath, dizziness, or abdominal stress, including diarrhoea and IBS-like symptoms.

Causes for anxiety can be external as well. So, in order to deal with your anxiety in a better way you need to find out whether your anxiety is caused due to an external factor or not. Any bitter incident which took place in your past life can be the cause or sometimes it can be an indistinct intuition that something is not right but if your anxiety is due to some external factors then you should work towards dealing with it. However, there is no obvious external cause for anxiety reactions to life.

Often-times, people may be prescribed medication for other conditions they have, which may also be associated with having anxiety. They may or may not have disclosed this to you. Having anxiety does not make someone a 'bad worker'. Nor does it stop them fulfilling their workplace obligations.

Your employee may also have other co-existing conditions which exacerbate or are exacerbated by their anxiety. This can be incredibly debilitating (Mellifont, 20190.

In the wrong workplace, though, one which is not supportive and in which the environment does not support the needs of that individual, that individual and their neurodivergent way of thinking and responding to the world, may not be recognised as a productive worker. People with deeply ingrained anxiety may have chemical imbalances in their brains for improper registration of neuro chemicals.

The usual symptoms are prolific sweating, 'lump in the throat', palpitations, twitching, dry mouth, chest pain and shortness of breath or wheezing. Sometimes, if a person is in an environment that repeatedly is unable to fulfill their needs, for instance, someone who is required to work in an open-plan office day after day and is 'okay' (though still only just coping with it, due to their neurodiverse needs), but one day, the whole office gets told that they must work on a hot-desk system. This might be the last straw for the employee, as having their own space was the only aspect of working in that environment that kept them feeling grounded and feeling 'safe' and secure.

Australian Workforce Statistics

I want you go back to those statistics we looked at earlier, for a minute, to put things into perspective.

→Approximately 1 in 70 individuals is deemed to be on the autism spectrum, up to 1 in 7 is deemed to be neurodiverse. (ABS, 2006). That is, their brain does not function in the same way that neuro-typical brains function. This is approximately 14 percent of the population. In Australia, that equates to roughly 3.4 million people. Across the planet, that equates to roughly 1 billion people.

To simplify this to its most basic elements, for the majority of individuals who have brains that function in a neuro-typical way, they can think in a logical, systematic, methodical sequencing pattern, on a regular basis.

For those who have neurodiverse brain-functionality, their brains function in a more diverse pattern, often called "creative" or dynamic ways of thinking. This is not the same as left brain/right brain thinking, although there are some correlations and linkages that could be made in identifying characteristics of 'types' of thinking. However, this is a bio-physiological non-neurotypical way in which the brain functions.

→In terms of literacy and numeracy levels, global and Australian-based statistics show some curious, disturbing and surprising results for Austrians aged 15-74 years of age.

According to the Australian Bureau of Statistics (ABS), 2006:

- around 620,000 (3.7%) Australians had literacy levels at **below Level 1** English Language and Literacy skills level

- a further 1.7 million individuals (10%) had Level 1 literacy skills (roughly Year 7/8 Australian standard);

- a further 5 million (30%) of the working age population had Level 2, or Year 9/10 equivalent literacy skills.

That is a total of 43% of the working age population (those who are able to attain an apprenticeship or traineeship; or have left school) who have a less than acceptable competence in literacy levels; and who need to be able to enter our workforce and engage in meaningful, purposeful, contributions to the workplace, who are not able to effectively utilise their literacy skills.

This leaves an average of 40.3 percent of the working population with only an adequate, or average, competence in their literacy skills and a staggering total of almost half of our working population with less than suitable standards of competence in literacy skills.

It is also shocking to note that less than 16% of the working age population had skills higher than Level 4/5 (University level competence and Higher Professional levels of literacy) (ABS, 2006).

As a key reference point, to highlight this even further, if we assume the Australian standard of Level 1 literacy and numeracy skills equating to approximate literacy levels of an 12 year old, and Level 3 literacy and numeracy levels to be those of someone who has successfully completed their entire school-based education with high level results, we can assume a benchmark for the above.

Now, if we take our earlier calculations, that roughly 27% of Australia's working population is employed in an office-based environment (based only on the industries I looked at in the referenced Table 1), we can determine that this extrapolates out to approximately 1.4 million of our overall working population has up to adequate or average level reading skills, and/or literacy skills. This is Year 9 level, or age 14-15year old reading skills.

** Whilst these statistics were taken from the ABS (2006) ALLS Survey, ABS statistics from 2014 and OECD statistics from the same period indicate that the percentages across prose literacy, document literacy, numeracy and also problem-solving/critical thinking have not shifted in Australia, by more than

2% for L1 and 2-3% for L2/L3, with a reduction in numbers for L4 and L5, across the past decade or so.

This is scary stuff for a 'developed' country!

Not just because of the numbers, but because these numbers represent real people, who will have REAL issues when it comes to the workplace, because they will not be able to engage as readily, effectively, or as actionably, in terms of their contributions, and may well fall through the cracks of society, again.

So, where are we failing ourselves?

Because, I -am- talking about us. This is our world, Our country. Our planet. This is our workforce. Our schools. Our workplaces. Our jobs. And, not surprisingly. Our whole society, at stake here.

A shortfall in human capital is expected, even in contemporary times, according to Australian Government sources. As far back as 2003 , the Australian Government stated that the country would require new strategies to alleviate the following: developing a more diverse workforce; mentoring and coaching new employees to develop and enhance their productivity; increasing education and training for existing employees; attracting and retaining workers diverse workers modifying the workplace and tasks so that they can be performed by employees with various levels of disability and diverse needs and requirements; and health programmes to encourage and support healthy lifestyles and to promote healthy lifestyle and an ageing population (AG, 2003).

This is not just an Australian phenomenon. It is happening all across the planet.

International Statistics

OECD statistics provide almost identical information from Europe, Canada and the USA. (OECD-UNESCO, 2003). OECD statistics indicate that there are currently 7.8 billion people globally. There are 3.5 billion adults aged 25-65 years. Of those the ones who are aged over 18 years of age and employed are estimated to be 600,000 million people across the OECD region, which is 197 countries. (Not all global countries have been included as the OECD only has information concerning the countries included in the OECD region. NB. All OECD signatory countries must contribute relevant statistical information about their in-country employment, health and demographic information to the OECD for compilation, on a regular basis. The USA, UK and Australia are all signatory members of the OECD). In 2017, the OECD indicated that 2.3 billion adults were working across their region (ILO, Asia Pacific Employment and Social Outlook, 2018, p. 8).

Australia only has 12.8 million adults in the workforce and up to 27% of those have some type of neurodivergence, based on the summary of my findings. If we did the same extrapolation of the working population given by the OECD across its region of 197 countries, we would see huge numbers of a neurodivergent workforce population, globally.

For humankind to be able to become truly inclusive in re-ordering and remodelling societal systems and structures, we need to explore new ways of setting up classrooms, workplaces, town centres, cities, and key economic centres, so that we can more fully and successfully address that changes we need to make, to collaboratively alleviate our embodied exclusion of some of society's richest and most innovative assets and future thought leaders. This is where the alchemy truly begins!

If we transfer this from a child at school, (Child A), to someone who has grown up and is working, or wanting to work, now (Adult A- let's call him Bob). Bob has a job, but finds it really hard to concentrate from 9am till 11am as his colleagues like to 'catch-up' with each other right beside his desk.

Correlations to Employment and Employability

It was very clear that low levels of literacy and numeracy had correlations to the direct impact on employability and capacity of an individual to engage in the social and brooder world we live in. For instance, if someone is unable to write to a certain standard, in Australia, this would be a Level 1- roughly Year 7/8, or the age of 11 or 12, then they will be significantly impacted in their access to employment, variety of employment opportunities, capacity to make an income to support a family, may be unable to read and/or write documentation for any of the many points in time we each may need to do this.

Whilst low levels of literacy and numeracy are not directly related to having a disability, there is a correlation shown in some research between low levels of literacy and conditions like dyslexia or ADHD, which are both forms of neurodiversity. We all know someone who has ADHD, or maybe someone who knows someone who has ADHD. We often talk about children who have ADHD, but rarely do we discuss the impacts on adults. In school, many people have support dealing with' their ADHD and associated impacts on health, memory and concentration, to name a few ways in which being neurodiverse in this way can impact on someone. People may have medication, they may be given special accommodations to enable them to concentrate more easily, in a quiet space, or without distraction from others. They may also be given extra time to complete tasks and assessments. What we don't do in our society is provide those same accommodations once someone becomes an adult and starts a new job.

That person who was once a child, who either missed out on additional supports because they weren't identified as someone requiring support, or they were 'tagged' as someone with behavioural issues' because they most likely couldn't learn in mainstream ways, got 'bored' or distracted or couldn't be bothered and so went looking elsewhere for stimulation, and were then deemed to be ' the naughty one'. Now, I am by no means stereotyping. I am clearly stating that as an educational system in a first world country, we often let our children down by only providing them with parts of the pieces that make up the whole of the support system they need to flourish. AND, we do the same in the workplace!

This has become quite a bug-bear that niggled away at me for many years, as more and more people crossed my pathway, each with different personal stories, but all pretty much saying the same thing, overall, in relation to support they were given to be able to access and then achieve their life and career goals- the education system let us down and now the workplace is letting us down too!

HOW could we get this so wrong? Surely, as a conglomerate of workplaces, we all want the same things? I have completed several business qualifications and nearly made it to the end of my MBA (that's a story for another time), so I have done a lot of research on organisational development, business analysis, systems and processes, and also what truly makes a business tick. In addition to my learning and development, teaching and facilitation frame of reference, I have spent the past 25 years supporting businesses in one way or another. I have coached business owners on how to improve their businesses, how to maximise their sales and optimise their income streams, completed 360-degree business analyses on business structure, ROI, training and development, functionality, the business environment and the meeting the needs of employees and stakeholders. Do you know where everyone falls down? That's right, meeting the needs of staff.

So, while it takes more than just a bowl of fruit on the kitchen table to meet the needs of your employees, to be able create a space where employees want to come in to the office, feel safe enough to share ideas and valued for their own personal expression and ways of working, it is possible, with a small budget that can be off-set as part of your deductibles, to create a nurturing, safe, stable and secure space where your employees will want to achieve! And, ultimately, where they will begin to flourish, as you show them how valued they are, by listening to their needs, acknowledging their neurodivergence, appreciating their unique set of skills and knowledge, and establishing an environment that enables them to not only collaborate more effectively and innovatively, but also provides new opportunities to increase your business productivity, reduce sick leave, retain great key staff, and build a solid and power-house workforce to be reckoned with!

Refocussing on...

Literacy and Written Communication

Why am I talking about literacy and written communication? Because it ranks so highly on the pie chart we saw in Section One, outlining neurodivergent conditions such as executive function issues, information processing, dyslexia, dyspraxia, low levels of literacy, social anxiety and other challenges with communication are often associated with literacy and written communication.

For the most part, someone who has these 'issues' in this way at school, will also continue to have some kind of literacy or communication challenge into their working years and beyond.

These conditions do not go away. Children with them become adults with those same needs for support and encouragement to continue in their endeavours to maximise their potential. They also still require adjustments and accommodations, so that they can participate as fully as they want need and have a right to do so, in society and the workplace.

As I mentioned before, a lot of individuals try to find alternative strategies that help them to achieve, on these levels. For those who can, and do, they are also usually the ones who find and stay in employment.

Some people were not included in the mainstream learning opportunities in a school-environment (for whatever reason that was) and because of this, they missed out. They were effectively 'running behind the train' for the rest of their lives. Whilst I was teaching adults English, language and literacy skills, ultimately, what I found was that 99% of those who were in my classes and came to me for support, needed that support because of one, though usually three or more of the above.

Many of these individuals were either not in employment, in unskilled employment (they told me that they felt guilty, ashamed, felt unworthy, were 'let go' because they couldn't read and write), or were working for themselves, because they did not feel confident enough to present themselves to a manager or supervisor, knowing that they had low levels of literacy, potentially were neurodivergent and/or may have a diagnosed condition that also made them neurodiverse.

And so, we can see that even literacy levels can hold someone back in the workplace. When we look behind why someone might have some challenges with their literacy, we can unusually find a mind that works a little differently than the neuro-typical mind. And, therefore, needs a different ways of approaching learning new things and absorbing information, in order to be able to first be interested in it, curious enough to stay focussed whilst learning it, then retain that information in the short, medium and long-term, as well as being able to pull it out of our employees' memory packages and apply it again, when required.

Initially, and with people who aren't creative in their way of thinking, these employees may be left by the wayside. In our modern-day workplace, we have the capacity to think through this a little differently.

As managers and supervisors and CEOs, it is much more inclusive to think about our employees having a whole variety of needs, on different spots on a round rainbow spectrum, rather than one that is linear and goes from left to right, with greater or lesser needs available. With our former version, it looks a little like the colour option wheel on our font colours. Have you ever looked at your fonts and decided you wanted to pick a different colour? Have you ever thought, "Hhhhmmmmm.... I don't want one of the basic colours, I want a bespoke colour", and gone to have a look at the colour wheel? If you look at this colour wheel, you can see that there are many different variants of colour, even in the oranges, the pinks, the purples and the blues. No one blue is exactly the same as another blue. This is the spectrum of needs that I am referring to, whenever I talk about employee needs and meeting the needs of our neurodiverse needs of our employees.

I am not talking about the 'rainbow' in a way that is referring to fairy-tales and lollipops. It is one of the symbols for neurodiversity, as is the infinity symbol. These are symbolic of the conceptual multiplicity of needs that neurodivergent individuals have and the many ways in which they can be accommodated. I am using it here to represent the many different ways that you, in your own capacity within the organisation, can come together and collaborate with your employees, to develop more congruent and coherent neurodiversity policies and practices.

My aim to is encourage you to step forward and become an ambassador for neurodivergent employees across the country, who need our support, to be able to become healthy, productive, collaborative, innovative and flourishing participants in our workforce. And, I want you to seriously consider becoming an advocate and spokesperson for the people around you who are neurodivergent, those who may have been a part of your workforce in the past, those who are friends and family, and even for yourself, if you are part of our neuro-kin. We need you to stand with us.

We are skilled. We are knowledgeable. We are creative. We are innovative. We are funny. We are sociable. We like to laugh. We are courageous. We are determined. We are committed. We are excellent at what we are passionate about! We put our heart and soul into what we do the best! We want to support each other. We care about others. We want to connect with our peers. We have fantastic ideas! We can communicate, we may just do it a little differently. We do make connections with people; we make our connections in our own ways. We are amazingly caring, funny, intelligent, loyal, emotionally attuned people!

Verbal and Interpersonal Communication

We all communicate the same, right? We speak words and we also "talk" in a non-verbal way. We have been 'taught that approximately 7% of what we say is absorbed by those we speak to each day. We therefore know, by deduction, that means that roughly 93% of our non-verbal communication is non-verbal. And, if our assumption is that everyone communicates in the same ways, then we should all understand each other perfectly! (Grinder, 1997).

But, do we?

Do you understand yours friends all of the time? Do you understand you family all of the time? Do you understand your work colleagues all of the time? Then, why are we expected to understand everything we are told in the workplace, let alone all of the non-verbal communication that occurs?

Let me throw something else into the mix- for most people with a neurodivergent way of thinking, they communicate differently, anyway. They may use the same words, but they may utilise them differently. For instance, have you ever met anyone who is very concise in their verbal usage? Where you might ask everyone in the morning, "How is everyone today?", our work colleague, Rebecca may only say, "Hello". This may appear abrupt to some, or disengaged, or even hostile, to others. It most probably isn't, if Rebecca is neurodivergent. It is more likely to be a part of her communication pattern. She is only using words that are absolutely necessary. She also doesn't use 'small talk' or stand around the kitchen chatting at break time. This isn't because she is not sociable, or because she doesn't like people, it is purely because she doesn't find a use for small talk in her world.

Others in the office may think she is anti-social. However, 1-1 or in small groups where she is comfortable with the people around her, she is friendly and outgoing and likes to laugh a lot.

So, why isn't she like this at work? Firstly, she doesn't feel like she 'fits in' at work. She feels uncomfortable when she hears others talking about her and she knows that some of them don't want to talk to her because she doesn't participate in break-time chats. Her communication style is different than her neuro-typical work colleagues. However, it does not make her an unproductive employee. It does not make her a 'bad' person. And, it does not make her someone who does not want to create friendships. It only means that she communicates differently to others, utilises different communication patterns and sometimes may find it challenging to enter into an already established network of people. All of these elements will have an impact on whether she chooses to reach out to her colleagues, or continue to feel uncomfortable in the workplace.

The reality is, Rebecca is incredibly creative! She comes up with thousands of ideas every day. She is a wonderful problem solver and loves supporting the people around her to achieve the best they can. She is also very good at pulling ideas out of the sky and transforming a blank page into a colourful landscape of images and concepts that can be adapted to suit many different workplace projects.

One of her manager's is aware of these skills, however, she isn't very supporting and encouraging of Rebecca and does not offer her a space to shine. Therefore, whenever Rebecca has a new idea to share, the rest of the team never get to hear it.

What Underpins Common Behavioural and Thought Patterns in the Every-day Workplace

A. The assumption that everyone is the same, with the same needs, requirements, beliefs, standards and expectations
B. The belief that what works for one person will work for another
C. The belief that new accommodations for an employee will be expensive and require endless restructuring
D. The assumption that once accommodations are made, there will be continuing requests for further tweaks to new environment.
E. The 'fear' that nothing will change (retention, recruitment, productivity, sick leave), even if the business does make changes

F. The belief that accommodations and adjustments for employees will cost a lot of money

The Workplace Culture Iceberg

We have talked a lot about neurodivergent employees. We have talked a lot about you, as their manager, team leader, CEO or boss. We haven't really talked about your neurodivergent employees' colleagues and how they may respond to their peer.

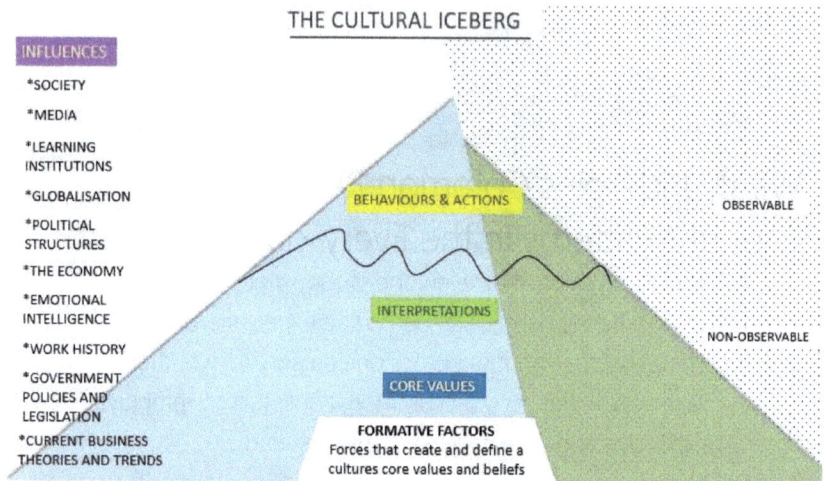

THE CULTURAL ICEBERG

INFLUENCES
*SOCIETY
*MEDIA
*LEARNING INSTITUTIONS
*GLOBALISATION
*POLITICAL STRUCTURES
*THE ECONOMY
*EMOTIONAL INTELLIGENCE
*WORK HISTORY
*GOVERNMENT POLICIES AND LEGISLATION
*CURRENT BUSINESS THEORIES AND TRENDS

BEHAVIOURS & ACTIONS   OBSERVABLE

INTERPRETATIONS

NON-OBSERVABLE

CORE VALUES

FORMATIVE FACTORS
Forces that create and define a
cultures core values and beliefs

IMAGE: 'The Cultural Iceberg'- Factors that influence the formation of workplace 'culture' and inclusivity practices Source: Adapted from LCW (2015).

The image above shows some of the formative factors in the development of culture, in a generalised sense. They are the formative forces that define your organisation's culture and underpin its values. These have nothing to do with me. And, for the most part, they may be something that you addressed very early in the establishment of your business, when you were setting up your vision and your aims and objectives. Pulling together your business and marketing plan and creating your business forecast.

These formative factors were in two parts: (a) those that were observable factors- organisational behaviours, words and actions spoken by you and your first employees; the actions undertaken by your employees in the delivery of service to your clients, etc. Then, there were those factors that were not observable: (b) what is acceptable and unacceptable within the organisation, what is thought to be 'good practice' and what is thought to be 'not-so-good' practice' or modelling, what is justified by the business values and what is not, what is the 'right thing to do' in the workplace and what is 'not okay' to do, on moral or ethical grounds.

Our interpretations of these all influence and impact on the unobservable workplace culture, as well. So, the CEO's beliefs about an ethical response to someone who has autism applying for a job but not passing through the recruitment process will determine whether or not s/he is willing to restructure the recruitment process to enable more neurodivergent employees an opportunity to work at your workplace, after reading this book.

For a Manager who thinks that it is 'everyone for themselves' and there is nothing 'wrong' with a standardised recruitment process that excludes certain members of the workforce, this may not be an issue for them. And, in a company that upholds an organisational culture that supports this set of beliefs and values, it will be unlikely that a *NeuroDiversity Works Here!* Program will be implemented.

For another Manager, who believes in equity for all, or in human rights, or in the provision of equality, or even, who would like to see what an neurodivergent employee, with all of their skills and knowledge and competence can do for the organisation, may want to create a more flexible recruitment system where potential neurodivergent employees can enter into the workforce with more ease and less barriers to participation.

For some, this may be uncomfortable. I don't mean it to be. But, it is worth getting out in the open, as it can have a direct impact on everybody's state of mind, responsivity to your new neurodiversity plan, to the way in which your overall workforce embraces or is resistant to the inclusion of one or more neurodivergent employees in your workforce, and also, how your current employees view any new 'programming' that may appear to favour neurodivergent employees.

This could be in relation to office redesign, inclusion of adjustments for your employees, accommodations granted for ND employees, new Talent Programs, the emergence of Wisdom Pods in your organisation, the celebration of the work of neurodivergent team members or the team productivity, itself. There are many ways in which there could be some negative as well as positive impact on your organisation, and it is wise to consider how this may be interpreted by your current employees.

How Does This Play Out in the Workplace?

So, what does "neurodiversity" mean when we are in our roles as a manager or team leader?

Some of you may have already heard this term prior to reading this book.

Some of you may be neurodiverse and not realise it.

Some of you may be well versed in the nature and multitudinous ways in which neurodiversity can display itself in your life.

Let me recap: the definition of neurodiversity is as follows: "A range of differences in individual brain function and behavioural traits, regarded as part of normal variation in the human population". To be 'neurodivergent' is to be someone who has a brain that functions in this way or who has these traits.

In reference to the workplace, it is an area of diversity and inclusion that refers to alternative thinking styles. I am going to include the reference to 'neurodivergent' in this article. Under the medical model, this term means that the individual concerned has cognitive abilities outside of the cognitive 'norm.' Under the feminist model, this term mean: All of our brains are unique and neurodivergence refers to those who sit in the greater field of neurodiversity than the previously conceived field of neuro-typical cognitive behaviour and thought processing.

What does this mean in real terms? It means that our brains each have individual ways of absorbing and processing information, as well as then interpreting it; and then expressing the influence and impact of that back out into the external world, via our actions and behaviours. For someone who is neurodivergent, they may feel challenged with some of the more contemporary ways in which managers and organisations have set up their organisational parameters, believing that they were pioneers in the forefront of the new technological age. When, in fact, they have been alienating tract after tract of employee cohort in their wake.

How have we managed to do this?

What's the 'Big Picture' on "Needs"?

We've just had a look at some of the internal socio-cultural factors that might impact on your neurodivergent employees. We've explored how you could redesign, rearrange and 'rejuvenate' the physical workspace. And, now, we can have a look at some of the less visible or overt ways in which your neurodivergent employees may have needs.

This Mayan Temple Model below has been adapted from Maslow's *Hierarchy of Needs*. Maslow realised that human beings had a set of psychological, safety, physiological, cognitive and what he called self-actualised needs, that were universal to the human state. He designed his original framework in the 1950s. Many researchers over the years have utilised his model in education, business, sociology and cultural studies, to illustrate the impact of environmental, socio-cultural, ecological, political and multi-dimensional factors on the human condition.

I have chosen to adapt it in this model, to illustrate some of the more substantive needs of neurodivergent employees in the workplace. They are ideas rather than a definitive list.

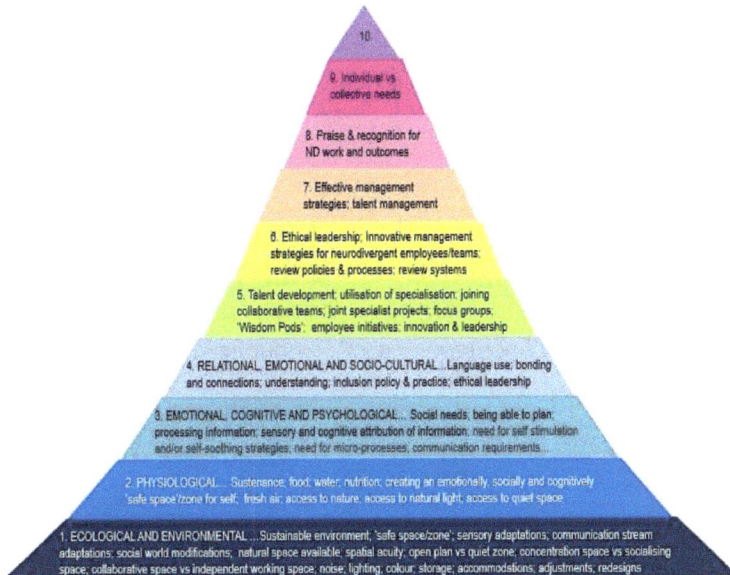

SOME EXAMPLES OF WAYS TO MEET THE NEEDS OF YOUR NEURODIVERGENT EMPLOYEES

The numbered layers in the pyramid above refer to the following:

1. Ecological & environmental
2. Physiological
3. Emotional, cognitive & psychological
4. Relational, social and socio-cultural
5. Collaboration and Social Working
6. Leadership, management, systems & processes
7. Management of specialist knowledge, skills, innovation and 'talent'
8. Praise, rewards, recognition and incentives – the neurodivergent way
9. Valuing the collective; valuing the individual
10. The neurodivergent employee as the 'evolved' person in your workplace

At the base of the pyramid, there is more need for support and sustainable input from external sources. The further up the pyramid a neurodivergent employee travels, the more self-sufficient they 'become'. In fact, they already will enter your workplace quite ready to 'be' fairly self-contained. Although, this does not mean that they do not want to interact, nor create friendships and bonds. It's just that the collective 'we' often have a different way of doing things.

And, so, we may require more support in creating and establishing an environment and an ecological space that works for us, at a foundational level. However, in terms of managing our 'selves', utilising our specific 'specialism' or 'talent', or doing things in our neurodivergent 'way', we will be quite independent and not require a lot of input from anyone, because it is 'just what we do'.

Essentials for Creating Workplace Harmony

In order to support your neurodivergent employees in the best way possible, there are some hints and tips provided in the image over the page. Once again, they are just a few ideas. There are many, many more that can be utilised. Each workplace and managers will have their own preference and best 'fir' for what works for them. I have chosen some of the more 'popular' and preferred options, from a neurodivergent perspective.

Just something to keep in mind, as it is always good to work with what works best for your employees, rather than what your own personal preferences are.

WORKPLACE ESSENTIALS FOR HARMONY

Use uncomplicated, concise and precise language to communicate

When writing job adverts, use plain English, only put in essential skills and knowledge required.

Utilise the specialist capacity and creativity of your neurodivergent employees. This is where innovation is born!

Provide tasks and workflow options in 'chunks' for ease of completion

Be open to actively listening to your employees needs and concerns

If possible, create a "quiet zone" (that isn't a meeting space), even in an open plan office.

Develop a workplace culture that is inclusive of multiple neurological processes and methods. Share them.

Communicate in all formats in Plain English. Jargon and technical reference only complicate communication.

Praise and reward innovative ways of 'doing' work and 'being' in the workplace. These are natural states for your neurodivergent employees.

Once we've explored what we can do to enhance and improve the situation for our employees, it is also important to assess the situation, to ensure that there are protections in place that offer 'protections' for our employees. This is from a legal and ethical perspective.

What Workplace 'Protections' Exist for NeuroDivergent Employees?

From an Australian perspective, the *Disability Discrimination Act (1992)* and *United Nations Convention on the Rights of Persons with Disabilities* (which was ratified by Australia in 2008) provide some protections for neurodivergent workers who are directly discriminated against in the workplace, if they have a diagnosed disability.

The definition of disability under the DDA is principally based on a model of 'disability' that includes physical, intellectual, psychiatric, sensory and neurological impairments, learning difficulties, physical disfigurement and the presence of diseases.

The term, "people with disability", as used in the *Department of Health Disability Action Plan* document, refers to people who face social, architectural, environmental and/or attitudinal barriers restricting their full participation in society due to the impairments covered by the DDA.

Whilst these are not personal terminology preferences, they are utilised within the documentation utilised by Australian Commonwealth institutions, such as the *Department of Health* and also by the *Australian Human Rights Commission* [AHRC].

The Australian Human Rights Commission (AHRC)

The AHRC is primarily occupied with ensuring that the human rights of all Australians are upheld and enacted appropriately, in all contexts.

In this context, the AHRC is the Australia's compliance body for discrimination in the workplace and in other areas of life.

What is an 'Action Plan'?

An action plan is a way for an organisation to plan for the minimisation of and aim towards the non-existence of 'disability discrimination' from the provision of its goods, services and facilities. This is relevant to not only employees, but all key stakeholders in your business, including your clients and customers, distributors and partnerships.

Although the Disability Discrimination Act (DDA) defines *Action Plans* in terms of service provision, it makes sense to include employment policies and practices as part of the writing of Action Plans and the principles that are embedded in the Action Plans. By implementing principles, ethical practice and applying these to internal and external relationships, organisations can more effectively and optimally address their responsibilities under the DDA, and more broadly, their ethical and moral duty of care under other business guidelines, such as Corporate Social responsibility, which should be applied internally as well as externally.

Developing and implementing Action Plans is a voluntary, proactive approach to DDA compliance. It benefits organisations, neurodivergent employees, clients, key stakeholders, internal and external relationships and overall organisational culture. They also create a wonderful platform for enhancing an organisation's corporate image, enhancing organisational reputation in the marketplace, broadening the buyer receptiveness to the brand/product/service and delivering services more efficiently and accessing a wider market.

The AHRC has approved all Action Plans and 'ticked the box' for organisations that have consulted with people with disabilities and/or their representative organisations. It is clear that these organisations have reviewed their policies and practices around diversity, discrimination, disability, inclusion, accommodations and adjustments, identified barriers for people with disabilities in accessing services, and planned strategies to eliminate these barriers, to at least some degree.

For someone who is neurodivergent or for 'people with disabilities', the implementation of AHRC approved Disability Action Plans has created a purposeful strategy that indicates that their organisation is considering their position and that eliminating disability discrimination is not dependent on complaints being made against organisations. In this way, the AHRC is supporting strategies to ensure that discrimination will be less of a factor in everyone's lives in the future.

Remember that these Action Plans are focussed on Disability, inclusion and diversity. We are speaking about neurodiversity in a broader sense, however the reality of discrimination from 'doing things differently', responding to the world in a different way', and 'being different', 'unique', approaching the world from an alternative standpoint are all part of the reality that many people who are neurodivergent face, in the workplace, each day.

The AHRC provides some great guidance for all organisations looking to get a head start on creating an Action Plan, to alleviate any concerns around this subject.

What is the link between the Australian Human Rights Commission, the United Nations and the Rights of Neurodivergent Employees?

Australia joined 29 other countries around the world aiming to promote a global community in which all people with disability are equal and active citizens. In Australia, the Australian Human Rights Commission (AHRC) promotes the development of disability action plans to reduce unlawful discrimination against people with disability. Internationally, the United Nations heads the empowerment of people who have been disempowered by others who oppress, violate, exploit and abuse the rights of others. The rights of neurodivergent individuals are protected within the **United Nations** *Convention on the Rights of Persons with Disabilities.*

Continuing On...

The *NSW Department of Health* refers to "sensory and neurological impairments, learning difficulties" as part of their definition of 'disability' which is in direct correlation to our neurodivergent employees.

Their reference to: "social, environmental, architectural and/or attitudinal barriers restricting full participation in society" clearly references the fact that if these factors are not addressed, then individuals who have these challenges will not be able to participate fully in those activities that they would normally be able to contribute their time and energy towards. Work is one of these areas of contribution.

The *Australian Human Rights Commission* has recommended that all organisations consider writing a Disability Action plan, so that they are compliant with DDA legislation. For international organisations, although these are international guidelines, it may be useful to have a look at what other organisations have prepared.

Personally, I have been looking at state-based institutions (county, regional and localised authorities, for some other countries), Commonwealth or Federal institutions, as well as private and public sector organisations, to see what they have developed as Disability Action Plans.

Adopting and Action Plan strategy that is integrated into an overall inclusion strategy for your neurodivergent workforce may be very useful in enhancing not only workplace practices and sprucing up your policies, but also in ensuring Quality Assurance, compliance and employee satisfaction.

NB. Whilst I have focussed on an Australian perspective in this particular section, this can be applied to an international gaze by exploring the United Nation's website. These ideas, concepts and documentation are all drawn from the *UN's Convention on the Rights of Persons with Disabilities.*

NB. For links to global resources, please refer to the Bibliography section of the Appendices.

The Impact of <u>Not</u> Addressing Neurodivergence in the Workplace

Overall, if neurodivergent employees are not effectively supported, they will eventually "fail", from a productivity and employability point of view. Someone who may be able to work very productively and at an optimum level and pace in one organisation, where they are supported and where adjustments and accommodations are made for their neurodivergence, may find that they are even put on a Performance Management Plan at their next place of employment, as this employer is not able to offer the same level of support and accommodations to this individual.

If we look at the situation objectively, in the workplace, what you may commonly "see" are the effects on the neurodiverse individual as them "negatively" performing. They may be seen to "need" a work plan of action, outcomes of "workplace productivity" may need to be addressed, and the overall "performance of the individual concerned may be highlighted in their annual or bi-annual reviews or appraisals. HR may also see a decline in the following conditions, illnesses, injuries, states of long-term health, and/or disorders.

It is something to think about, the fact that the impact of these *does not make it the fault of the individual.* This is particularly so, if they are unaware of what is occurring for them. However, even if they have this awareness, they are not in control of the divergent way in which their brain undertakes its cognitive and sensory processing and the demands placed upon it by day-to-day living in a neurotypical environment. However, any condition that creates an effect that is outside the parameters of control of the individual should not be blamed on them. If we were to do this, we would be discriminating against them.

If our workplaces are established for our neurotypical employees, which is the "standard" Western workplace, then we are doing a complete disservice to all of our employees. More importantly, we are edging towards some level of disenfranchisement of our potential, highly capable neurodivergent employees, dismissing our current neurodivergent employees and setting them up for "failure" (as our expectations for them are to 'fit in' to an environment that is not the 'right fit' for them and will never be "comfortable' not conducive to their workplace wellness nor wellbeing.), AND we are also placing ourselves in a legally precarious position of potentially discriminating against a whole community of individuals who, if we were able to make some small, simple adjustments to our environment, would most probably quite happily spend a lot of time working for us, way into the future!

As such, as employers, we have a responsibility to provide a more optimum working environment, to enable our participating workforce to achieve their optimum performance levels. This is in association with WH&S policy and practice, Human Rights Act and the *Fair Work Act* guideline, along with other associated workplace policies and practices with which we are all familiar.

Although these are Australian guidelines and legislation, there will be equal health and safety guidelines and legislation that equates to these in each of your countries. Some of these are listed at the back of this book, relevant to the year of publication.

If somebody's condition means that they are unable to effectively fulfill their role purely because the fluorescent lights shine directly on their desk-top, it is within our scope as employers, to change that on behalf of our employee. And, in doing this, enhance their workplace experience, increase the chances of an increase in their productivity and also increase their employee satisfaction levels in the workplace, due to our support and concern for their requirement for an additional adjustment.

Workplace Innovations

In the example above, Rebecca has a lot to offer her organisation. Her manager may know she has some very valuable skills. Rebecca may have quite a few under-wraps skills, knowledge and expertise available too. However, unless we, as an organisation, provide Rebecca with the right environment to flourish, it is unlikely that she will do so.

Firstly, she will need a conducive space for her to be able to relax, get into her creative flow, feel comfortable enough to generate innovative concepts and ideas and also be comfortable enough to share them with her peers and senior managers.

How can we do that for our neurodivergent employees? Well, as an example, Google has just discovered that they have an invaluable asset with their team technical specialists who are on the Autism Spectrum (ASD/Autism Spectrum Disorder/Autism Spectrum Condition- depending on where you are in the world). They have recruited people with autism (just as an indicator, many neurodiverse people these days prefer to use IFL (Identity First Language), which means that, in this case, they would be referred to as Autistic, rather than use PFL (Person First Language), where someone would be referred to as 'someone with Autism'. This is not a choice made by people other than the neurodivergent individual themselves. This is also a personal preference. Please ask if you are unsure of how someone would like to be referred to. Personally, I would rather you call me, "Leigh".

It may feel uncomfortable or unusual for work colleagues and others to change the way we think and refer to others in our realm. However, our terminology for people with various health conditions, illnesses, injuries and other factors influencing their lives has changed time and again over the years, so this is one more shift in your perspective.

Implementing Innovative Practices

Innovation and innovation practices requires a whole lot more than just setting up an R&D team and a couple of individuals who think outside the box. I'm certain that you are already on top of this, as a concept. You may already have a very deep understanding of what this means, in terms of your business. I'm in no doubt that you do.

Our businesses are vital, life-giving and of utmost importance to us and to the people we serve with our products and service delivery. That is a given.

In my way of thinking, I would be honoured to start to engage you in a thought process that begins with us thinking of alternative ways in which you could pivot, diversify, innovate or consolidate your business in a way that creates even more opportunities for you to meet the needs of your clients.

I am asking you to do this via your innovation practice. And, also, through the inclusion of your neurodivergent employees.

There are two ways of that managers generally thinking about including neurodivergent employees:

A. You have a business. You are happy and willing to 'include' some neurodivergent individuals., "as long as they do their work".
B.   You want to get the best out of your business and the people in it, including your neurodivergent employees, and you are hoping they can value-add to your innovation strategy!

I am hoping you are this far along in the book, because you are in "Group B!"

That's where I am too!

So, how are we going to do this?

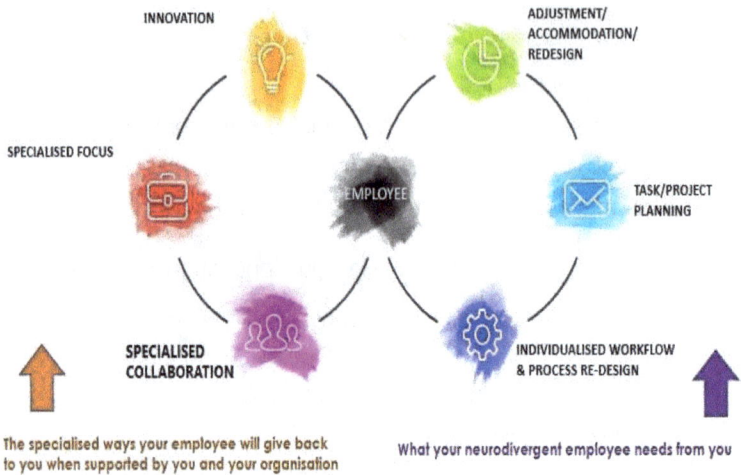

INNOVATION

ADJUSTMENT/
ACCOMMODATION/
REDESIGN

SPECIALISED FOCUS

EMPLOYEE

TASK/PROJECT
PLANNING

SPECIALISED
COLLABORATION

INDIVIDUALISED WORKFLOW
& PROCESS RE-DESIGN

The specialised ways your employee will give back
to you when supported by you and your organisation

What your neurodivergent employee needs from you

The Benefits to the Organisation
Providing Accommodations and Adjustments for Neurodivergent Employees

There are way too many benefits of having neurodivergent employees on-board in your organisations to go into in great depth. I have broadly covered some of the rewards and benefits for organisations above. Some of the key benefits that have stood out for me when I have been a manager have been the strength in thinking from a different perspective, being able to collaborate and enrich a collaborative project, being able to engage from another viewpoint that can be paradigm-shifting, and being able to address problem from a completely different angle.

There are also immense benefits for organisations who bring new neurodivergent employees in to fulfil job requirements that are more creative and require more innovation and expansive mindsets, as these can provide flexibility and adaptations within systems and processes that the organisation may not have considered prior to their arrival in the workplace.

SECTION FIVE

Productivity, Inclusion, NeuroDiversity and Innovation-How Does it all Fit Together?

Workforce Development: The 'Bigger Picture' and Its Impact

The concept of 'workforce development' has been one that organisations have primarily thought from an internal standpoint. They have decided on a set of ideals, features and attributes that they want from their team/s and have set about training and developing those associated individuals to suit their internal model. From a training and development perspective, whilst this works well in the short term, it does not address some of the more inalienable workforce development needs that have existed for the past 20 years, at least.

This has been due to the introduction of more advanced technologies in the office-based workplace, faster systems and processes, higher levels of expectations and requirements of employees, stricter workplace standards and more QA frameworks, WH&S/OH&S guidelines, regulations, legislation, and benchmarks being implemented. Whilst this is a priority for health and safety purposes, and an inherent part of the Quality Assurance and Quality Improvement Processes, this has also left a gaping hole in the generalised workforce development planning, development, training and expectations.

For many neurodivergent employees, there is often a sense that they are being asked to repeat something they have already been asked to do before. This can be perceived as a form of invalidation for what they have achieved prior. It also invalidates their previous experience and can register as a negation of their achievements. Whilst this is not always the case, I have had this feedback from many neurodivergent contacts of mine who have not felt comfortable talking with management about how out of place they have felt due to being asked to repeat these processes and procedures over and over again, across progressive workplaces. They have often wondered why there isn't some kind of transferrable 'passport' of a kind, that can evidence that WH&S/OH&S has been completed, and updated, if necessary, to a certain standard, that they can carry from employer to employer, as and when required.

It would certainly alleviate a lot of the stress and distress, and anxiety caused by the above, negating, experiences, that both invalidate, and also disharmonise the workplace.

It is certainly something to keep in mind, as we move forward into a space where we begin to look at some strategies and innovations you could start to put in place for your neurodivergent employees.

For every workplace that requires WH&S/OH&S training as a minimum standard, plus Induction, plus, an (often unstated) mid-range level of literacy. Plus, a level of social competence; plus, a heightened level of cultural competence, to be able to fit in' to the organisation. All of this, before anyone even starts their working life with an organisation, someone wo is neurodivergent could be led to assume that they do not 'fit in', and are not 'competent' and have 'not achieved' a high enough level to meet the needs and demands of their current employer, purely due to the design, delivery and facilitation of the above.

In all of my time in training and development and adult education, one of the key things I have learnt about people is that if you want someone to learn something, it is important to create learning materials (online and face-to-face) and the whole process of learning that are conducive to them absorbing that information. If I want someone to learn something, but I don't present it in a way that makes sense to them, they just won't absorb it (either, at all, or in a very limited way).

It makes sense, doesn't it?

However, when we are thinking about our neurodivergent employees, we rarely take on their perspective. Yes, we have become very adept at providing learning materials that meet the diverse 'learning' styles of individuals.

Did you know that this is just the beginning of understanding your employees and how they learn and take on board information?

I mean. Of course, it is wonderful that we have gained an awareness of basic learning styles. It is even more important that you get to know how this occurs for your neurodivergent employees, especially if they are going to become part of your innovation teams; and/or specialist team members.

We just don't learn like everyone else.

Even with the pretty pictures...

We need a reward, action, reward process, rather than a work, work, work, reward process, as indicated in this image, below:

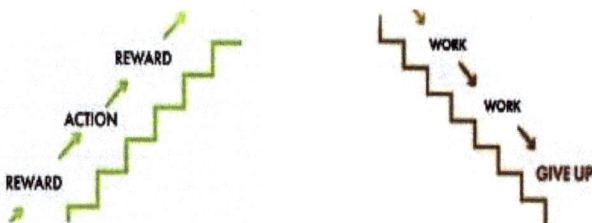

Reward-Action-Reward Motivators vs Work-Work-Work-Benefit Motivators: Impact on NeuroDivergent Employees

So, core parts of your HR processes, like *Employee Handbooks* that are 150 pages long most probably won't get read by a neurodivergent employee. Not because they are subversive or because they don't want to follow the process. They do.

However, reading that much, all at once, in a short period of time, is just going to be too much for some neurodivergent people. I'm not going to categorise them, nor say who they are. However, after 20 years of training, I know that my neurodivergent colleagues have been very upset when I have seen them in my facilitated groups and training sessions. They have stated that they have been very distressed because there has been an expectation placed on them that they are unable to meet, because of their neurodivergence.

If there was an alternative in place, they would have easily achieved an appropriate and relevant outcome.

And, yet, no other accommodation, alternative, nor adjustment was made.

Using the same example, it is very possible that we could have our *Employee Handbooks* on audio-file, so that employees could listen to them. We could prepare a *PowerPoint Presentation* [PPT] – a visual format, so that they have something pictorial to refer back to, in the future.

In relation to the image on the previous page, the 'Reward-Action-Reward' motivators vs 'Work-Work-Work-Benefit' motivators are far more strengths-based and conducive to getting the best out of everyone, really.

Neurodivergent employees are particularly responsive to these kinds of motivators, as they mirror their natural capacity to chunk things into smaller components.

To explain this a little further, if I am doing a smaller, micro-process and then my manager comes along, sees that I have completed my micro-process and then praises me for doing that, I will have far more of a sense of job satisfaction than if I did 10 days solid work, in deep focus, and was only then told , "Great!. Now let's get on to the next section", by my manager. The first is the *Reward-Action-Reward* motivator, the second is a limited version of the *Work-Work-Work-Benefit* (finish the task, not get praise) motivator.

Of course, as managers, we don't all have very much time to share praise every time someone completes a micro-task. I can fully appreciate that. I am asking you to consider ways in which you could embed strategies that complete this process for you, into daily and weekly workloads, so that your neurodivergent employees (and other staff, as they will benefit too) will be able to gain some extra "oomph" in their step and want to continue with that momentum, throughout their working week.

Workforce Development in the Western World

Going one step further and talking about workforce development from a broader perspective, in the past 20 years, across the Western World, research has been conducted in four areas pertinent to what we are about to delve into:

1. Workforce skills and relevant skills and 'talent' development
2. Organisation culture and practice
3. Innovation and productivity
4. Levels of language, literacy and numeracy

...required in order to be able to carry out minimum suitable levels of workplace competence within the growing knowledge society and information economy that is evolving in front of our eyes.

I have also conducted some further research into the following two areas, to round off my perspective on neurodiversity in the workplace:

A) Organisational culture and its impact on business innovation
B) How enhancing staff satisfaction can increase organisation productivity and ROI

Whilst this book is about neurodiversity in the workplace, it is also framed within a broad global business culture that asserts that we must all confirm with a set of 'standards' for business that provide limited lee-way to enable us to be flexible to the needs of our employees and overall workforce (CIPD, 2018).

If, as savvy business managers, we are looking to optimise our organisation's productivity levels, enhance client performance levels, develop deeper and more secure, long-term reciprocal working relationships with our stakeholders, enhance our quality improvement, enhance our overall reputation across a 360 degree spectrum, leverage our 'talent' and utilise our human capital to its best advantage, gaining us even greater competitive advantage, then, we must, as ethical, socially conscious, innovative and culturally competent leaders, provide a working environment for all of our staff, that not only addresses our business needs, but also enables them to thrive and excel in the workplace.

Globally, there has been a shift, in the past 5 or so years, in larger, more robust companies, who have been amenable to starting 'talent programs' that support the recruitment, development, training, coaching and leveraging of employees, new and current, who are neurodivergent. These programs illustrated in Harvard Business Review's online article, "Neurodiversity as Competitive Advantage' (Austin & Pisano, 2016), have outlined how these larger organisations have been strategic in their race to bring on-board neurodivergent individuals with specific skills sets and/or technical or job-specific skill sets, to do primary task and project roles.

These organisations include:

> ➤ SAP
> ➤ Hewlett Packard
> ➤ Deloitte
> ➤ IBM
> ➤ Dell Industries
> ➤ JP Morgan Chase
> ➤ The Department of Health and Human Services, Australia
> ➤ The Australian Defence Forces- Cybersecurity section
> ➤ Specialisterne, Europe
> ➤ Microsoft
> ➤ Google, UK

And many, many others.

As societal attitudes shift, workplaces who choose to engender and embrace ethical, moral and humane practices towards others, in embedding workplace practices that support new policies, processes, systems and management strategies to develop and enhance the working environment and lived experience of "work" from a neurodivergent employee's perspective, will ultimately hold the Ace card. Neurodivergent employees will come to make strategic choices in who they want to work for and with. They will choose who has the ethical framework that meets their needs and standards as someone who is part of the neurodiversity community.

In the not too distant future, neurodivergent employees and their advocates and allies will eventually move away from employers who do not fulfill their needs, nor accommodate and make adjustments for their neurological variances. They will instead choose to work for employers that have met a benchmark 'standard', just like those individuals who are part of the LGBTQIA+ communities who are on the look-out for the *Rainbow Flag* at their future workplaces, those who want to work for organisations who take care of their customers, staff and stakeholders, who want an Investors in People [IiP] employer, or individuals who may want to work for environmentally friendly organisations and look out for the Reduce, Reuse, Recycle emblem in their workplace. Each of these says something about you as an employer and also about the way you lead and manage your employees in the achievement of your business objectives.

With the right environment, neurodivergent employees can achieve at 'good', 'excellent' and masterful levels. With the 'wrong' environment, they will falter and maybe even fail to produce at a level that is productive for your organisation. That is the same employee. The same employee in a different environment.

If you are a neurodivergent employer, advocate or ally and would like to know more, please visit: www.neurodiversityworkshere.com. This book supports the NeuroDiversity Works Here! Campaign and is an ally and advocate for all neurodivergent employees, students and non-working individuals, globally.

For many neurodivergent individuals, myself included, our difference is not obvious, nor visible, at first glance. This can make it challenging to distinguish why we may need adjustments, even if we have asked for them. It may also make it appear that we are asking for something that others may feel we have no 'rights' to, or that we are asking for something above and beyond what we are entitled to have.

In addition, for those with a recognised disability, in the workplace, we have entitlements to adjustments under the Disability Discrimination Act [DDA] (Australian Government, 1992), if we have a diagnosed condition, illness or injury and can provide evidence of this to our employer. Details on this may vary slightly from country to country. So, please check with your legislative body in country and/or region, for more finite details.

However, there is legislation in place that protects the rights of people who have illnesses, are injured and moving back into the workplace, and also those with long-term conditions that may affect their overall capacity to work. In terms of neurodivergent and cognitive variations, sometimes these have not been diagnosed, sometimes one aspect of the condition is diagnosed buy other neurodivergent factors also impact on the individual's capabilities, or the impact of their environment upon them.

For all of us, we have entitlements under the Human Rights Act, to be treated fairly and without discrimination, under the Act (AHRC, 2020). In

Australia, we also have some protections, in the workplace, under the FairWork Ombudsman's jurisdiction, so it is worth checking in with them, if you find yourself floundering a little. As well, there are Occupational Health and Safety standards (and/or Workplace Health and Safety guidelines that meet both regional and national standards). These will be familiar across countries, even if named slightly differently. They will highlight the minimum safety standards for workplace conditions.

As a manager, I want you to think about this, in terms of OH&S/WH&S- minimum standards are just that. Fulfilling minimum standards is the bottom of the rung in terms of health and safety of your employees. I know because I used to conduct WH&S training. I have also been an Emergency First Responder trainer where we had to cover all of the MSDS guidelines, hazards and control measures and SWMS. If you are patting yourself on the back because you have achieved a minimum standard in safety in the workplace, I want you to go back and revisit your WH&S strategy. I want you to look through it with fresh eyes. Eyes that might have some of the environmental impact concerns that we have talked about so far.

In relation to neurodiversity and neurological variations, it is important to consider what you can do to promote ethical work practices that are inclusive of all employees, that engage and utilise the core skills, talents and capabilities of your workforce, and the engender strategies and methodologies that enable you to effectively lead, support and engage in the continuous improvement and leadership of your human capital.

Nurturing Your NeuroDivergent Workforce

Evidence has shown how enhancing and increasing your neurologically diverse workforce can provide huge benefits in the following areas:

➢ Business performance
➢ Productivity
➢ Increased measures of success

- ➢ Optimising ROI (human capital)
- ➢ Enhancing competitive advantage
- ➢ Shifting internal cultural perspective
- ➢ Increasing staff satisfaction with workplace environment
- ➢ Enhancing customer perception
- ➢ Boosting stakeholder management
- ➢ Creating innovative leadership and management models and best practice

Admittedly, the business world is filled with professional justifications and overt quantification of "performance". It is rarely 'person-centred', filled with compassion, caring nor nurturing. However, we vow to adhere to a set of ethical and moral principle, in running our business. We agree to comply with national, global and local policy, legislation and best practice, in order to be compliant with contemporary business practices.

What we don't do, is accept that our workforce, our employees, are human. Just like us. Yes, we employ them. We want them to do what they said they could do when they passed the test to get through the front door.

We have put our faith in them to achieve their established daily and weekly tasks, outputs, projects targets, milestones and overall business objectives and KPIs. If they are not able to do that, what can we do to effect change?

Ultimately, workplace cultures that engender inclusion and diversity, including neurodiversity, that promote and embed organisational innovation, generate open productivity flow and encompass an evolutionary approach to business development and growth, will come through the next decade intact (Herring & Henderson, 2014).

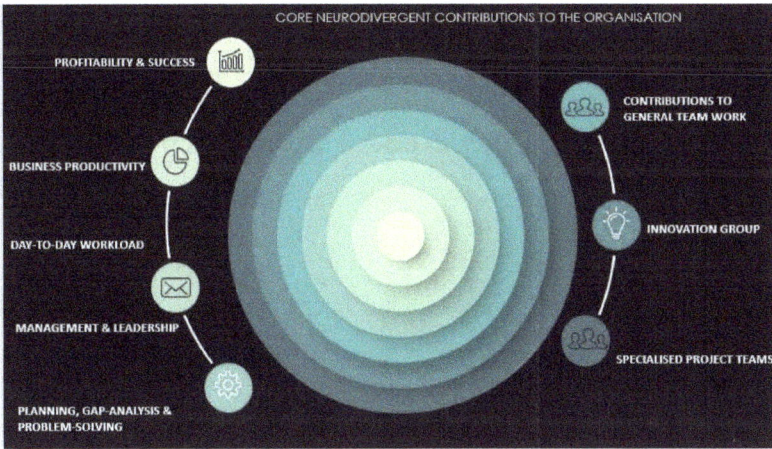

CORE NEURODIVERGENT CONTRIBUTIONS TO THE ORGANISATION

PROFITABILITY & SUCCESS

BUSINESS PRODUCTIVITY

DAY-TO-DAY WORKLOAD

MANAGEMENT & LEADERSHIP

PLANNING, GAP-ANALYSIS & PROBLEM-SOLVING

CONTRIBUTIONS TO GENERAL TEAM WORK

INNOVATION GROUP

SPECIALISED PROJECT TEAMS

In the Knowledge Economy, We Have Let Ourselves Down

Whilst the information about low levels of literacy and numeracy above, is somewhat frightening, it is not too surprising.

In 2006, ABS statistics show almost 80% of people with higher than average incomes also had literacy competence levels at L2 or higher. This is compared with only 57% of middle-income level earners; and only 37% of lower level income earners. (ABS, 2006).

We **need** a strong, solid and enduring workforce, but we have not put the correct foundations in place to be able to grow and nurture it, from the start. Our school system is not equipped to deliver both a rigorous curriculum AND a solid employability development program. And, most of all, we have not established a safe, structured, well-designed space for individuals to be able to explore and flourish. Particularly those who did not fit well into the school system.

Researchers in education, such as Siegel & Valtierra (2019) and O'Regan (2003; 2020b) and others with a broader scope of the social world and neurodiversity, such as Silberman, (2016) have come to the conclusion that when absorbing information, when "learning" (and as an employee who is 'learning', in a workplace context), one can make contributions in diverse and meaningful ways that may sit outside the standard norms. However, these are still valid and meaningful contributions. They affirmed that institutions and workplaces that have a disposition that validates the individual are far more likely to achieve higher levels of productivity and personal and interpersonal satisfaction, as well as engagement. This is also affirmed by the initial statements framed at the beginning of this book, where I stated that the GALLUP Soft Skills Survey (2019) concluded that 70% of employee engagement was attributed to the quality of leadership of their management and leadership team.

Considering the numbers stated above (those who are neurodiverse (an estimated 14% of the population) and those with lower than 'workplace suitable' literacy, numeracy and critical thinking skills (almost half of the working age population), we have a lot to develop in order to effectively secure the trust of those who look up to us as leaders, role models, managers and designers of the rest of their working lives- an average of 50 years.

So, back to my original question- where did it all go so wrong?

And, is there a way we can shift some of this mess, so that we can begin to make changes in the way our world functions? So that we can more comfortably invite the new Knowledge Age in through our workplace doors?

In 2000, the OECD, under its guise as the UNESCO Institute of Statistics [UIS} completed a series of research on literacy skills across its 188 participating nations. The UK, USA and Australia being just three of them. The findings were published in a Report (UNESCO, 2003), which outlined how these countries could develop their education systems to prepare their students, so that global workforce development occurred at a more coherent rate and in a more collaborative manner.

Whilst this could have been viewed as an idealistic approach to globalisation, it was actually a very clever and compelling incentive for all participating countries to join together and create a united front, so that literacy and numeracy levels did not continue to decline.

What came out of this process was a group of countries that set about mitigating the effects of social disadvantage caused by inequality, social disadvantage and non-equity of resources, opportunity and access to resources.

One of the key ways in which a manager can create this reciprocal developmental approach is through mentoring and coaching. Whilst many people may view mentoring and coaching as 6 week of lazer-style "zinginess"- aimed at 'fixing' your newest 'issue'. I have been working with individuals and groups to develop and enhance their mentoring and coaching programs, in a wide variety of contexts, since the late 90s, in a global economy.

That is 25 years of 'wizened' (just don't call me old) experience to draw from. From an employability perspective, in working with the long-term unemployed, when skilling up the under-employed and those who society sees as having 'limited skills' (but who are eminently willing and wanting to work!); and, in a globalised business marketplace that has seen at least two economic downfalls, and in which I have personally witnessed the upturn and downfall of many, many businesses, across three countries that I have resided in, for those periods of time.

Another format for mentoring and coaching is that of peer to peer relationships. This can have its pitfalls when utilising it with neurodivergent employees. However, it can be a useful way of pairing employees for learning projects and collaboration. Risquez, (2008) states that this form of mentoring "offers a useful orientation to a mentoring system, involving a degree of social responsibility to the community in ways that attempt to confront and reverse an ever-increasing individualistic, competitive approach to career, education, and life development". This affirms the approach offered by O'Regan in her Final Evaluation of the European Social Funded (ESF) Transnational E-Mentoring Program, which came to the above conclusions, after the application of e-mentoring in 5 European countries, across 5 differing contexts and with five diverse audiences (O'Regan, 2006).

This was a ground-breaking, multi-year project, at the time and from it developed many further e-mentoring, mentoring and coaching programs, which are so popular in developing, enhancing and promoting motivational strategies that boost productivity in educational contexts, and business, across the globe, today.

Productivity- What Does it Really Mean?

In the context of this book, we are talking about human capital, what they can produce for profit and the influence and impact of our neurodivergent employees on this production, in a positive way. We have discussed the many variants and variations in presentation of these employees, noting that these are mere examples. The diversity of neurodivergence means that there will be an ever-emerging array of examples that may present themselves in our staff, managers, colleagues and even those around us in our social worlds. I have merely presented the examples in section one, to provide you with some real-life case studies as representations of individuals already in the live workforce Beardwell & Thompson, 2010).

In relation to human capital, our employees and their capabilities, we are now discussing how these correlates to our organisation's productivity and ultimate profitability, it is important to take into account the significant link between an organisation's human capital, how this can provide a distinct competitive advantage in the marketplace and productivity (Chowdhury, Schulz, Milner, & Van De Voort, 2014).

How Does Inclusive Practice Tap into Productivity?

By utilising the capabilities of our neurodivergent employees, taking competitive advantage of their specialised skillsets and providing access to spaces, teams and resources that empower our employees in a way that creates more flexibility in the overall organisational system, to allow them to develop, design and create, as well as nurture and be responsive to the shifts and changes within the organisation as well as externally, in the marketplace, we are ultimately 'going with the flow', whilst ate same time utilising our neurodivergent employees as specialised team members (Honeybourne, 2019).

Why is Innovation So Important in This Space?

We will link into this further, a little later in the book. However, at this point, it is important to link innovation to the utilisation of human capital, in this case, neurodivergent talent, and especially specialised talent, to exercise competitive advantage. By engaging in innovative practices, this will highlight and compel the individuals, teams and organisation forward in a more progressive and innovative manner.

The negative correlation here is that without innovation, the organisation may become stagnant or even stuck', meaning that not only the neurodivergent employees, but everyone else is left in a 'bit of a rut', hole or completely buried, under the weight of a minimally or non-performing organisational 'tonnage'.

How Can Neurodivergent Employees Support this Process?

If you have been developing a respectful, trusting working relationship with your staff, then there won't be any issues with a mutual and reciprocal support process, when it comes to the development of new and innovative workplace practice, systems, processes and policies.

The best people to bring on board, as we established before, are the ones who you will be a part of this process. Asking your neurodivergent employees to assist with the development of the above is vital, so that they can participate in the consultation process, take part in the decision-making processes about them and also speak to decision that are being made about them, at an organisation level. It is also useful to hear what neurodivergent life and workplace experiences are like, straight from the mouths of your employees (Krzeminska, Austin, Bruyère & Hedley, 2019).

It may be challenging to hear at time, but it can, in the end, be the most rewarding and transformative experience your managers and organisation will take part in

In addition, you employees can support the process by:

- o Sharing their own specialist knowledge and skills
- o Creating new strategies, models and processes
- o Sharing their specialist skills and innovations
- o Engaging in focussed work for the organisation. i.e. research and development, creation of resources, rewriting policies and procedures
- o Engaging in consultations

Identifying Employee Strengths

All employees like to be appreciated for their contributions. For a neurodivergent employee, some employers can find it a challenge to identify core strengths, as those that usually rise to the forefront of an employers' mind are not always those that are present in a neurodivergent employee, at first glance.

That is why it is important to approach the assessment of neurodivergent strengths form an alternative perspective (Mellifont, 2019; O'Regan, 2020b).

I have developed a simplified assessment tool to support the assessment of neurodivergent strengths that can also be applied to all staff and also to managers and leaders. It looks at strengths not in areas of competence, but in realms of application. For instance:

-Cognitive

-Emotional

-Socio-cultural

-Environmental-Ecological

The assessment is conducted on a personal level, to assess each individual's strengths.

The areas that are assessed are personalised. This is so that assessments are not compared from one person to another. The reason for this is so that there is not a commodification of employees.

There is a rationale for this that I outline in the full training provided for this assessment.

The short version is that your neurodivergent employees are human beings. They have their own individual strengths and these are unique to them.

COGNITIVE REALM	SOCIO-CULTURAL REALM
EMOTIONAL REALM	ENVIRONMENTAL-ECOLOGICAL REALM

The Four-Part Matrix: Assessment of Neurodivergent Strengths

Use the four-part Matrix over the page and the two examples provided below to assess your collaborative team of two neurodivergent team members. The idea may seem a little complicated, but basically juxtaposes a series of strengths over the top of the matrix to assess strengths and core areas of strengths.

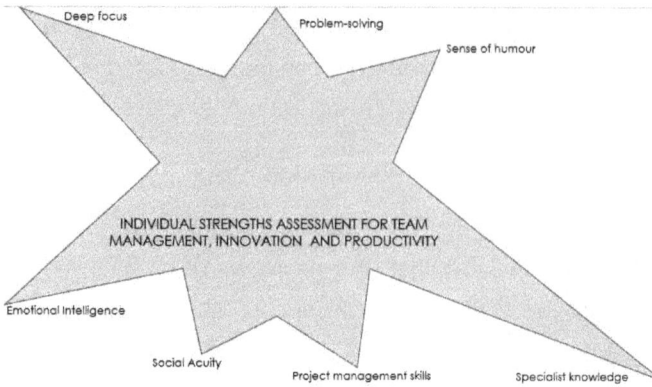

Deep focus Problem-solving Sense of humour

INDIVIDUAL STRENGTHS ASSESSMENT FOR TEAM
MANAGEMENT, INNOVATION AND PRODUCTIVITY

Emotional Intelligence

Social Acuity Project management skills Specialist knowledge

Example 1: Assessing Individual Strengths Against the Matrix-
Assessment of Neurodivergent Strengths

In the example provided above, you can see that the individual has
some strengths in their area of specialist knowledge and deep focus, as well
as in emotional intelligence. In the example below, the individual has a
differing set of core strengths, with training and development skills,
organisational skills, sales and marketing skills, and a few others.

By juxtaposing the two examples over The Matrix, you can see that
there may be 'gaps' in this team collaboration. However, by not 'comparing
strengths against strength, the individuals are not made to 'feel' competitive,
nor is a situation created where one person feels 'lesser than' another.

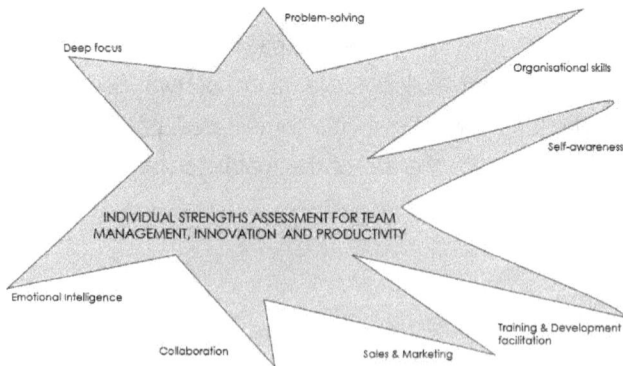

Problem-solving Deep focus Organisational skills Self-awareness

INDIVIDUAL STRENGTHS ASSESSMENT FOR TEAM
MANAGEMENT, INNOVATION AND PRODUCTIVITY

Emotional Intelligence

Collaboration Sales & Marketing Training & Development facilitation

Example 2: Assessing Individual Strengths Against the Matrix-
Assessment of Neurodivergent Strengths

As you can see from this team's analysis, this team has a reasonable range of strengths, between the two individuals. They may require some support with initiating the project and also with monitoring and reviewing progress. Although, one team member has stated excellent project management skills, we do not know the scope of those. That would be worth exploring in more depth.

These are neither personality profiling tools nor diagnostic tools. They are-strengths-based assessments aimed at identifying gaps in team strengths and enabling managers to rationalise why teams may be "under-performing" and why that may be the case. That is, which area is not being addressed (and also what they need to do to strengthen team performance).

You can see though, how this small innovation can provide an easy snapshot of how you team may complement each other, individually, or where there may be gaps in skills and expertise.

I have found this style of assessment much more useful than standard psychometric assessments, which can be quite confusing for neurodivergent employees, and which are also pitching one individual against another, in a competitive way. This is a far more complementary approach that enables a manager to assess gaps (and I love to do gap analysis!) and then look at innovative ways to fill those gaps without disturbing the equilibrium of the established system or process that is already working.

Creating Collaboration and Ownership of Projects

One of the key ways to engage your neurodivergent employees in the process of innovation at a fundamental or grassroots level is to give them some ownership over it. When someone feels as though they have a direct part to play in the design, development and overall equity in a collaboration, they are far more likely to give their all than if they are only asked for minor input and contribution. This is even more the case for neurodivergent employees, who want to show you, as their manager, what they are capable of achieving. Some of the more common key attributes that come along with being neurodivergent, which we haven't yet discussed, are a sense of loyalty and commitment to those you are connected to; a desire to contribute, a level of integrity, a high-order value system, an internal moral compass that cannot be swayed., a strength of character, a fantastic ability to assess other people's character on sight, and a 'connection ' with others that once made, will only be severed if there is a distinct betrayal of trust (Bewley & George, 2018).

Surveys that have been conducted with longer term employers of neurodivergent employees in the UK have indicated that they are the most loyal, committed, dedicated, and long-term employees in many organisations, as once established in an organisation and settled, they do not often leave their employer (Hacque & Gilroy, 2016).

And, so, for neurodivergent employees, having a piece of work that they can take on board, truly make their own, have some ownership over and put their heart and Soul into can be highly beneficial to their overall contributions to the organisation. It can also showcase their key contributions to their employers and also to key stakeholders in the business, building the organisation's external reputation and delivering organisational innovation and productivity both internally and externally.

Neurodivergent Employee Motivation During Enhanced Productivity

We have been talking about all the different and alternative ways in which a neurodivergent mind works, processes information and sensory input and approaches the 'world'. So, it is inevitable that the neurodivergent employee will also potentially, and in reality, be motivated by different and alternative methods and incentives and rewards as well.

Since we are talking about enhancing and optimising productivity and exploring ways in which to increase profitability of your organisation, it would be a useful time to explore how you might adopt and adapt your current motivational strategies to further motivate your neurodivergent employees.

One of the key things I want to emphasise here is that of internal or intrinsic motivators. I am sure you are aware that all of us are motivated by either a primary extrinsic (external) motivation source, or by an intrinsic (that is, internal) motivational source (Amabile, 1993; Moody & Pesut, 2006).

Just as a recap: these motivators could be many things. Here are some examples:

EXTRINSIC

Money (payment for service)

Status

Power

Payment/salary

INTRINSIC

Integrity

Values

Moral compass

Satisfaction

If someone is extrinsically motivated, they are unlikely to take the initiative and contribute their time and effort to a task or project, outside of the scope of their daily assigned work tasks, unless they have some buy-in for completing or engaging in it.

Whereas, someone who is intrinsically motivated will be more inclined to participate in a project or task if they can gain an inner sense of moral, ethical or emotional sense of satisfaction from engaging with the project.

There are many research papers that indicate that neurodivergent people tend to lean towards being intrinsically motivated and therefore will willingly participate in extramural projects, collaborations and tasks if they can see the benefits on a personal level.

It is worth exploring this as a management and leadership team when deciding how you structure your incentives and rewards and also on how you engage your participants in collaborative work, as your neurodivergent team members may be motivated very differently than your non-neurodivergent employees, who may be more drawn to extrinsic motivators such as status, recognition and payment.

Utilising Innovation to Fill the Productivity 'Gaps'

At the end of the day, innovation is purely a new, alternative or different way of doing something in a way it has not been done before. This book is innovative, because no-one has written about neurodiversity in quite the way I have written about it!

I know that you haven't come to be in your position as a team leader, business owner, manager or CEO because you are no good at problem solving, creating ingenious ways around what seems like an impossible situation, or adapting something that just wasn't going to work into something that fits just perfectly!

That is you, right?!

I know it is. Even if you haven't done that kind of thing for a very long time.

Your neurodivergent employees are those kinds of people too! They feel like they are flying high when they can use their abilities, capacity, skills, knowledge, specialism and focus, to create, design, develop and innovate!

I have been emphasising this all the way throughout this book.

If you can find a way to merge these abilities, qualities, strengths, skills, knowledge and uniqueness with your product or service so that your organisation ends up with something even more special than it already has going on, then you will have created a business unicorn!

Reframing the Workplace for Higher Levels of Productivity

How Can You Encourage and Motivate Your NeuroDiverse Workforce?

The most powerful concept in being able to persuade and motivate someone is in the way we frame what we say. When we look at the overall, big picture we can see most everything we do and say as a 'frame'. When I suggest examples based on neurodiversity, neurodivergence, environmental rights and wrongs in the workplace, I'm not endorsing one side or another. I'm simply showing there are blind in our thinking and in our ability to think about the needs of others. These blind spots sometimes make it hard to see what those needs are. Generally, as a society, we don't always do so well at this. In our workplaces, we have come to believe that everyone is exactly the same. That everyone will be okay with working at a desk, with a certain amount of light, underneath fluorescent lights, with up to 100 telephones around them, with conversation all around them, with printers and photocopiers in their vicinity, with opening and closing doors, and generally, with exactly the same environmental situation as everyone else who works with us. It's just not true (Cassidy, 2018; O'Regan, 2020b).

Unfortunately, where our blind spots exist, where we have holes in our 'arguments' for or against something, we often believe we have made the right choice, the right decision, the most equitable, person-centred choice. Once again, it is not always the case.

This is because we can usually only see what is happening, in our home, in our workplace, in our society, from the 'frame' of our own experience. So, for instance, if you have never experienced a 'difficulty' with a manager over a working environment, you may not believe that anyone could have an issue at work, over whether or not they could have a lamp next to their desk. It happens, more than many of us might want to know.

And, if you think that your way is the only way, then you will most probably not have gotten this far into reading this book.

I think you are wanting something more. I think you are looking for an alternative solution to something that isn't quite working in your organisation. And, I think you don't quite know what that is.

It's okay. No-one is watching. They haven't seen you pick up this book. Purchase it at the counter. Put in in your bag. Take it home. And, start reading it. They don't know that you are a third of the way through it. Learning something new. And, a little bit intrigued.

You are, aren't you?

What I am saying hasn't been said before. Not quite like this. Not quite in this way. Not to you. Not to your manager friends. Not so that it makes sense like this. Right?

So, whatever you may have fervently or fanatically believe in before, whatever was the "blind side" of the issue. It's okay.

Not everyone knows everything. And, not everyone knows everything and everything!

The ability to reframe is to tell our truth, life the way we see it. It requires us to repeat things deeply carving neuro pathways that show us what to think in any given situation, with any given group or idea, in any setting.

Without naming names, think of the major coffee chain, the one that's taking over the world. They're responsible for putting little mom and pop cafes out of business. They charge A LOT. They may even be slightly overrated. AND yet, they are fair to their employees even providing part time workers with health insurance. They buy their product from sustainable coffee growers in 'developing' countries. They also have a delicious organic iced decaf mocha.

It's possible all of these statements are true at once. Maybe it doesn't matter a one iota to you either way. But they are beliefs and as a result, they are frames.

For those of you still 'umming' and 'ahhing'. I have absolutely no interest in changing your deeply held beliefs. My goal is to simply point out that all of these beliefs, ultimately, are different frames. There are different ways that people's minds work. This is a scientific fact. It has been proven many times over. And, what this means for you, in the workplace, as their manager, team leader, boss, CEO, HR representative, is that you have a duty of care, of some sort, to support them in having their alternative and neurodiverse needs environmentally accommodated.

Opening Up the Mindset of Innovation

In today's contemporary society, many progressive words are bandied about, in relation to our workforce development, utilization of space and transition into new and more innovative work practices: collaborative practice; think-tanks; hot-seats; eco-friendly work-spaces; sustainability in the workplace; open-plan offices; and so on. We have become focussed on technologically advanced workplaces, where information systems and process are primarily driven, firstly by the rate of technological advancement a business can afford to bring on board; and secondly, by the degree of market demand for their product or service.

Of course, as astute business people, we realise there are many other significant factors involved in the maintenance, sustainability, and even evolution of a business, which I will abstain from adding to my conversation, here, in the event that it sullies the waters of what I truly want to focus on. And that is, have we lost our humanity, our human touch, our curiosity about and our compassion for, the people that make up our enduring workforce?

I know many of you will state that "we cannot do what we do without our people" and "they are the lifeblood of our business", and "we take care of our people, so they take care of us". And, of course, as people who want to believe that we are caring individuals who care about the people who work for us, of course we don't want to face up to the fact that, depending on the research source, up to 75% of our global workforce has some level of discontent, that relates to where, how and with whom they work. In terms of workplace wellbeing, and the care and maintenance of our employees psychological and mental health and wellbeing, this is incredibly significant!

If we want a 'sick' workforce, we're certainly heading in the right direction. Although there is huge value in collaborating, both internally, within our organisation or sector, as well as externally, in order to gain new ideas and engender new partnerships, collaborative working often: takes more time; requires more reporting back to overseeing bodies (SMTs; committees; Board of Trustees/Management; Line Management; project management etc). Open plan offices, although conducive to conversation and ideas-sharing, can create, rather than reduce, chaos for many staff. Employees who require quieter space to work at optimum productivity will falter. Phone calls will be interrupted by too-loud laughter and conversations that may have just been short 5-10-minute catch-up conversations will continue on through the day, disrupting other workplace tasks. Without wanting to sound like the workplace Grinch, this could be catastrophic for workplaces who rely on high-productivity (Griffiths, 2020).

SECTION SIX

20/20 Vision and The Paradigm Shift- Managing and Leading Your NeuroDivergent Workforce

Managing NeuroDivergent Employees

Many employees think, and respond to the world around them, in what is called a neuro-typical way. That is, their brain follows particular cognitive and sensory patterns in thinking, processing information, sensing, responding to, communicating with and feeling into the world. Other people have a more diverse way that their brain works. It means that their brain works in a more divergent manner. That means they think in ways that are not the same as neuro-typical thinkers. It also means that their brain is physiologically hard-wired differently. So, they do not respond to the world, at large, in the same way that people with neuro-typical brain patterns do. These individuals are neurodivergent and belong to a neurodiverse community of people.

What does this have to do with the workplace?... I hear you all asking.

Well, what is really interesting, and incredibly interesting to me, both personally and professionally, is that, as a society, we have established our workplaces, particularly office space, and teaching environments, to be really great for individuals who are neuro-typical, but not work so well for people who are neurodivergent.

For instance, what works really well for someone who is 'neuro-typical' is to have a fast-paced, ever-changing, loud, open-plan office, with over-head fluorescent lights, end or desk-line conversation pods, limited quiet space, clear-desk policy, last minute changes to projects, limited break time/space, frequent changes to meetings, limited opportunity to engage in create methods for planning, preparation and evaluation and be able to more easily 'cope with' a go-go-go atmosphere, at work. That was just framed off the top of my head!

Now, some neurodivergent individuals may be able to work 'okay' in that environment for a period of time. However, they will eventually come to a point in time where their productivity will start to falter and they will begin to take time off work due to niggly (or maybe major) health issues, as they begin to be affected by sensory 'overload', cognitive 'overload', classic symptoms of 'environmental 'overwhelm ', and so on. This will all be happening inside the neurodivergent employee and may not be visible to anyone around them, until it all becomes too much. It's a little like when you have just gotten home from work, you passed a major accident on the road and it was a little emotionally unsettling for you, as soon as you enter your house, your partner and 3 children all want your time and attention, the dog wants a pat, your best friend rings, the neighbour knocks on the door and all you want to do is go and have a shower and chill your mind a little bit. Just for 10 minutes or so.

Usually, after a short break, you are back on track and able to focus on everyone else's needs. Right?

For someone who is neurodivergent, they may be mildly, moderately or significantly affected by any one of the above elements of the workplace and in their social realm. I have seen it take hours and even days for someone to recover and recuperate after a significant disjuncture in their equilibrium caused by a scenario like this. It is what a friend of mine calls a 'complete discombobulation!"

Because it feels as though everything has been turned on its head. And, it is very challenging to come back from that in a short period of time.

For this book, I've chosen an office just to illustrate some of the core areas in which neurodivergent individuals have some major challenges in the workplace, which are either dismissed or continually challenged by their employers.

I will delve into this in much greater detail as you read through the book. However, for now, I want you to imagine how it might feel for you if every time you walked through the door at work, the lighting affected your ability to concentrate on daily workplace, because the fluorescent lighting gave you a migraine every day (even at current *WorkSafe* (WH&S/OH&S) guidelines for lumens). And, when you asked you team leader if you could have a lamp next to your desk, your Team leader did one of three things:

- Laughed and said that WorkSafe guidelines were being followed, what is your problem? (and nothing else can be done)
- Told you to take some preventative migraine medication
- Said "No, you can't have a lamp next to your desk... that would look silly/you have a clean-desk policy in place/the boss wouldn't like it"

Our employee struggled on for a couple of months, with her migraines getting worse and worse. She went to see her GP (and then a specialist) about her migraines and was eventually given preventative migraine medication. She found that the migraines over those few months were so severe that she had difficulties concentrating, so her productivity fell. She was co-ordinating a few different projects at work, and her team leaders decided that both her sick leave accumulation and her "attitude to work", along with her drop in productivity must mean that she didn't care about work. She was put on a *Performance Management Plan*. In the end, she decided to leave. She did not feel as though her Managers and team leaders understood that it was the environmental impact on her that was creating these barriers to her achieving a high-level productivity. All they saw was her 'failing' as an employee.

Imagine living like that every minute of every hour of every day. Imagine entering into spaces to work for 7-10 hours every day, 5 days a week, where the environment has you feeling on edge constantly and not feeling comfortable enough to really relax into your work enough that you can be fully productive, engage with your colleagues in such a way that they feel comfortable or you feel comfortable, and others around You know something is a little off kilter, but nobody quite knows what that is.

I am talking to you as a more senior member of staff, assuming that you are neurotypical. Maybe you are not. Maybe you also fit into the neurodivergent community too. Maybe you are aware of this, or maybe you are not.

What I'd like you to consider is this: just like not all children learn the same way- some love to take part in learning, getting fully involved, getting right in there amongst the learning, in order to take on board what they are learning; others want to sit by the sides and just take it all in, before they are willing to venture into the 'practicing' anything space; and others again, want to hear all about how they do that new thing, again and again, before they want to do it. Some also want to read what they are meant to do, but these young ones are usually few and far between!

Using this analogy above, I want you to think about your employees and your team members in the same way as these children. Some employees will really take to the workplace environment you have created, as it is highly suitable to their neuro-type (their neurotypical way of thing and being in the world). Others will find it very off-putting and incredibly uncomfortable to be in and a part of.

This does not mean that they are being difficult. This means that when they are in your work space, they will not be able to function as well as an employee, as the environment will be having a mild, moderate or significant impact on their cognitive, emotional, social or psychological responses to the world around them. This is not anything they have any 'control' over, and many of them may not even be aware that they are neurodivergent, so may not recognise that this is happening. Not everyone will respond to the different elements in the workplace in the same way. They will all find some of those elements I mentioned above either absolutely fine, or very, very uncomfortable to be around.

From a personal perspective, neurodivergent employees will be searching for workplaces that will be conducive to meeting their needs, have already made accommodation to meet their needs, or are willing to listen to what their needs may be (ACAS, 2020; AHRC, 2020; AND, 2020; EEOC, 2020; HSE, 2020; UK Govt, 2018; US Dept of Labor, 2020: Workplace Fairness, 2020).

One day, my greatest hope is that all workplaces have a space for their neurodivergent employees, that is created specifically to accommodate the needs of their neurodiverse workforce.

I hope you will be more willing to recognise these needs of your own workforce, after reading this book! And, I hope that if you recognise yourself in any if what I have said about living in a neurodivergent world or being a part community, that you reach out and find some support. The world is a healthier place when we support each other to live our lives in the best way possible!

Addressing the Issues of Neurodiversity and Inclusion from a Manager's Perspective

To be a successful manager in today's world, you need to create an environment of inclusion where people feel valued and integrated into a company's mission, vision and business strategy at all levels. When employees' skills and knowledge are recognized, appreciated and utilized they are more engaged in contributing to an organizations' success. They are more willing to go the 'extra mile' and share ideas and innovation. They spread the word that your organization is a great place to work. They are enthusiastic about recruiting their talented colleagues to fill open positions who bring new ideas and diverse ways of thinking, solving problems and expanding market share

Creating a neurodiverse workforce means a massive shift in perspective, for some. For others, maybe you are already in alignment with new ways of thinking about your workforce. I want to highly commend you on making this paradigm shift. We have entered a new dimension of workplace design and workplace and workforce development. The ways in which we used to 'do' things will no longer work for us. For a whole range of reasons.

Now is the time to take on board new information about how we can take what we are already doing, make some tweaks, and create something a whole lot better!

By fully accepting that not everyone does everything exactly the same. Not everyone's brain works exactly the same way. And, acknowledging that the vast majority of most workplaces are filled with neurodiverse individuals, who have needs that are not currently being met (meaning- and this is the key to your business development and growth, so lean in and listen carefully- ... meaning that, if their neurodiversity needs are not being met and they are being adversely impacted upon by their working environment, there is NO WAY they will be able to voluntarily offer you the best that they can give you, as an employee.

Does that make sense?

Imagine if you, yourself, were asked to "do your best" in a small, dark, walled up room, with a hard seat, limited lighting, no stimulus and asked to "do as much as you could", without a time-piece to keep track, no extra support, no 'bonus' when you did something "right", and no ongoing encouragement.

Try that for a day, a week, a month. Try working like that for a year, a lifetime.

It is an extreme example I have given you, but these are some of the areas that people who are neurodivergent are often challenged. They have sensory issues, they have cognition issues, they are under or overstimulated by noise and lighting and hardness/softness of their environment. They may be responsive to daylight, have time keeping issues, due to executive functioning constraints, and so on.

None of this makes them a "bad worker". It purely means that their environment is not set up to enhance the optimisation of their working capacity.

This is not your employee's doing. It is your responsibility to ensure that they are able to excel and meet the demands of their workplace, under all inclusivity guidelines (and, if appropriate) any relevant Disability Act guidelines. I know some of you will say, "we are meeting the minimum standard" of (fill in the blank legislation, policy, government guidelines).

So. Are. Your. Neurodivergent. Employees.

If you commit to supporting them to your fullest capacity, they will most certainly give you all they've got. I promise you!

But, no-one, and I mean NO-ONE, is able, capable or has the capacity to willingly go beyond mediocre (without adverse pressure on their health and wellbeing, over time), without support. That means both structurally, in policy, processes and practice, as well as in the implementation of environmental adjustments and additions that will be able to meet and accommodate their needs.

It is truly as simple as that.

Mission

Stepping Out- Neurodivergent vs 'Neuro-normative' Thinking

Sequential or methodical thought processes have often been explained as left/brain cognitive processes. In fact, we can explore some of the reasons why someone might have a neurodiverse way of thinking. I have referred to this as 'neuro-normative thinking'.

In addition to the above reasons that may give rise to neurodiversity, individuals with ABI (Acquired Brain Injury), those recovering from brain-related injury (not classified as ABI) or brain-related illness, individuals with learning challenges and those with low level literacy and numeracy levels may also often display significant signs of neurodiverse ways of thinking and processing information, from a teaching and learning perspective, and must, therefore be included in this grouping of individuals.

If neurodiverse individuals don't tend to start from step one and then move to step two and then on to step three, in a sequential manner, and this then does not appear to those who are not neurodiverse, let's call that group of individuals or 'neuro-typical', then the processing of information undertaken by the neurodivergent individuals may appear to be one of the following:

→ illogical

→ 'incorrect'

→ ill-formed OR unformed/piecemeal

→ 'confused'

→ 'under-developed' thinking

What is Actually Happening?

1. There has not been enough time to process and/or assimilate information and produce and answer/outcome/product that is in alignment with neurotypical cognition. However, the neurodiverse mind is in the process of sifting through every possible outcome, conclusion, and answer relevant to the situation. So, it will take a little more time.

One of the key things people close to me find incredibly funny at times (they are close to me, so I let them find humour in some of my uniqueness), is that if they ask me mid-thought process, they will often get a 'stream of consciousness' thought sequence from me, which in effect makes little sense to them. Although they have learnt that this means "Come back later, Leigh hasn't fully processed yet", in a workplace situation, I have received some very scathing feedback when in a similar situation and called in to an urgent, off-the-cuff meeting and asked to explain where I was up to with a series of complex project delivery milestones.

From feedback, I have been told that I can sound as though I don't know what I'm talking about. Or, that I haven't grasped and idea. Or that I am unable to effectively communicate or articulate what I mean or am feeling about a situation, task, concept or idea.

What is really happening for me (and, I know from interviewing and asking my neurodivergent friends, family and previous working colleagues, they have felt the same) is that I have either:

-been interrupted before I have fully processed the information at hand (therefore, the information in my brain is unstructured and in little packages), and usually found in different parts of my brain. For instance, I may have a part of the information stored in my long-term memory. If I haven't fully processed some information that requires that 'package' of information from my long-term memory, then I won't have gone to pick it up yet. So, it will be a missing piece in my information trail. In addition, if I require both analytical and emotional information pulled from my cognitive system, they are also 'stored' in different 'pods' and in different 'packages' in different parts of my brain. So, if you want me to explain something in an analytical way, I will draw from that 'package'. I may then appear very unemotional about it. This has really thrown some of my colleagues and managers, at times, as I have explained that my grandmother has just died, or my father has just had a heart attack. In giving the information, I have delivered it from an analytical package, as I am sharing medical information stored in my 'medical knowledge' section of my brain. This is insight I don't usually share with anyone, as it has taken me a very long time to gain this level of awareness about how I think and why I sometimes appear incongruently to what I am trying to convey and share with others.

If you want me to delve into the emotional effects of my father's heart-attack, then I need to access a different 'package' and that requires me not speaking from an analytical (in this context, read, information medical sharing) perspective. I would have to access my emotional repository. As you'll have noticed, this is stored in a completely different storage space inside my cognitive realm. This is also often an interesting space for me to access, unless I am actively feeling something at the time.

-   I haven't yet assimilated the information, from an information processing point of view. For any of you who know how a computer works, my mind works in a fragmented mode of operation all of the time. If I tried to defrag it, I would end up in chaos, as I am well aware of where pieces of information and knowledge is stored. What I can't do is speed up the retrieval process. So, if I am not able to have enough time to assimilate information, i.e. Pull it together from all of the regions from where it is kept, then my articulation of what I know will sound 'bitsy' and uninformed.

- If I have been working on focussing on one stream of concentration, let's say, writing this book. And, then, I am interrupted and asked a question about the organisation of the Business Development Conference in September, my mind will not easily be able to switch tracks. I may appear to be uninterested (I am not), dissociated (I am not, just rapidly trying to gather information from a very different pod than the one I was just in deep concentration mode, delved waist high in concentration with), or I will appear blank. This may be the case, for a second or two, until my brain does switch tracks. But I am not in control of this process. Please bear with me!

Always remembering, my brain is hard-wired differently than some of yours, and I am doing my damnedest to ensure I am fulfilling my obligations to you and the organisation. It just might take me more time, more energy, more unusual methods or ways to achieve what others appear to achieve "easily"!

So, being placed in a position of having to do an on-the-spot analysis was neither pleasant, not comfortable for me. Had I been given notice of the meeting, asked to deliver a presentation I could have prepared for, or even given an hour or two to get my thoughts together, I would not have seemed so incompetent and ineffective as a project co-ordinator. The sad part about that situation is that I had only recently disclosed my neurodivergence to my Manager and had been very upset about it and its implications, as I had realised that many things I had thought were 'deficits' in me were actually now easily explained by my condition. She then utilised my disclosure in publicly humiliating me in the workplace. Not a tactic I would suggest for any manager with a heart.

2. The employee has a highly 'creative' and non-linear cognitive approach to problem-solving, which is perceived as 'outside of the box'

For Managers who appreciate innovative and quirky natured employees, this is a huge bonus. In Silicon Valley, many IT companies are recognising the value of neurodiverse employees, as they have the micro-focus, long-term commitment to getting the job done, specialist knowledge and skill-sets, in-depth research capacity, high levels of productivity (when given the *comfortability parameters* we discussed earlier) and genuine loyalty to their workplace and employer, when happy in their workplace.

3. A 'masking' effect, where it looks as though everything is okay and then everything goes to pot, all of a sudden. This has been shown to be more common amongst women, but not always.

Many people 'mask' in order to 'fit in', hide an aspect of themselves that does not 'conform' to something which is considered a 'social norm' or a workplace 'norm'. For instance, many people with Autism or ADHD do something called "stimming". That stands for self-regulatory self-stimulation". What that means is that people do involuntary movements, gestures and sometimes vocalise, in order to self-soothe. It can happen often and regularly. It may be something that a person does to show they are excited or happy. But it may also be something that a person does when they are anxious or concerned about something. The individuals who do this are often unaware that they are doing it. It is known that to stop someone 'stimming' is actually non-productive and can be dangerous, if they are particularly anxious, as it is a sensory and emotional regulatory measure for the Central Nervous System (CNS). Without it, the individua's CNS will not be able to cope with cognitive or sensory input and it will 'shut down', if the individual is overwhelmed completely.

Providing people with space, time, opportunities and meeting their environment needs, by making adjustments and accommodations will all serve to minimise any potential Central Nervous System shutdowns. Also, allowing space for someone to 'stim' is a valuable way to support some who needs to self-regulate and self-soothe in this way.

Overall, this uninformed assessment of the neurodiverse cognitive process does not allow space for us to explore the immense wealth and value that this group of individuals can offer to society and to our workplaces.

Creating an Alternative

I know you still want your employees to be able to do the following (that's a given):

→ Communicate with you, their colleagues and to your clients and other key stakeholders

→ Get their work done by the set deadline

→ Follow instructions you or others in leadership and management provide

→ Be productive

→ Contribute to the organisation's profitability

→ Work as part of the overall "team" or workforce

→ Be compliant with everything that requires it (WH&S/OH&S; HR policies; safety guidelines; technical standards; etc).

In identifying the above, we can start to see how differences in cognitive resonance afforded by neurodiverse approaches may actually present much more innovative ways of:

→ resolving challenging issues

→ approaching decision-making

And, taking it one step further, in a workplace context:

→ exploring project design, development and even project management

Individuals who are neurodivergent can bring new perspectives to your organisation, support the development of new models, new processes, adaptations of current processes and systems, and also see the 'gaps' in areas that neuro-typical minds are not often able to see so easily. These individuals are fantastic at identifying and assessing patterns, which means they would be wonderful at customer behaviour analysis, business analysis and system analysis. It may also be why many neurodivergent individuals are drawn to job roles that require the identification of patterns and the meta-cognition skills used in analytical and critical thinking skills, problem-solving and systems analysis.

For individuals with skill sets that relate to development and resource creation and innovation, these individuals will find it relatively easy to design, create, assess and evaluate resources for the organisation. This may be particularly useful for HR and training and development roles. It is also highly relevant where there may be 'gaps' in organisation knowledge that needs to be 'filled' with information packs. This is also true of policy and procedural guidelines. These are all roles that would be suitable for someone with this range of skills and knowledge.

Many neurodivergent employees will be easily able to assess a social situation and tell you what is occurring between the individuals concerned. This is often a surprise to others, as this is an area that is not often promoted as a classical skill-set or capability for the neurodiverse community. However, there is a level of emotional attunement and sensitivity that enables neurodivergent people to be able to 'tune into others emotions and feelings, without being distracted by external stimulus.

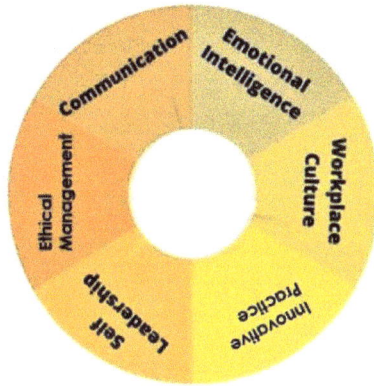

MANAGING YOUR NEURODIVERGENT EMPLOYEES

From the perspective of your neurodivergent employees, if you are aiming to be the very best manager and/or business owner possible, it is vital that you take the following as some helpful guidance (Goleman, Boyatzis & McKee, 2001; O'Regan, 2020b; Pedler, Burgoyne & Boydell, 2013;). Looking at this from a management and leadership perspective, it is paramount to consider the following:

Ethical Management

Do you have an ethical framework? Does it include strategies specifically for your neurodivergent employees? Have you considered implementing ND specific strategies? Are your managers neurodivergent-friendly? Have your management team completed training and development to bring you up to date on neurodivergence and what it means for your employees?

Communication

Are you aware of the many nuances of neurodivergent communication? Have you done any training and development that relates to this? Do you know where to send your staff for this training to minimise any issues relating to unconscious biases, limiting beliefs, discrimination of neurodivergent employees, disability awareness specific to this topic...? Would you be able to navigate your way through a new communication model with a neurodivergent staff member? Would you be challenged if a neurodivergent employee couldn't understand or comprehend something you were trying to communicate? What would you do to alleviate this barrier?

Emotional Intelligence

Do you know what Emotional Intelligence is? Have you read any books on it? Or completed any training or development in this area? How competent in this area do you feel you are? Would you be able to apply EI strategies to your management and leadership? If so, how confident are you that these would be appropriate and relevant to your neurodivergent employees? If not, would you know where to access training and development that could guide you to do this effectively? (Goleman, 1995)

Workplace Culture

The culture that your employees work within will only uphold them and be valuable to them if it provides them with the following: a sense of certainty, safety, security, stability, social connection, contribution, support, benefit, value and meaning.

If your organisation cannot do that, then your employees will leave.

Innovative Practice

For neurodivergent employees, it is an imperative that they are able to show their 'flair' and contribute in their own 'unique' and inimitable way.

Finding ways in which to 'showcase' your ND employees will provide them with a platform to deliver their expertise, specialist knowledge and skills and offer their own constellation of professional 'gifts' to your organisation in a way they would not generally do, if just sat at a desk, plodding away at day-after-day tasks.

I know of one organisation that has enabled this space for their ND employee by showcasing her as their key marketing 'face' of the organisation. She is now the international "face" (and superstar, I might add!) of the organisation. She also likes to wear unicorn horns to work, gold lame dresses to train business executives, peruse business documents through Dame Edna Everidge glasses, clothe her neck in feather boas and has her own particular fashion style and catwalk flair. Instead of maintaining an office-based, back-office, desk-based approach, this organisation has enabled this employee to shine and in doing this has created a new organisational brand that is making them BIG money in the global marketplace!

Self-Leadership

Leading a team, versus leading and organisation versus project leadership versus leadership of oneself are all differing aspects of leadership. It is vital to be able to identify and define the core elements of each. It is also particularly important to know how you, as a manager or team leader, e=approach each kind of leadership, especially in relation to your neurodivergent employees. This is because they will have different requirements of you in your management role compared to your leadership role/s. They may be distinctly different, depending on the task, project, their expertise of that task/project and also how well equipped they are to complete it.

It is something to consider.

Pioneering Work in Neurodiversity Leadership and Management

On-Boarding New Staff

Many, many neurodivergent individuals do not find the application, interview and pre-assessment process for on-boarding at all comfortable! We've briefly discussed this in Section Two. However, just to reiterate, this is the first impression that a neurodivergent employee has of your organisation.

If I was coming to work for you, or wanting a job at your organisation, and all I could see or felt during my experiences when applying for a job with your organisation was one where I was excluded, marginalised, felt alienated, uncomfortable or even outright discriminated against, I would not feel very positive about your organisation.

My experiences would most probably lead me away from your organisation, at this point in my life. However, at earlier parts of my life, I often 'fought' hard to gain and keep those jobs, no matter what. Which was to my detriment. As I was not in the right environment, on that was safe nor a conducive space for me to work.

Many, many neurodivergent individuals have similar experiences.

Now that you have come this far in the book, I know that you have started thinking of alternative ways you could be proactive and do things a little differently.

Some of you may already be doing things a little differently. And, for that, I applaud you.

The business world needs to shift their perspective a little to understand that in order for someone to be included, you actually have to open the gate. Secondly, you have to open the gate wide enough that they aren't impeded in any way from entering. And, thirdly, you have to ensure that if you are inviting them into your zone (your workplace, right?) that you have a space that is just right for them. Not a metaphorical wonky chair that you pulled out of the back shed. It won't be suitable for the job you want it to do. And, if you expect them to sit on it while they are in your space, they may not be able to complete the "work" you want them to do while they are there either, as they don't have the correct resources available.

Do you see where I'm heading?

If you can support that first and second and even third step into your realm, that is a great start!

Creating 'Low-Arousal', 'Low-Stimulus' Working Environments

Although some neurodivergent individuals do like to seek out stimulus, this can be managed individually, in that they can monitor and control their need and 'go and find' a space to access that stimulus' in the workplace. It is a far better strategy to create a 'low-arousal', 'low-stimulus' workplace environment, such as the ones that HOK design, which adhere to free-flow spaces, with quiet zones adjacent to low-footfall areas and 'high-arousal' areas closer to more 'social zones' such as kitchen and meeting points.

With redesign features such as these simple factors in mind, even relocating someone's desk to the far end of the office, not to isolate them, but to offer them optimum opportunity for minimising noise and distractions will support innovative strategies within your organisations, at the most fundamental levels, even if you have limited funds and are unable to redesign your workspace.

Mainstreaming In-House NeuroDiversity Programs

Creating in-house neurodiversity programs that are inclusive of everyone, rather than creating sub-groups of "all of the ADHD people". It also helps to form more cohesive and organic bonds between co-workers and start the process towards the development of Wisdom Pods', if that's where your organisation is heading.

Segregating your neurodivergent workforce only serves to further isolate and alienate your workforce and further stigmatise those who have a neurodiverse way of doing things. Since that is not the focus of this book, we will be refocussing you onto more supportive, eco-system-based models for an all-in support manner of creating diverse, adaptive, dynamic and High-D, (high development), collaborative teams that can energise quickly and begin task or project-based work much more efficiently than they might have done in the past.

Just to be clear, this isn't segregating your neurodivergent employees into 'zones' or 'teams' as some organisations have done. It is purely for the purposes of utilises your team player's specialised skills and knowledge to the benefit of the larger group or organisation.

Scaling NeuroDiversity Within Your Teams

One of the key ways to do this, if you are low in numbers, of Neurodivergent to non-neurodivergent employees, is to scale. The suggested ratio is 4NT:1ND (where NT equates to non-neurodivergent employee and ND equates to neurodivergent employee).

In this way, you can have the input of someone who has a neurodivergent perspective and the other skill-sets encompassed by your NT team members. That compilation of skills, knowledge, specialised competencies, attributes and talents can be highly beneficial for team-based projects.

Quality Efficiency Programs Led by NeuroDiversity-led Best Practice

Krzeminska et al, (2019) found that there were lower levels of product and service defects and much higher levels of quality assurance, quality systems management and generalised quality improvement processes and

QIP management, once a neurodivergent team member or team leader was taken on. These QA/QSM/QM assurance models. In my own experiences of managing teams and in my consultancy work with small businesses, I have also found this to be the case.

Embedding 'Wisdom Pods' for Collaborative Innovation encourages complex collaboration, embeds best practice models for Wisdom Pods, establishes supportive social and cultural framework and modelling for other teams. As stated in the section above, re: scaling, the addition of one or more neurodivergent team members has been shown to enhance productivity, innovation, divergent problem-solving processes and also solution-based R&D in many companies.

Many neurodivergent individuals have an ability to specialise in certain areas that they have an interest in. It may or may not have anything to do with their specific job. However, it may be something that could benefit your organisation. Their capacity to hyper-focus, utilise investigative skills, deep-dive into research materials and also come to more radical and innovative solutions has repeatedly proven their value in both teams and organisational contexts.

Whilst this is not the case for all neurodivergent individuals, many do have these skills and abilities. In the workplace, they are often under-utilised and often times find themselves in positions and job roles that do not allow them to be as creative as they have the capacity to be. This is where your talent scouts and talent development sections of HR could develop your neurodivergent employees, utilising their skills, knowledge and abilities and enabling them to develop beyond some of the lesser skilled occupations that many neurodivergent individuals find themselves in, purely due to unrecognised environmental factors negating their value within the organisation.

Establishing Innovative Talent Management Programs

Amending 'talent' criteria to include neurodivergent 'talent' and the many different manifestations of this that your organisation may benefit from having on-board. It is important to establish here, that 'talent' is not a standard. Not everyone with 'talent' fits into a box. In fact, most people with 'talent' do not fit into a square receptacle, nor do they want to be squeezed into one.

This is also the case with neurodivergent individuals. In fact, it is probably more so the case.

For us, we want to be able to showcase our skills, knowledge, talents and expertise in a way that is true to who we truly are.

Whilst we may want to work for your organisation, we also have needs. As human beings with needs, we would like these needs met. As our employer, you have some obligation to meet these needs. If you want us to perform to the best of our capacity, capabilities and competence levels, then it is also in your best interests for you to ensure that our environment is optimised, so that we can give you the best that we have to offer.

Because, if we are in your workplace already, chances are, we actively want to do that.

Because we do things a little differently, our talent may not look the same as someone else's talent. However, if you look a little more closely, in a non-conformist way, you will uncover a treasure of richness and gemstones!

How Can We Do This in a More Cohesive and Coherent Manner?

In this context, having our organisational Managers (that's you), be the cheer-squad, leader, provider and enabler of space to be able to flourish, grow, maximise their potential and show their 'true colours' in a positive and delightful way!

One of the elements of implementing a more conducive environment for your ND employees is to put the three conditions of quality in place.

Those three conditions are:

a) It is important to keep a focus on empowering rather than disempowering your employees. Many organisations aim to do this, though end up facing the entirely opposite way, as they are conflicted in implementing quality assurance and quality improvement strategies and systems, performance management procedures, ensuring that employees are bound to employment policies and processes, and working in compliance with local, regional and national regulations and legislation. It can be challenging to remember that your employees are human beings who are just like you and have lives and families and are faced with all sorts of issues in their every-day life.

b) I know you realise this on an intellectual level, however, embedding this into your overall working policies and practices can prove challenging, especially if you are retrospectively doing this.

c) The image below represents some of the ways I have seen organisations go horribly right and also horribly 'wrong' in trying to find the 'right fit'.

DISEMPOWERING YOUR EMPLOYEES

STOP/START PROCESSES/MECHANISMS

'CHASE YOUR TAIL' SYSTEMS

THE 'TOO MANY MASTERS' SYNDROME

LADDERLESS HOLE PROCEDURES, PROCESSES AND STRATEGIES

THE 'FOGGY DRIVE' ORGANISATION

MENTAL 'PARALYSIS' & COGNITIVE TWISTER PROCESSES AND PROCEDURES

ISOLATION STATION ORGANISATIONAL CULTURE

'HOPIUM" INJECTIONS WITHIN YOUR ORGANISATION CULTURE

'MOUSE-TRAP' HR & MANAGEMENT SYSTEMS

EXPECTATIONS THAT NEURODIVERGENT EMPLOYEES 'JUST KNOW'/'JUST DO'

ASSUMPTIONS/BIASES/PREJUDICE/

MICRO-AGRESSIONS AND BOUNDARY VIOLATIONS IN THE WORKPLACE

Or, you can choose the alternative, which are to empower your neurodivergent employees, as shown in some of the examples provided below.

EMPOWERING YOUR EMPLOYEES

CONSISTENCY, REPLICABILITY, CERTAINTY & RESPONSIVENESS

REGULAR WINS, REWARDS & PRAISE FOR ACHEIVEMENTS

ABLE TO SEE THE BIRD'S EYE VIEW, SO THE DETAIL CAN BE DEDUCTED

APPRECIATION OF BIG PICTURE VISION AND DETIL & FOCUS

NORMALISING CHANGE AND CHANGE PROCESSES

CREATING AND OPTIMISING POSITIVE FEEDBACK LOOPS

DESIGNING & CREATING SUSTAINABLE AND EFFECTIVE COMPETENCE LOOPS

OPTIMISING SUPPORTIVE AND NURTURING COMPETENCE LOOPS

CELEBRATING MOMENTUM

ALLOWING TIME FOR 'REST' AND PROCESSING

CELEBRATING THE PRINCIPLE THAT COMMUNITY IS CARING

PROMOTING PRINCIPLES OF COMPETENCE IN CREATIVITY, CULTURAL EXPRESSION, COLLABORATION

I call this, "Playing Snakes and Ladders", after a popular game from my childhood, as it is reminiscent of the trials and tribulations that can often face each one of us, as business owners, team leaders, and managers, in trying to get things right, when working with our teams. We cover each of these in our in-depth training, if you are interested in finding out more about these areas.

Fundamentally, it is vital to do the following for your neurodivergent employees:

1. Create a need-satisfying environment for your employees.

a. **Employees need to feel connected to each other**, management and the organisation's mission, vision and values.

b. **Employees need to feel empowered by having their opinions sought out and listened to and having their work respected**. You can do this easily, by celebrating their uniqueness and also by giving them a 'voice' within your workplace.

c. **Workers need to feel safe on the job.** This pertains to their emotional, psychological, as well as physical safety. Providing a mentor, workplace 'buddy' system, someone to talk to, or a workplace counselling service, are all ways you can engage not only your ND employees, but everyone, in this process.

d. **Workers need to have the ability to make choices, be self-determinant** and exercise some independence and autonomy within the definition of their job roles.

By allowing employees the space and opportunity to ask for workplace adjustments and accommodations, to adjust their working environment to suit their sensory, cognitive, processing, psychological and functional needs, you are enabling them in this way.

e. **Workers need to experience some fun and learning on the job.** Working with your ND employees to figure out ways that they can learn productively and in learning chunks that are conducive their learning styles and patterns will only benefit your organisation.

2. Workers must only be asked to do useful, purposeful and meaningful work.

If this is not clear, management must take the time to explain it if quality is what you are seeking. Clarity, concise directions or instructions and tasks with meaning or purpose are all a purposeful and meaningful work is a valuable part of the employment experience for neurodivergent workplace experience.

3. Finally, workers need to be asked to self-evaluate their work. This self-evaluation component is far beyond the scope of this article, but suffice it to say that two main components are required for employees to be able to accurately and honestly self-evaluate, and also provide this open feedback to management without fear of repercussions or fallout.

4.   **Also, there must be a very clear and definite matrix of what 'quality' is and what it looks like.** The employee must have an ideal with which to compare their work. For neurodivergent employees, this is particularly important in relation to time-related quality measures and also in reference to any nuances related to quality measures. These must be spelled out, even if you, or your QA team, do not feel this is necessary. For ND employees, this could be the difference in understanding why something is important to the context of their work or its completion and them not doing that thing, or not doing it within a certain amount of time. (Believe me, this has tripped me up a number of times, when I have been unaware of the importance of a quality measure, or its existence... and then found out later that it was part of a Critical Success Pathway!)

When these components and others are added to the workplace, you can expect:

5.   **Increased employee satisfaction.** Employees will be taught that they have the potential, capability and responsibility to personally get their four basic needs met.

This awareness will result in a decrease of a sense of victimization and complaining, because employees will be focused on solutions and resolving misunderstandings, they can implement instead of the problems that exist.

6. **A unified approach to conceptualization of problems, designs, issues, concepts and other innovations.** Once all your employees understand this, they will be conceptualizing problems in the same way. This unified approach will decrease a lot of competition among your employees and will result in the creation of a unified, cohesive and committed group of workers who believe in the direction your company is headed.

7. **Make room for individuals' strengths and unique approaches.** This framework encourages people's personal expression. Employees will be able to include their unique and creative talents, as long as they don't conflict with neurodiversity and its inclusion principles.

8. **Create space for more effective communication.** When everyone in your company understands the basic framework for conceptualizing human behaviour, then communication is enhanced. There will be fewer misunderstandings because all are speaking the same language.

9. **Find creative ways to decrease employee stress.** Many employees experience stress on the job. This usually comes from a lack of understanding about responsibilities. With this level of support and acknowledgement from their management team, ND employees in your teams will understand that the only person they can control is themselves. Once people stop expending energy trying to change people or circumstances beyond their control and instead begin to focus on what adaptive response they can take, stress levels dramatically decrease. Managers who do this will also come to see that in supporting their neurodivergent employees through adaptive measures, they will generate a far more productive working team and more overall productivity.

10. **Utilise neurodivergent employees to optimise benefits from a significant decrease in employee turnover.** Creating a need- satisfying environment for employees, while holding them accountable for their work will enable ND employees the opportunity to take the bull by the horns and really embed

themselves into your workplace. This grounding will generate a dedicated and committed workforce, as people who feel wanted, listened to and valued will always fare better and be more committed than those who do not. Ultimately, when people are in environments that meet their five basic needs, there is motivation to stay in that environment.

11. Optimise creativity to enhance and stimulate increased creativity and innovation. When employees work in an environment created by their employer that allows for self-expression and encourages personal power, limitless creativity is unleashed, which often results in business improvement and expansion. This can only be enhanced by the inclusion of the Wisdom Pods and the Talent Programs that celebrate and emphasise the inclusion of neurodivergent talent within the organisation.

12. Redesign organisational culture to enhance workplace relationships. People who have their needs met without interfering with others meeting their needs are the happiest in the workplace and in society. When this happens, the status of their current personal and professional relationships improves both at work and at home. The possibilities, and the potential, is unlimited!

13. Build on the Reward-Action-Reward Motivators to Decrease Resistance/Increase Cooperation. When this process is implemented in the workplace, employees become less resistant and more cooperative because they are being heard. When we stop pushing people in the direction we think is best and focus instead on building better relationships, resistance is decreased and cooperation is increased. This is one of the key factors in providing effective and conducive adjustments and accommodations in the workplace, for our neurodivergent employees. It also underpins the Wisdom Pod experiential collaborations and it is a very tried and true methodology for flexible-thinking organisations who have tried-on an ecological framework, in adaptive modelling and organisation planning (Daughtery, 2013; Griffiths, 2020; Mellifont, 2019; O'Regan, 2020b; Virgin, 2020).

Embrace Inclusivity and Full Organisational Innovation shift from efficiency-based competition to innovation-based mindset

Implementation of inclusive and innovative selection processes, practices and protocols that allow for more flexible recruitment

Implementation of Neurodiversity-friendly strategies and practices for recruitment, and more flexible retention strategies

Implementation of Wisdom Pods, collaboration through scaling teams and enabling of 'focus time' and space for specialised

Organisational integration of neurodivergent employees via neurodiversity inclusion policy and practices, training and culture shift

Managing and providing leadership and mentoring to neurodivergent employees through talent programs, leadership programs & accommodations

Implementation of Wisdom Pods, Interdependence Model of Neurodiversity, talent development programs and leadership

Shift in organisational mindset and Success Measures

Innovative Employee Selection Processes

Flexible Recruitment & Retention Strategies

Social integration strategies and management

Organisational integration of neurodivergent employees

Managing Performance

Innovation and Productivity Enhancement

IMAGE: Developing an Integrated Diversity & Inclusion Strategy for Neurodivergent Employees that Enables New Innovations Enhancing Productivity

The Practicalities

Phase One: Creating a Workplace Sanctuary

This may or may not be appealing to some of you. However, we can all sit and think about where our most appealing space to be might be. It may be real or it might be imagined.

I want you to think about your ability to create a space at work, where you could have your desk in a position where it was best-placed for you to work with the window in the right position, the sunlight present/not present, natural light/no natural light (believe me, there are people who do not "appreciate" natural light!). A space where you were either surrounded by noise (because you love to be in the midst of it!), or in the quietest space in the whole office (because you love to hunker down and just get your work done). A space where you could put your feet onto tiles, or run them across carpet, or even floor boards, or other sensory surfaces (yes, I'm heading into sensory, neurodivergent zones, now).

The optimum for all of us is a space where we could have full control over what it looks like, its colour, lighting, size, positioning, floor covering, noise control, 'atmosphere', heating/cooling, desk size/placement, seating, computer positioning/height, screen size, and so on. All of these play a factor in the daily working lives of neurodivergent individuals.

So, most of us don't have full control of our office or desk space, where we sit, or how our 'space' is managed and accessed. So, how can we, as managers, accommodate this for our employees with required adjustments and accommodations?

The easy answer is: create a solution that works for everyone. But, that would require money, a complete restructuring, no doubt, and also a whole new rethink about space and design, for your office. I have no doubt that you have either an open plan office with a kitchen at one end and a storage room-cum-photocopier room, plus a Manager's office or two, enclosed and at one end for "privacy". Or, you have a succession of individual shared small room spaces along a corridor of sorts and a "meeting room' or two for collaborative events.

It doesn't get much better than that!

Except that neurodivergent employees probably won't tend to flourish in either of those environments. For a number of reasons. Most of them, you may have been able to garner by now.

Space is Not Just "Out There"

Space is not just 'out there'. For someone who is neurodivergent, space is also an internal world.

Now, we all have internal worlds, and we access them at various points in time. Some do it when they are meditating. Some do it just before they fall asleep and they are 'remembering' things, recalling the day's events, or reminiscing. Others do it when they are daydreaming or planning.

For someone who is neurodivergent, there are many portions of the day when I spend the majority of times, 'inside my own head'. And, after talking to thousands, maybe tens of thousands of other ND individuals, I can guarantee that this is the case for them, as well.

I have come to know this as my 'cognitive inner space'. It is where I go to think.

If I am in this 'inner space', or need to enter this space, it can be very confronting to not feel it is supported, environmentally, socially, cognitively or emotionally.

If I can manage or control my environment, I have the best chance of being able to enter into that space. If I can plan my surrounding desk space and 'head-space' to accommodate what is required of me (for the task, for the day, for the period of time ahead) then I can accomplish whatever is ahead of me.

If I am not able to do that, or am not supported to do that, then, I will not be as competent, or fulfill my duties to my best capabilities, as I am not in an optimum state of being.

There are other 'inner spaces' where I go to process my emotions and feelings, but I will not be discussing those here, except to say that these are somewhat compartmentalised for me, in my state of neurodivergence, and I know that it is for many other people as well.

There is both internal and external space. I am not going all woo-woo on you! Stick with me, okay? We all understand the concept of external space. In a workplace environment, that is where we put the chairs and desks and plants to make everyone 'feel good'. It is where the phones are placed and the doors are positioned and the office walls are. It is where the windows face and the reception desk are positioned and the Manager's office is. It is also where the photocopier and scanner are placed. It is where the toilets are located and the kitchen is found. You get the picture. This is all part of the office environment (externally space).

For individuals who are neurodivergent (and for everyone else, too- it's just that sometimes, neuro-typical people aren't always aware of their non-active inner space). As we discussed just before, we often have very "active" inner space. We might have a very active inner 'voice' that talks us through tasks. We may have a checklist of activities to do every day, that we cannot shut off. We may also find ourselves in a repeated cycle comprised of repeating song phrases, words that come and go when we are highly anxious, names, dates and phrases that are repeated to ensure memorisation or recall. Sometimes, 'inner world' happenings occur as part of 'self-stimulation', for individuals who have ADHD, ADD, or Autism. It is often a form of relaxation that occurs as a part of self-regulation of emotions. It can be visible or internalised (Benton& Barkley, 2010).

Sometimes, we may 'do' this whilst we are concentrating on a task at hand. It may be quite challenging for us to pull out of our heavy concentration when interrupted, as we are so very deep in concentration, that it is almost like we have a "Do Not Disturb" sign on our head! I have had previous colleagues laugh at me for being in this 'state' at work, when I am in development mode. I can spend hours and hours with my head down and not bothering anyone, whilst I just get on with whatever is on front of me. It also often means I appear to be ignoring others around me (I am most certainly not! It is that I am in my own world of concentration and only able to focus on that one element whilst I am in -deep focus mode). So, if you, as my Manager, want me to complete this task at hand, you must accept this is my modus operandi.

If I am disturbed or interrupted, even by extraneous noises or conversation that has nothing to do with me, music or laughter, I often lose the thread of what I was doing. Is this my 'fault'? No. It is part of my *executive functioning* capacity, my *neurodivergence* and my *interoception* working a little differently. These are fun concepts for you to get to know. You may find that one of your children does this. Maybe your partner. Or even you, yourself, may find you have this pattern of focus (Benton & Barkley, 2010; Brewer & Cook, 2016; SPD Australia, 2020; VCASP, 2012; VCASP, 2014).

What you will notice is that at least one of your employees will more than likely also 'do' this.

They may or may not be aware that they have this neuro-cognitive pattern. It is always wise to let your employees disclose their needs to you, first, rather than approach them. However, if you want to be support and do notice that someone may be sitting in a thoroughfare, yet having to concentrate on multiple projects, and that they are often immersed in this state of deep concentration (and keep getting 'thrown' out of it by external stimulus, you could always offer an alternative room or space for them to work in, whenever they are required to do this deep concentration work.

They will be very appreciative. And, you will find that they are able to complete their work tasks a lot more quickly. They will also feel more productive, as they are not constantly being drawn out of deep-thinking space and having to re-engage their mind back into it (which takes a great deal of effort, from personal experience. Others who also 'do' this have also told me that sometimes it can take them days and days to get back into the 'flow' of deep thought and concentration they were previously in! Imagine the effect that would have on workflow, for your organisation, even if you just made that small change for that one employee?)

You would be a superstar!

Creating a Stress-Free Environment for Everyone- Is It Possible?

Stress is a serious business. The subject is often in the news: we know that it causes the loss of more working days than physical illness and can lead to serious conditions of the heart and significantly affect other organs. Stress is taken so seriously these days that employers have a legal duty of care towards their employees (Mellifont, 2019).

You might think that neurodivergent employees might have more stress than other employees. This is not the case. Although. ND employees can have overall higher levels of anxiety in the completion of a specific task or project, day-to-day stressors on individuals in the workplace are the same.

The media has put far less emphasis on the natural antidote to stress: relaxation, fun, enjoyment and laughter. It might be useful to remind ourselves what relaxation actually means.

Far from merely being the absence of tension, relaxing actually requires a positive act of will. Many people believe that jumping in the car, with the kids and driving 70 miles to go camping is relaxing. It may well be. Once you have gotten over the traffic jams and the road accidents and the congestion just getting out of the city. That three days is almost half of your week- long camping trip. By the time you have started to 'relax', you are starting to think about the next phase- your journey home, all the things you have to get before you go back to work next week, visiting Granma for her birthday, on your way back down the coast, picking up lunch for the kids, for when they return to school, buying a gift for your partner, because it's their birthday. So, you only really get a maximum of 1 day's 'relaxation', if that, right?

Just as a composer writes rests in their musical scores - indicating silence – which we need to take heed of, as carefully as the notes played by musicians; we need to decide when to relax and how to do so. Just think of the expression 'To compose yourself'.

It's most definitely the techniques that help.

We know of many techniques and disciplines, some of them very ancient, that help us to relax. Meditation has been described as 'Increasing the distance between thoughts', a way of emptying the mind of its usual chatter, regret, worry and aspiration. Yoga can help us to achieve a similar inner calm through focusing on the body and how it breathes. In both cases, the emphasis is actively on focusing our attention on the here and now, rather than reflecting on the past or thinking ahead.

As with any other conscious decision, we need to focus on what we are doing if we want to succeed - and here, for many of us, lies the difficulty. If we want to benefit from these disciplines, not only do we need to endure the slow process of learning new techniques that feel strange and unfamiliar before enjoying the benefits, we also have to overcome an instinctive objection from our own bodies.

What tension does.

The trouble is that when we are experiencing stress, we become tense: our muscles tighten and adrenaline and cortisol flow through our systems, making it even harder to relax. Even sitting in a quiet darkened room doesn't guarantee success – if your mind is buzzing, you'll feel over stimulated. It's easy to understand why we seek easier, more instant ways to calm down. That's why we sometimes confuse relaxation with distraction - especially in a time when so many distractions are available.

What does or doesn't relax us.

'I feel stressed out tonight. Let's just relax in front of the TV.' Unfortunately, most television programmes are designed to engage us by arousing our interest in some way. The sound tracks are especially effective in stimulating us emotionally, so that the net result of our attempts to 'switch off' turn out to be merely 'changing channels' with our attention. We swap one set of stimuli for another - and we have even less control over the content than when we are wrestling with all the details of our own over-busy lives.

The active choice.

So. Relaxation is an active choice, but it can seem too difficult and time-consuming to learn how to use the techniques that work. How can we actively choose to relax easily and effectively? William Congreve wrote 'Music hath charms to soothe the savage breast, to soften rocks, or bend a knotted oak.' and throughout history gentle music has been a favourite way to change the way we feel. This is because the vibrations that reach our ears do more than just please us as they cause our own internal rhythms, like heartbeat and brain activity, to synchronise with the music.

If you have ever tried turning off the sound track of a scary movie you know how flat it can seem with only pictures to keep the mood going. Anyone who has seen what happens to baby boomers at a party when someone plays a Rolling Stones record has experienced the power of music to move people.

Type of music that relaxes.

Naturally, the result depends on the type of music being played. A growing number of composers are choosing to focus mainly on the effect their music has on the listener.

Making Appropriate Accommodations and Workplace Adjustments

This book is being written from an Australian perspective. However, it is completely applicable all over the world. I have some awareness of the legalities and requirements for some regions around the globe, but not all. I have lived in the UK for 13 years, so I have some understanding of the systems and legislation that is in place there. I have also spent some time in the USA, so equally have an awareness of US guidelines and protocols. I will give a few examples here, to inform you, as readers, rather than to be directive or prescriptive.

However, I do not have the full scope and awareness of all that is available globally, nor in the three countries I have mentioned, as government policy, social policy and practice, services and agencies that apply these policies and address the needs of individuals, are all shifting and changing on a regular basis.

So, if when you are reading this book, you find something that is no longer relevant, go and do some up-to-date research. At the time of writing, everything was as I have referred to it.

Suffice to say that there are guidelines in place in various parts of the world that recognise that parts of the workforce require different support systems and structures in order to be able to fulfil their work tasks, projects and business objectives (AHRC, 2020; Australian Government, 2010; UK Equality Act, 2010; UK HSE, 2020; US Department of Labor, 2020).

In Australia, we do have a State by State set of workplace safety guidelines that organisations and businesses need to comply with. These are regulated by our WorkSafe/Work Cover bodies in each representative State. WorkSafe would cover workplace issues such as the brightness of lighting, the loudness of worksite noise, any structural issues that could pose a health and safety issue, and/or any other issue which may present as a direct WH&S or OH&S issue (UK HSE, 2020; OSHA, 2020; Safe Work Australia, 2020).

In Australia, *Safe Work Australia* (2020) deals with OH&S issues such as risks, hazards and control measures, lighting and noise, first aid, building site induction compliance, and remote working and working at heights. As well, it oversees issues in the workplace, such as leadership and culture, good work design that includes factors that optimise job satisfaction and business success, issues that may affect mental health of employees and bullying.

We also have the *Office of Fair Work* (2020) and the *Office of Fair Work Ombudsman* (2020), who both seek to maintain and uphold a balance between organisational practice and employee rights and responsibilities. If there is a perceived breach of Fair Work Practice, then the employee has the right to approach the OFW and/or the FWO office for further consideration and potential mediation of a workplace dispute. The FWO may deal with issues such as non-payment of wages/salary for work completed, non-payment of other due benefits, incorrect application of workplace standards, unionised protections including *Enterprise Agreements* and so on. Finally, Australia has the Human Rights Commission (AHRC, 2020), which handles calls directly relating to workplace bullying, harassment, discrimination on the grounds of a protected characteristics, such as gender, disability, age etc.

Whilst Australia has some protections for individuals who are directly discriminated against on the basis of their disability, health condition or medical illness or injury, there vis b=very little in our legislation that sets out what workplace requirements are for organisations to effectively and ethically accommodate for the needs of their employees who are neurodivergent, in a pro-active manner.

This could be seen as an unfortunate glitch in the system by some. Personally, and professionally, I see it as an entire nation letting down a huge proportion of their already working population, and not being proactive in offering our children and young people who will soon be entering the workforce a strong start in employment.

These could be your children, your teenagers, your nieces and nephews, or grandchildren.

And, that is only the start. If workplaces were more accommodating of the needs of individuals who are neurodivergent, in Australia alone, we may reduce the numbers of unemployed neurodivergent individuals from the hugely disproportionate numbers that they currently stand. It deeply saddens me to think that so many highly talented individuals are not able to get a job because so many organisations are not willing to give them a chance and make a few adjustments to the working environment, so that they can be accommodated.

Both the USA and the UK provide legislation that protects the rights of people with a diagnosed disability. Other countries may also have a protective legislation like this, I am less familiar with it. Please apply it in the same way for your own country, if it is applicable, when I am referring to the *Disability Discrimination Act (Australia, 1992)*.

NB: Not every country has the same protections for its individuals.

However, for those of you familiar with the United Nations and its Declaration of Human Rights, one of the areas covered by the Declaration and its Conventions is that of protections for individuals with a disability. The *United Nations Convention on the Rights of Persons with Disabilities* (UN CRPD) is the first binding international human rights instrument to explicitly address disability. For countries that are a signatory to the UN Declaration, you can find out more information here:

Office of the High Commissioner for Human Rights,10th Session of the Committee on the Rights of Persons with Disabilities (12 November 2013), Retrieved from: http://www.ohchr.org/EN/HRBodies/CRPD/Pages/Session10Old.aspx on 19th September 2020.

This is internationally applied legislation that covers the countries that are signatories to it.

Whilst I said at the beginning of this book that I wasn't going to refer to people who were neurodivergent in a way that limited them to having a diagnosed disability, unless they themselves identified in that way, I am needing to be inclusive and welcome those individuals into our neurodivergent group, who are diagnosed and who are able to make claims under the Disability Act in their own country.

I will just reiterate again, her that not everyone who is neurodivergent or part of the neurodiverse community has a diagnosis, and nor is everyone recognised as having a disability.

Apart from specific legislation that focusses on promoting and protecting the rights of people with disabilities (e.g., the UK's Disability Discrimination Act [DDA], (now known as the *Equality Act (2010)* in England, Scotland and Wales) and the USA's *American Disabilities Act [ADA]* (1990), the participation of people with a broader range of disabilities is still lagging when compared to their able-bodied peers (Kruse & Schur, 2003; WHO, 2011).

In the UK, *Equality Act (2010)* goes some of the way to providing a solution to workplaces. While things have improved, I am still receiving feedback that many individuals still find it difficult to find, retain, maintain and thrive in their jobs, due to non-accommodations, different ways of working, non-understanding of different methods for, judgemental attitudes and other poor management (Bewley & George, 2016).

In the USA, "the *American Disability Act* (ADA) covers employers with **15 or more** employees, including state and local governments. It also applies to employment agencies and to labour organizations. The ADA's non-discrimination standards also apply to federal sector employees under section 501 of the *Rehabilitation Act*, as amended, and its implementing rules" (EEOC, 2020).

However, since the introduction of a more comprehensive way of perceiving diversity in the workplace and the inclusion of neurodiversity as a valid area for consideration, not just in terms of 'making accommodations and adjustments', as many research studies have focussed on, but also as a way of fine-tuning teams and really providing fuel for organisational innovation and a shift in workplace mindset. This paradigm shift, towards positive leadership, the expression of emotional intelligence in management and leadership can bring maximum results to your business via the undeniable utilisation of employees to optimise productivity and innovation in the workplace, via the adoption of their specialised skills-sets and capabilities.

However, there are still gaps in understanding about individual capacity, functionality, ability to undertake tasks, and apply themselves to tasks in the workplace, meaning that many employers still will not consider anyone who is perceived as having extra or additional needs (read, "Please could I have some adjustments so that I can do my work as effectively and efficiently and productively as possible for you?"

The United States *Department of Labor* has developed a set of guidelines that can assist the owner, operator or manager of an organisation or business to accommodate a broader range of conditions, illnesses, disabilities, injuries and so on, under the ADA. More information on these guidelines can be found through the *Occupational Safety and Health Administration (OSHA)* which is an agency of the U.S. *Department of Labor* (2020.

When it comes to workplace accommodation, there are different types of suggestions made by the *Department of Labor*. For example, one of the areas that people with chronic fatigue and weakness could have accommodations around the following:

-Reduce or eliminate physical exertion and workplace stress

This can be done via staff mindfulness programs, the introduction of relaxation techniques, stretching, workplace wellbeing and/or personal proactivity

-Schedule periodic rest breaks away from the assigned workstation

-This could include time separate to standard breaks, or include team meetings that are held outside of the office, or team meet-ups on the roof, or other innovations for team bonding, personal development in the workplace and maximisation of cultural development

-Provide for the employee a more flexible work schedule and a more flexible use of leave time

-This is an important part of the UK *Access to Work* program, where employees are provided with adjustments to their working environment, desk space and also have accommodations made, such as a scribe, use of assistive technologies etc.

-Allow or permit the employee to work from home

-For many employees, post-COVID (certainly in parts of Australia), this has already been occurring for the past 7 months. Indicators have shown that workers have increased productivity, higher levels of engagement and longer retention, when they are able to have flexible workplace arrangements and also when they can negotiate work-from-home arrangements that can accommodate their needs.

Whilst this has, in the past, primarily been a consideration for carers and those with children, in Australia, this can be applied across the board. Pandemic conditions in Victoria, Australia have shown that more than 50% of the workforce has been able to work from home, with little or no extra resource demands nor repercussions for the employer.

Some employees have also found that they are suffering from fine motor impairment, fibromyalgia, CFS/ME, musculo-skeletal issues as a result of spinal injury or neurological damage, etc, have found some of the following useful:

-Implement ergonomic workplace and workstation design

-Provide alternative telephone and computer access for the employee

-Provide arm supports on chairs and/or for wrist rests

-Provide grip and writing aids

-Provide a book holder, place-keeper for books/articles being read and a page turner

-Provide the employee with a note-taker

-Provide ergonomic workplace tools and other ergonomic adaptations

(OSHA, 2020)

Phase Two: Systems and Structures
Systematic isn't automatic, for everyone!

As we noted above, in our chat about my family member, systematic does not work for everyone. I can fully appreciate that your entire business may be automated and systematised. However, people are not robots. We have our own quirks and idiosyncrasies at the best of times. Any expectations that we will all do something in exactly the same way is quite ludicrous, from where I stand.

Of course, the business objectives and their achievement are of primarily importance and must be a priority. However, they will not be achieved with the people in place to energise and sustain the momentum.

How can we do this, in your business, whilst still accommodating the needs of our neurodiverse workforce?

For some employees, this really is about going back to pen and paper.

I remember one of my employers was absolutely adamant that I not use notepads, ever. Never, ever, ever! EVER!

I didn't really understand it. My employer said that it was a waste of paper and they would appreciate it if I could just comply. I explained my need. They stated that as everyone else was being asked to comply, I was too. And, if I did not comply with instructions, I would be given a warning, as the office was working under a renew, reuse and recycle policy.

All good. I love it! Corporate Social responsibility in action! Brilliant!

However, that had nothing to do with my own needs and the fact that if my employer was not able to financially afford to accommodate my needs, I had even offered to pay to do it myself. As long as I was given the accommodation and enabled the adjustment- being able to take notes in my own personal (symbolic) way.

I understood, from their perspective, what they were saying. I also knew that without note-taking, I would not be able to remember anything. At all. Zilch. So, I tried to explain again, and even suggested that I could buy my own notepads and pens, if that was more convenient, as I appreciated that I was utilising more office resources than other staff.

I had developed a certain way of note-taking that, for anyone who knows me is both creative, colourful, quirky and incredibly symbolic! However, without this note-taking regime, I am literally 'information/knowledge-blind". I can't describe it any other way. My sensory processing plays a part here and so does my executive functioning. There is no way around the fact that if I don't take notes, I can't remember what I've just learnt. Notes which are written in a standard format (i.e. written from top to bottom, left to right, across a lined page) generally don't work that well for me. Why, because it isn't starting the information processing process in my brain. It's kind of just depositing information in a holding bay. And, no-body comes back to that holding bay, so that information just stays there, endlessly (O'Regan, 2020b).

Whereas, if I clump the information into groups, matching information I am currently learning, connecting it with information that I have previously learnt, and also highlighting key information in stars and circles and flowers (each one has a different level of significance and meaning for me), and I create my page on a blank, Artist's Diary page (white sheets, no lines), using different colours to signify different things, it is so much easier to differentiate which ideas take priority, what I need to action first, where I have made connections, and what has piqued my interest or needs to be followed up on. This is my "way". It is how I do what I do. It is the only way that works for me. I can appreciate that it may looks strange or out of the ordinary to some people. Some of my colleagues have laughed away my need for creativity in this way by stating that I'm 'drawing pictures and colouring in, again". They have completely missed the point, and they are being derogatory and dismissive of my own personal accommodations.

Going back to my employer, at the time, their answer was still a 'no' and I was placed on a "Warning" for not following a manager's instructions.

This was a little confrontational for me. This wasn't a choice for me. It wasn't something I could leave out of my day and just do something else. I had to take notes in this way. Otherwise, I do not remember what I am learning.

Does this prevent me completing my work? No. Does this mean that I am not competent? No. Does this mean I am not the right worker for the job? NO! If I have applied for a job, it means that I believe that I have the capacity and capabilities to do it to the highest of my ability.

What my boss saw was someone who was making trouble, "trying to 'doodle' their way through meetings", and "unable to think for themselves without a prompt".

Mmmmmm.

I have mentioned a lot about changing perspective. I have mentioned that often-times, we need to assess things from a different standpoint, including more information or awareness than we initially had. I was, admittedly, very angry with my boss, at the time. I could not find a way to get them to collectively see what I needed. Even when I asked for additional support, through our *Employee Assistance Program* (an employee counselling program, for those of you outside of Australia), they suggested that I work on compliance or find another job.

I did find a way through and out of this situation, but I did not stay with this employer. They were not open to listening to my needs. They were averse to even recognising that something could be done differently to their particular way, and they were also hell-bent on proving that I "was in the wrong".

I wasn't. there was no way that I could be. I have a viable need for accommodations and workplace adjustments. I had made my own adjustments to my working practice to ease any discordance with communication and information processing that might show up in the course of the day. And yet, they were doing everything in their power to strip me of my own self-accommodations, as well as discriminate against me for having valid needs for alternative measures and workplace requirements, in the first place.

In the end, not only were they breaching the Disability Act, but also discriminating against me for a protected characteristic under the Human Rights Act (AHRC, 2020; UN-DESA, 2020).

We are in the paradigm shift section now. This is your time and place to think a little differently to my old employer.

How Can We More Effectively Support Our NeuroDivergent Workforce?

It's a question you may have been generally asking, in relation to your whole workforce and intra-organisation team development. You may not have thought as specifically as considering your neurodiverse workforce and including more individuals with neurodivergent talents, skills, knowledge, traits and qualities.

Generically, it would be wonderful to focus more on your people investment and your ROI for the recruitment and retention of staff. By being more strategic and less generalist in your approach to on-boarding, you may find that you can more readily 'fill the gaps' in knowledge and skills that your organisation requires. I know that you are already doing this to some degree, but let me take you down a pathway, just for a minute.

Many organisations have implemented wellbeing programs that aim to enhance and promote healthy lifestyles for employees. For example, work–life balance programs, flexible hours, professional development training, leadership training, the implementation of organisational culture change programs, inclusion and diversity programs, safer workplace programs, and health and wellbeing programs. All of the above are not only beneficial to the organisation and Managers, but also the employees, as they serve to increase performance and productivity, enhance employee experience of the workplace, reducing absenteeism and enhance retention of employees. Ultimately, they also aim to promote healthier lives for staff (Burton, 2019; COMCARE, 2010).

In the business world, it seems that every 10 years, the landscape changes and there is something new on the horizon. There is a new 'fad' or trend. There are stacks of books that come out following a new theory or practice, and we are all asked to take part in it.

This runs through the business world in terms of supervision and in the world of diversity management, outsourcing, innovation, R&D, diversification, knowledge resourcing, leadership, organisational culture, generational work conflicts and the information/knowledge age, things are even more complicated than ever before.

No longer does a one size fits all leadership model really work. We can't treat everyone the same and expect that everything will just "work out" somehow. Managers and leaders must have a framework with which to manage their workers in a way that honours everyone's unique and specific position on the job.

Empowered leadership is the way to do just that. Empowered leadership shares the power between management and the workers, thus empowering both groups. I have been sharing some new ideas with you on how to do this, in this book. They are not just applicable to your neurodivergent employees. However, they have come from the mind of a neurodivergent individual who has spent many years analysing the workplace and why it just doesn't work for neurodivergent employees.

A new kind of leader and manager is required to be able to see the potential for their workforce, in the inclusion of, development, training, talent management and optimisation of neurodivergent employees as a key human capital resource.

I have been promoting the meeting of individual needs, so that your neurodivergent employees can feel more secure, safer' and therefore more able to fulfill not just their basic work obligations, but also show you what else they have up their sleeves!

And, we need a certain type of manager and leadership to be able to draw the best out of us!

Conventional wisdom tells us that when those in power relinquish some of that power by sharing it or giving it to their employees, then they would lose something when in actually, they gain.

Think about it. When people rule with an iron hand, they generally instil fear in those who work for them. Do you do your best work when you are afraid? I don't know about you but I will attempt to comply because I want to avoid negative consequences but it certainly won't be my best work. The absolute best a manager can hope for (with coercion) is compliance. If compliance is enough, then coercion might work.

No one works well under either of these kinds of pressure, in the workplace, no matter how well you may think they are 'performing' for you. It is just that. And, at some point, it will all start to unravel. Especially if your employee is neurodivergent.

You will eventually end up in a situation where you feel as though your employee isn't giving their best. You may have even decided to put them on a *Performance Management Plan*, because they are 'failing' at their duties.

You will then find that your employee will rarely have a kind thing to say about you, as their employer and at every available chance they will seek corroboration for how they feel about you. This kind of cultural 'slide' only serves to spread the "us" versus "them" mentality.

This is exactly what I don't want for you, your managers and your workforce. Why? Because, as I've been saying all along, you have some amazing people there!

And, many of them are neurodivergent.

It is very important to state, here, that I am pro-empowerment of employees, both neurodivergent and for everyone at work. Yourself included. We all need to know that we have a place, that we do our work to the best of our ability and that, if we need to say something, that we are listened to and that action is taken, in relation to what we say. It is also very important that we have a space in which we can contribute, outside of our daily work tasks and that we are given praise and 'sustenance' that creates a space we want to return to, every day. This is all environmental and based in the emotional/psychological landscape of our workplace.

Much of it has to do with our own emotional intelligence and the way we use our own mindset and our emotional landscape to navigate through our day, with our colleagues and with our employees.

Stay with me here.

When leaders and managers seek to empower their workers, they will gain their loyalty. Workers want to give their supervisor their best when they are listened to and respected. Without fear, their minds can be creative and innovative.

When managers are willing to accommodate special requests and it doesn't interfere with product or service delivery, then their employees will be sure to give back their best in return. Giving away power only increases a manager's power.

Now, I am not talking about being a total pushover and only advocating for what employees want. As a manager, you have a two-fold job—you are to represent your employees' desires, opinions and suggestions to management while at the same time communicating management's issues, concerns and expectations to your employees. This is not an easy line to walk.

Mutual and reciprocal respect in the workplace is paramount. That is true.

And as a manager and a leader, you have the responsibility to create a need satisfying workplace for yourself and your workers. You cannot emphasise one to the exclusion of the other without there being undesirable consequences.

When you focus on production only and forget the human capital, you will end up with resentful, resistant, angry workers. On the other hand, when you only focus on the people end and allow production goals to be compromised; you will have workers who do everything they can to take advantage and to get out of doing the work. After all, if you the manager don't value production, why should they?

Somewhere in the middle, when you are walking that very fine line between relationships and production goals, you are practicing empowered leadership and that's where you will get the most from your employees.

Inclusive NeuroDiversity Communication Strategies

Communication in the workplace is very important but with so many people involved, all with different personalities and varying levels of understanding - communication can be difficult and misunderstandings can arise.

Workplaces can be hectic places where messages are flying left, right and centre: that's prime territory for miscommunication. Try to avoid that by following a few simple guidelines.

How you need to communicate in the workplace varies a little according to your job responsibilities. Those differ sometimes in whether you have responsibility for and authority over certain other staff members. It's important to realize that you only have authority in so far as you can get people to follow you. How successfully you get people to do that comes down to communication too!

Communication is vital in any workplace and here are some of the essential ingredients for good communication in the workplace:

1. Give clear instructions

You save time in the long run by taking time to give even simple instructions clearly and make sure they are understood. Leave a pause for people to ask questions - or invite them to do so. It's much better if a task is understood from the start rather than you having to go back and do work again because it was done wrongly the first time.

2. Be constructive, not critical

Supervisors and managers can be a little harsh at times, especially if they do not fully understand the big picture.

Often people who have tried to organize their work or solve workplace problems themselves have been severely criticized for the solution they have implemented. Is it any wonder then why they don't bother trying to sort anything out again? That's not an efficient way to organize a workplace.

One of the main issues is the natural response of someone who is being criticised is to switch off and not listen. Nobody learns anything or moves on in that way.

The other side of the coin is that when employees are empowered to make some decisions themselves, managers get more time to get on with their own job and really progress a business. For this to work, people need to feel safe to explore alternatives, give suggestions and ask questions.

Managers also need to make sure they ask the right questions to inspire their employees and to help them to think through solutions.

3. Broadening people's horizons- letting them in on the 'bigger picture'

What are you all aiming for? People will work harder and smarter if they know how the work, they're doing contributes to an end product, they will have more buy-in and gain an interest in it and then be more engaged in why they are contributing to that part of its development/delivery.

4. Communicate messages effectively (don't leave out the details, especially if someone's comprehension is reliant on knowing the details)

Workplaces often have many people working there. Messages need to be passed on efficiently through whichever medium - face-face, Zoom, Skype, CRMs, telephone, e-mail etc.

If you have a message to pass on, make sure you do it accurately, to the right person - and in a timely manner. If the message is long - type it rather than relying on your memory.

5. Give people the freedom to organize a portion of their work

If people are clear about what needs to be done, they can understand and set a list of priorities for their own work. This keeps people motivated to work hard, but also, it makes them work more efficiently as they know what has to be done and can switch between tasks accordingly. There's no need for them to stop work having hit a snag when they can get on with another project.

6. Establishing clear expectations

End a conversation with something like, "So, am I right in thinking that you think the project will be completed by the end of today?"

Then, if people anticipate a problem, they have the opportunity to tell you if there's going to be a problem with that. That gives you the chance - and responsibility - to help them.

7. Treat people like individuals

Everyone has different needs and different personalities. Different people will all react well to slightly different approaches. It's good if you can find out what approaches work well for your colleagues and employees; that way, you will get the most out of each interaction and everyone will be happier.

It all comes down to communication skills - or lack of them. It's completely your responsibility for making yourself understood - no matter how many times you have to try - and it's the other person's responsibility to let you know every time they don't understand something: communication in the workplace relies upon it

None of us like to be told that we aren't communicating effectively, or clearly enough for someone to understand or comprehend what we are saying. However, it happens every day.

Some of us may feel we are effective and competent communicators.

In some contexts, within some formalised groups, we may be. However, across the board, I'm sure you will agree that we all muck it up sometimes.

Being able to provide clear and explicit structure to our communication is vital to the other person understanding. Assuming that what we say should easily be understood by someone else is a faulty way of thinking. It is also a default mindset that many people have.

You are this far into this book; I want to believe that you can see by now that not everyone communicates in the same way. Because of this, not everybody understands everyone else, either.

That includes you, as their manager.

You may not understand them and they may not 'understand' you.

The easiest way through this is to ask questions, have discussions and try to get to know the other person, what their motivations are and why they do what they do.

You may not have enough time to do that for each and every one of your employees. However, I am hoping that this book has given you some valuable insight into the reasons why some people may not respond to you, their colleagues, the workload and also their working environment in the way/s you might expect.

Now we are looking at some innovative ways in which you can work together to create a powerhouse of new ideas, concepts and frameworks, for the whole team and workplace's benefit!

This leads us back to communication. Discussion is like conversation in that it is a free-form dialogue without any direction. Each person responds to what the last person said. While this can produce entertaining party chatter, it seldom leads to agreements or decisions.

In fact, in a meeting, discussion can even make things worse. For example, suppose you said:

"We need to talk about the budget."

And then someone says:

"Is that the one we approved last month?"

"And my department is doing fine."

"Oh yeah, what about the new computer that you just bought."

"Did you hear about the new operating system?"

"My dog had an operation last week."

And so on.

Many ND individuals will respond to communication directed at them in a literal way. So, if you ask, "Have you completed the task?" They will respond with "No, I haven't", as this is the truth. It does not, however, expand on the fullness of what is happening behind the scenes, which may be that they are almost complete and have started a side-project that they are going to propose to you tomorrow, at the same time they present their full and complete proposal you have just asked about. Your staff member, Jennifer's, answer implies that she has not only not completed her set task, but also sounds like she may be nowhere near finishing it. Her direct and honest answer could be misinterpreted as incompetence or low performance, which it actually isn't. For Jennifer, she is merely responding to what you have explicitly asked. If you had asked a different question or framed your own question in an alternative way, she would have answered that directly as well.

Unfortunately, for Jennifer, her direct and non-expanded answer could lead to negative workplace consequences. Would this be Jennifer's "fault" (if her Manager's perceptions of her self-initiative, commitment, competence and capacity to work efficiently and effectively were inaccurate)? Or is this an issue that is directly related to a mainstream approach to workforce management and development?

From a neurodiversity perspective, having heard many different variations on similar streams of miscommunication between Managers who don't appear to 'understand' their staff and their employees' ways of competing work, those who make assumptions on information not given and those who assume that information not given means information not available, are interesting to consider, from a management perspective. It is important to remember that our neurodivergent employees have different 'hard-wiring'. They do not think in the same ways as people who are not neurodiverse. They will not respond to others in the same ways in social and cultural situations. They will not communicate using the same communication patterns, gestures and responses. It is important to remember that issues that arise due to differences in the way someone communicates in alternative ways to you (due to those neuro-developmental differences and alternative cognitive wiring we discussed earlier) are never the "fault" of the individual.

From a personal/employee perspective and through the eyes of someone who has experienced this on many occasions, being placed in a position of having to "explain your style of communication" to the team, because it was so very different to everyone else and (according to my supposedly personally aware Manager, "no-one understood my way of doing things", was quite demoralising. It made me feel disheartened, devalued as a team member, excluded from 'the team', humiliated in front of everyone (as my differences were highlighted in a not very pleasant way), as though I 'didn't fit in', and, ultimately, over a little more time and more stigmatisation and exclusion from the social norms of that organisation, I began to feel 'less than' and quite unworthy of my job role.

You may be asking, is that really a managerial issue or concern?

Well, yes, it is.

I went to work every day. I was committed to achieving the organisation's objectives and I followed all workplace procedures, policies and practices. Sometimes, I did things in my own way, as it was more internally 'comfortable' for me, due to my own neurodivergent condition. My employer was not initially aware of this, and initially appreciated my creativity and innovations. It was only when I disclosed that I was specifically challenged by one workplace environmental aspect and asked to have it changed slightly due to my neurodivergence, that everything started to go pear-shaped.

Who would have thought, hey?

In this day and age, when workplaces are in a prime position, following Workplace Health and Safety (WH&S/OH&S) guidelines to ensure that they are compliant with safety requirements, including mental health and wellbeing, it seems unheard of that there would be an organisation that would not be interested in upholding a space for the wellbeing of their employees. Right?

Especially those whose rights aren't generally taken into consideration. Like, those who are individually neurodivergent and collectively, exhibit neurodiverse characteristics, strengths, skills, knowledge and a worldview that could potentially benefit the organisation 100-fold!

What Are We Doing Well? And, How Can We Do It Better?

Well, firstly, let's look at the way we assume everyone communicates.

In every organisation I've worked for, whether it be government-based, Not-for-Profit, large or small, every week or so, we have a meeting. Are they productive?

Personally, not particularly.

Why do I say that?

Mainly because they are generally not well facilitated. Secondly, because they are facilitated to suit the agenda of primarily one person and everyone else must sit and listen. Thirdly, participation and interaction in the meeting are very, very low, meaning that for those of us who are neurodivergent, we will tune-out pretty quickly (looking like we are bored, that we don't care, are uninterested in the person speaking and/or the topic, would prefer to be somewhere else, and/or are daydreaming). None, some or all of those may be true. However, not because we are 'bad' employees!

It is the opposite, in fact!

We feel 'bored, but that is because we aren't engaged, or are not being kept stimulated or interested in what is being conveyed during the meeting. Things that might stimulate us might be visuals, interactive participation, being asked our opinion on something, being asked to present, and so on. most likely want to be somewhere else getting our work done. We are rarely uninterested in learning new things, although, sometimes, especially if we have been focussed on something for a long time, we may not want to be away from that task or project. So, this may be at play, whilst we are sitting in meeting number 3 for the week (whilst still trying to complete that very important task for our Manager, with a deadline of tomorrow morning).

And, as for day-dreaming, this is a form of self-stimulation or cognitive relaxation for many individuals with Autism and ADHD, which is often perceived as a 'time-waster' but actually, in effect, is vital to assist them in self-regulating and getting their internal system and bio-physical system back on track, so that they can continue working for the remainder of the day. So, sitting in a chair for an hour or more seems non-productive, inefficient and even down-right ridiculous to us!

So, for the majority of individuals who are neurodivergent, although a well-throughout, well-planned, structured and well-facilitated meeting is vital to continue inter and intra-office communications, a poorly managed, poorly run and unintegrated meeting can pose a real diversion from day-to-day self-management and also completion of tasks, projects and overall organisational objectives.

This happens because 'discussion' and meetings generally are divergent processes. Each idea elicits a response from someone else. It's like a conversation where no specific result is expected. For someone who is already operating from an alternative paradigm, that is, not thinking in the same way as the neuro-norm, this can be very distractive and even detrimental to the completion of their daily professional management.

NeuroDiversity and Equality- It's an Interesting Discussion

Firstly, do you know who your neurodivergent employees are? If you do, do you know what their baseline daily needs are? If you do, do you know how to meet those needs, on an environmental level?

If you've answered 'no' to any of these questions, I want you to have a think about why this might be the case.

It could be possible that your neurodivergent employee/s do not want to disclose. There are a number of reasons for this. I won't go into all of them, however, negative previous experiences with employers can often play a part in whether or not to disclose to a current employer.

It is also vital that you are aware of your employee's daily baseline needs, especially if they relate to environmental concerns and are issues that can be resolved with accommodations and adjustments. This can most easily be addressed by opening up communication and feedback channels and establishing equitable relationships with your employees.

Finally, knowing how to meet requests for accommodations and adjustments without saying 'no', being reticent, or being resistant, and also knowing what your employer responsibilities, accountabilities are is paramount, if you are to be a successful manager and ethical leader.

Managing Sustainable vs Time-Limited Achievements

For many neurodivergent individuals, time-limited, or time-constrained options are going to create a stressful situation. No-one is going to tell you that, because you are their boss. However, it is true. Deadlines, milestones, "emergencies", "crises" and "things that just have to be done right now!" are all stressors to someone who is neurodivergent. Why?

Well, aside from the fact that they create stress for all of us, time limitations for lots of neurodivergent individuals put a clamp on lots of other aspects of processing that require neurodivergent 'time', which is non-chronological.

This is a little hard to articulate, but basically, sometime, a neurodivergent person needs "time" that just can't be defined as an hour, or a day.

It is more that they need to move through a process or a set or series of sensations or sensory processes before they can then resolve whatever is going on for them. Then, they can fulfill whatever comes next. Thus, it then becomes, "time" for the next step.

So, if you wanted me to complete some work. And, there was a deadline attached to it. And, I asked for a separate space, so that I could focus on completing that work. Because it required focus. However, I was not given that space, but had to complete it in an open plan office, where there were lots of sensory distractions. Keeping in mind that I have a sensory processing disorder, where I can become overwhelmed by an overload of sensory input.

By the time the middle of my day is upon me, I may be unable to "function" any longer, due to 'too much' sensory input. I will need some "time" away from all of the distractions.

How much "time"? That will be dependent on how long my system and my brain takes to regulate again. It may be half an hour. It may be an hour, It may be the rest of the day.

So, whereas I could have had the task completed and all ready to go, with the accommodation in place (a quiet room, no distractions),; I am compromised and unable to fulfil my workplace objectives dur to a time-limitation and a non-accommodation which has impacted on me due to my neurodivergent condition.

Sometimes, it is better to try a new approach when dealing with a situation that is new to you, or which you have not had experience of managing before. Managers often get caught up in the management of the details and forget the big picture. Or, alternatively, focus on the attainment of smaller goals, but leave the more strategic management to more senior managers.

It is becoming more and more clear to me that the management of both long-term, sustainable objectives, as well as short-term, micro-objectives is in order, so that neurodivergent employees feel as though they are achieving something in the workplace.

One of the core strategies we utilise in education, which has a transferrable component here, in a business model, is that of 'scaffolding.' For those of you who have anything to do with training and development, HR or R&D, you may already know what I am talking about. I will continue on, for those who don't.

The idea of scaffolding is to create a block of knowledge, expertise or skill about something. In the future, that knowledge, expertise or skills will be developed and built upon, in a variety of ways, to create something larger. Education at all levels now utilises the concept of scaffolding to enable learners to develop core and foundational knowledge.

In this context, let's assume that we are scaffolding a component or block of 'task/activity competence', instead of knowledge, skill or expertise.

Let's continue and say that competence is to do with writing an email using Outlook. So, your employee, Jane, has been required to write a morning email to 10 other employees asking what their task list for the day is. Jane is using Outlook to do this. She has a pre-determined template to use. She learns how to use this template and is using it daily, and successfully, for 3 months.

Jane has achieved a 'Time-Limited Achievement', which she achieves every day, now. You, as her manager, want to know if she can scaffold her knowledge and achieve a sustainable achievement.

You ask her to write a monthly report, utilising all of the information received back from the 10 colleagues, each day, for 1 month. You want her to write a productivity report in this for you and for your Senior Manager, Max.

You think this should be an easy task for Jane to complete, because Jane said she can use Excel and Word.

Jane appears very stressed for a few days and is very quiet. On the third day, you ask her why. She states that although she knows how to use Excel, and can create a graph from the information provided from her colleagues, she does not how to interpret this into 'management information' that would be useful to you and Max.

Interestingly, this is a common occurrence and a regular 'mistake' that managers make in assuming that just because employees understand A and B separately, they can add A+B to =C. Unless people are shown the way, via scaffolding, they rarely are able to fill the gaps themselves.

So, whilst Jane was able to achieve a 'Time-Limited Achievement', your assumption that she could automatically achieve a 'Sustainable Achievement' was incorrect and also require some input and support from you as Jane's manager.

The value of working on a scaffolded system of learning, from my perspective, has been that I can often identify where something is missing in comprehension, absorption or recall or understanding, for someone.

If, as a manager, when I utilise those skills, I could have established quite quickly that Jane had a gap in knowledge about something, so she was unable to achieve my objective. Because she did not know exactly what that 'gap' was, she could also not effectively articulate that to me, directly, either. In addition, she felt self-conscious about confessing that she could not achieve the task I had set her.

For someone who may already have some challenges identifying internal processes (if they have sensory processing issues), with information processing (if Jane had an Information Processing Disorder), have anxiety (a range of neurodivergent conditions), any issues with her executive functioning (often associated with ADHD and Autism/ASD/ASC), but other neurodivergent conditions as well), this simple task allocation from me, as Jane's manager, could have turned Jane's world upside down.

However, if as Jane's manager, jane had disclosed her anxiety, IPD, SPD and ADHD and needs around executive functioning to me, because we had established a respectful, ethical and open working relationship, this whole scenario would have been a whole lot different.

I could have walked Jane through the Excel sheet data, once she had compiled it and turned it into a graph. I could have provided her with headings and subheadings of what kind of information Max and I were looking for, so that she would extrapolate that from her raw data and also manipulate the data to produce a graph that was representative of the information we wanted to produce within the report.

In this way, Jane is still learning a new skill. She is building on her expertise (scaffolding is at play, here, as I am taking her base skills and knowledge, and her 'competence block' of being able to write and email and extract data from her colleagues on a daily basis). I am also guiding and leading Jane towards the next level of her skills and knowledge- that in which she can support me in report-writing.

Can you see the difference?

As managers, we have a responsibility to our employees to nurture them in this way. If our employees come to us with a particular set of needs, based on their neurodivergence, we are accountable for making those adjustments. And, as organisation leaders who are ethical in our practice, we have a responsibility to provide a workplace where our employees can learn and develop in a safe, open and 'scaffolded' manner, just as I've highlighted for you.

So, What Works?
Strategic Team Development

How do you 'develop' a neurodivergent team? In general, a strong, positive teamwork is defined by a leader who has a vision and the ability to inspire his or her team to work toward the realization of that vision. This is the same with any team or similarly minded working group. Whenever your neurodivergent employees are working within a team, they will find their own balance.

In order for them to excel, you may choose to provide some supports and interventions that are of a higher order than those you may provide for your non-neurodivergent employees. What you do is entirely up to you.

However, the more direction, focus and motivation to engage and achieve an outcome your team has the more your will optimise your chances of achieving an overall outcome. This is true for everyone.

Some specific interventions and focussed supports you may want to put in place are:

-A mentor/coach

-Talent development group participation (separate to the 'team' participation)

- 'Participation in Wisdom Pods'

-Participation in scaled team collaborations (4NT:1ND as previously suggested)

Furthermore, if a leader is not threatened in the least by the expertise and diversity of his or her team, the team can flourish to a higher degree, with or without input or 'check-ins with the leader. An effective team leader engages his or her teammates in in-depth discussions about what quality is, what it looks like in theory as well as in practice, differing alternative strategies for achieving quality, what is needed to perform and complete the job/task/project at hand, and what the team needs (specifics) to empower it. All of this will ensure that the team members always strive for quality improvement.

Let's break all that down into its component parts. The first is a clearly defined leader. I believe every team must have a leader. There must be someone who is in charge and makes the ultimate decisions.

In a 'Wisdom Pod', team members may take turns being the leader everyone knows what the guidelines are (these will be different for each of your organisations, so don't be too concerned that I am being a little vague about it here. If you are interested in knowing more, please contact us).

As long as everyone is clear who the leader is on any given day, the running and facilitation of the group dynamic should flow smoothly under their leadership, for that day/session. For individual projects, another variation of that theme is to have certain people be the leader for projects that are, in their area of expertise. Just ensure that everyone knows who is leading for that day, project or task. Clarity is the key, here.

Stephen Covey (1989) said: "Begin with the end in mind."

A focussed leader needs to have this vision clearly at the forefront of their mind. They also need to convey this to their team. It is important for the person in leadership to have the concept of their vision in mind and be able to not only conceptualise it, but manifest it. That is, bring it into the real world.

It is not good if you are just an ideas person! Ideas are great! Don't get me wrong. But, they will not make you, nor your business, any money, unless you can monetise them. That means turning your and your team's ideas and concepts into a valid, viable process, system, structure, standard, service or product. A true leader creates the end product twice---once mentality and then in its actual form. It is impossible to lead toward a fuzzy vision. People are simply not inspired to follow uncertainty.

Certainty is where the money is!

At least for neurodivergent employees.

If you want them to be productive...

This is why your neurodivergent team members can be one of your greatest assets. They can more often than not see the big picture and convey it to everyone. They can also go in-depth and find any gaps in what might create a barrier to its achievement (and then help to fill these gaps!). They can also support the development of the system, process, structure, standard, service or product. Finally, they can work steadily and systematically towards the end result, with a laser-focus that few non-neurodivergent individuals have.

And, that's just the start of some of the specialised skills that a neurodivergent team member could have on offer for you!

So, having the vision is not enough to inspire teammates to strive toward the same goal. A good team leader knows how to help each teammate see how the end product or service will be useful and what, exactly, their individual contribution is toward that end. Knowing how to get the very best out of your neurodivergent employees and team members will play a vital part in ensuring your overall organisation's success in modelling proactive leadership and employee empowerment. It will also be a key driver for your innovation program and pivoting for future success.

Another component of being able to inspire one's teammates is having a clearly defined mission that everyone, preferably, has had a part in developing, but if not, then at least team members can agree to the previously established team mission.

The other advantage of having a mission that has been agreed upon by all team members is that it can enhance cooperation. There can be petty inconsistencies in work practices and an overall competitive spirit that can kill the cooperation of the best team. Most neurodivergent individuals tend to find this kind of power-play and workplace dynamic uncomfortable at best and may shy away from these kinds of situations. This is not anti-social behaviour, but a need to stay away from emotionally charged situations that do not appear relevant to them. Having a Mission Statement for your organisation and also for your team may help to minimise this potential for disaster.

The Mission remains the focus that everything else is compared to. An individual's action is means to comply with the mission and support its achievement. The group's goal must always be placed above any individual's desires.

A good leader is in no way threatened by the expertise and diversity of his or her team. The best leaders are always seeking information from the front-line people who are doing the actual work. Without information from team members, the leader's hands are tied behind his or her back.

It is also critical to use team members in their areas of expertise. Leaders can't know everything about everything. There will be team members who have skills and abilities that surpass those of the leader in certain areas. A good leader will ask for help when it is prudent.

This is also a time to value diversity and the specialised skill-sets and knowledge base that individual employees have. Creating a team made up of people who all do the same jobs in pretty much the same way really has no value. One person could more easily do the job than assembling a homogenous team. This is also where the real and dynamic value of a neurodivergent team member can come into play, as they will be able to think in ways that the majority of employees will not. This will provide a definitive edge to your team and its ability to produce and end result (Krzeminska et al, 2019).

The value of a team comes from its heterogeneity. Getting feedback and suggestions from people who do things differently is what will spark the creativity and the genius of the team. This is what masterminding is all about. Tap into the wealth that is already there.

Finally, a good leader holds the bar high. He or she does not ask his team to be average or mediocre. Average and mediocre can be easily replaced. The leader asks his or her team to collectively do their very best and when they are done, the leader asks them to always strive for continuous improvement. The team should always be evaluating and improving what has been produced implemented and be comfortable making suggestions for ways to do it even better.

In addition, I mentioned that a good leader empowers his or her teammates. Creating a need-satisfying environment does this. This whole book has really been about doing just that. You, as a manager, are really the leader of your greater team. Whether you are the Manager of your company, or the manager of a small team of one or two people. It doesn't matter. Your ability to lean in, to actively listen and then take action, and to be effective in meeting the needs of your neurodivergent employees can only bring benefits to your organisation.

At a minimum, team members must get along and know that the leader and the company have their best interests at heart. They must feel important, listened to and respected. They must have the freedom to make choices within the context of their assignments and they must have some fun in their work.

It is also critical for team members to feel safe. This means that they are not fearful in any way. The team leader is critical in fostering this environment for the empowerment of the entire team.

We are going back to a safe, secure and nurturing environment. If you haven't already had a look at their site, go and take a look at HOK. They have offices all around the world. They have been designing office spaces for neurodivergent -friendly workplaces for a few years now. You will see how their leadership in the design field has paid off for the employers who had utilised their services. Their key focus is the environment effects of a workplace.

The influence, impact and effects of a poorly designed workplace are core to the reason for me writing this book, as I stated in the early pages of this book. As a leader, your ability to nurture the talent and capabilities of your employees via the optimisation of workplace design and creation is one of the best gifts you could give them!

By the way, I have no connection with HOK. I came across them while doing research for this book. I do think that workplace design is at the forefront of architecture (a secret passion of mine- I have my "draftsman's" certification, from a long, long time ago!). And, I believe that from a teaching and learning/training and development perspective, we have already started to look at classroom and university design in this way. Now it is workplace design time.

Key Leadership Lessons for Those Managing NeuroDivergent Talent

1.Create certainty where there is uncertainty

Even a skinny pathway is better than no pathway. It's a starting point. Having a focal point to start from is a great anchor and far more relevant for an innovation team than having a blank-bubbles to start with.

2. Refuse to "lose".

Innovation is about trying different things until something sticks. Neurodivergent people do this every day. Many of them do this all day every day, in fact! It is second nature to some. Not that it is preferred, it is just familiar. That is why 'innovation' and ingenuity' come as second nature to many of us. We have always thought 'outside the box', as there is no 'box' for us. We've been thinking of alternatives, sometimes many hundreds or thousands of alternatives, all day, every day!

3.You must be willing to do what has never been done before

Resistance is futile! Commitment to the process of trying something new is essential to being a leader sand to modelling positive and empowering leadership. As far as your team is concerned, they will be doing this for themselves anyway. They may well be very used to doing things in a different way or in ways that things 'haven't been done before', so this will not be too much of an effort.

However, keep in mind that change or the process of change or shifting through different mindsets can be jarring for some neurodivergent individuals. It may take them a little while to shift tracks. Once they have done that, they will be back in the game again. It is a little like watching electric trains change tracks versus steam trains. We don't have too many steam trains left in Australia, but I know they do in the UK. There is a build-up prior to the track change. Sometimes, for some ND individuals, this needs to occur prior to a change, as well. was tested a few different times when his top leaders, letting human nature get the better of them. For your organization to excel past all others you must be willing to think outside the box.

You must be willing to look at your job and organization in a totally new way. It is certain that your organization (even your life) will face challenges this year. How you view these challenges will determine your future success. While at the same time, how you view your organization (the values, vision, and mission) will determine its success.

4.. Your focus must be flexible in order to have your preferred future
Flexibility, both in practice and also in mindset, is vital!

Without it, you will not be able to move with the flow and navigate with and for your team, as and when it is required. Also, this adaptability is necessary to keep up with the ever-changing landscape of the business world. No matter whether you are running the whole organisation or only a small part of it.

'Loops of Competence'
Creating opportunities for small "Loops of Competence" by starting a project, volunteering, or getting a part time job to build their skillset and self-

esteem in a way that doesn't involve large opportunities for failure. Basically, when you are first starting, make it impossible to fail. Creating 'loops of competence' for people enables them to build on the skills they have and also to share those with others, in a way they can then develop and enhance their transferrable skills, by engaging in multi-disciplinary projects, alternative team development and innovation teams.

'Wisdom Pods'

This is my personal concept "baby". Okay, I've had a few. But, this is my key one for this book. I have utilised this model in a whole range of settings and environments and it has worked a treat! I thrive on working with groups, and I have a deep passion for bringing my compassion, warmth, passion, curiosity, humour and creativity to clients and colleagues.

One of the keys to a successful and productive 'Wisdom Pods' is the relationship we establish with our clients before meeting up with them, and also, before they have their first group session. We work closely with the client to understand their organisation's needs, the needs of the individuals attending and to effectively create the appropriate theme and platform to frame the discussions. We do this by establishing non-negotiables, a set of 'must haves', and a 'blue-sky' set of 'probable's, possible's, do-able's and maybes.

The theme is the only frame that in these externally run, participant-based sessions see. Often-times, our initial Wisdom Pod events can appear chaotic, unmanaged and unstructured. They are, however, run to a format and therefore, highly structured. They are allowed to flow within these pre-established parameters to enable innovation and creative 'flow' during the sessions.

There are four unusual principles and one law.

The principles are:

1.No-one is specifically invited to attend. Whoever is present on the day is the right person for the event, on that day

2.Whenever it starts is the right time.

3.The compiling and logging of information and ideas and concepts is recorded as and when the group decides. If this is pictorially, that is okay. If it is completed symbolically, that is okay. If it is digitally, that is okay. There is always more than one person compiling the information, in more than one way, so visually, by recording, by drawing, by writing notes, etc.

4.When the meeting finishes, that is the end. It may take one hour, it may take four hours, it is the creative content that we are interested in and its' 'capture', for future use.

5. The organisation's 'Wisdom Pod' owns copyright over the ideas. How this is managed internally and externally is an organisational decision.

If more than one 'Wisdom Pod' exists within an organisation, then participants are free to move between them, without needing to 'ask for permission' to do so. This is free space and a sharing of ideas unfettered by the normalised parameters of working space, environment and duration. The law of mobility invites participants to move from to another group or elsewhere if they are not learning or contributing. Moving like butterflies and insects.

'Wisdom Pods' are like gardens that can be cross-pollinated and also act as zones of growth and nourishment for the small or larger teams you have in your workforce. People can place an idea or problem into a Wisdom Pod and watch as the participants work to resolve it.

Using the theme and principles, and taking into consideration the "givens" or non-negotiables, participants identify issues they find personally relevant. When all issues are collected and written on sign-up sheets displayed in the room, participants are then invited to choose the issues they want to address.

'Wisdom Pods' are productive and have accountability due to group ownership and also because of the co-creative elements present within them.

The collaboration, knowledge that ideas developed will be acknowledged as individuals and team owned concepts, and also the ethical approach to collaborative workplace all make this a fabulous way to bring dynamism and innovation to your workplace!

The space is productive because it operates on the concepts of accountability, ethical practice, passion, reciprocity and responsibility. Passion engages people and responsibility ensures that tasks are accomplished.

Organizations going through transformative change often experience chaos, confusion and conflict. This is not only a powerful approach for engaging people in change management, but is also a dynamic way of engaging teams in innovative practices and productivity growth mechanisms.

It can also work for teams that are experiencing cultural confusion, and who are undergoing fluctuations in cultural identity, no matter what the reason, whether that be a shift in organisational branding, diversification, external pressures from the marketplace, or a global pandemic, as is occurring at the time of the publication of this book.

Ultimately, utilising Wisdom Pods is a fantastic way to introduce and expand new leadership models, engage employees in new structural processes and systems, a way to share leadership within the organisation, an innovative way to include all employees in R&D, a great way to engender staff empowerment, a great platform for showcasing diversity and finally a wonderful way to ensure that organisational 'issues' have a place where they can be openly passed around the table and considered more broadly than just in the Senior Managers' offices!

It can only be a win-win situation!

Strategic Leadership as Part of the Overall System

For the leaders of organisation there are two levels at which workplace stress must be addressed. Firstly, at corporate, strategic level, where a degree of stress is inevitable, given the pace and frequency of change that businesses of all kinds are experiencing today. Political, economic, environmental, social, and technological changes combine to make it essential that the organisation is equipped to respond to or, better, to forecast and prepare for change. In this book, we have mainly explored the social and environmental impacts of leadership on the overall system. However, one of those impacts, on the performance of human capital, can play out in an economic way, which we have been alluding to all along. That which affects innovation, the ability to pivot when change occurs, and also the productivity and profitability of your organisation.

Without strong, empowering and effective leadership, the organisation will not survive the tumultuous nature of a global crisis, nor the ups and downs of a global economic marketplace, in the long-term trajectory. Therefore, the need to manage change successfully adds to the complexities and pressures facing the leaders of the organisation (AIM, 2020).

Secondly, at the operational levels stress which affects the managers and operational staff can be caused by many factors, not least the behaviour of the operational managers themselves. This is mainly where we have been focussed in this book, as we explore the operational nature of what it means to have neurodivergent employees on board. We have looked at how we might recruit them in alternative ways that reduce excess stressors that marginalise and negate their experiences, to the point that they may not even apply for our jobs. We have looked at ways in which we can be more inclusive within our general workplace practices, providing adjustments and accommodations to neurodivergent employees who require them. We have looked at proactive strategic management, from the standpoint of environmental design and how a shift in workplace design may invite more conducive work practices and also more optimum work performance from both our neurodivergent and other employees, recognising the power and influence of environment to workplace productivity.

In addition, we have looked at how we can strategically utilise the specialised skills and knowledge of our neurodivergent workforce, both individually and collectively, to optimise workplace organisational culture, productivity and profitability, via mechanisms such as 'Talent Management' programs, team-based innovation-led 'Wisdom Pods' and the development of individualised 'Competence Loops'.

There are a few more things we've also covered, but they have been more operational and information-based, so useful, indeed, but not strategic in nature.

I just wanted to pull us back into position, so that we can see how relevant everything has been, that I've been talking about.

The strategies we use in business tend to be very sequential, step by step and methodical. The very nature of innovation is almost the complete opposite. It is lateral and diverse in nature. Innovation is creative and flowing! It does not follow form, but flows and is organic in its development.

Neurodivergent minds often think like this, as well. Although some of us can think in a very formalised, structured manner, there are many of us who fit very well into an innovative, lateral-thinking 'world'. And, as you have seen, your ability to utilise these skills, capabilities and specialised knowledge packages that we all have can only bring benefits to your organisation.

How you choose to strategically manage this process will be an interesting journey.

To date, "management" has been fuelled by set processes and procedures that often do not fit well with the needs of neurodivergent employees, as you may have picked up from some of the examples I have provided in this book.

Your capacity to be more fluid, adaptable and dynamic in your approach to management will enable to you to more appropriately and sensitively manage your neurodivergent staff, in a way that both meets their needs and those of the organisation.

Whilst managing performance has traditionally been about ticking of a series of boxes to provide evidence that the 'job was done' and 'done well', managing a neurodivergent employee may sit a little differently with both operational and strategic managers.

You may find that you are called to 'manage' us a little differently'. And, that is okay. We are not being 'different' to challenge you' or try and call you out. We want to work with you to create a more enhanced, empowered, enlightened and innovative workplace. One that, maybe one day, will also influence and empower other workplaces to work in a flexible, adaptable and organically managed way, showing true empowered leadership.

Without doing this, you may find that there is friction and/or stress caused by your own, your own manager's or the overall organisation's inability to shift gears.

The Big C- Change and Stress

The leaders of the organisation are responsible for the way in which the organisation responds to the threat of negative stress, at both strategic and operational levels. In fact, it is often the behaviour, the actions, the style of the leader(s) that causes the stress. Some of the most common areas in which the negative behaviour of the leader(s) can cause stress are described below.

Successful leaders ensure that their organisations are appropriately resourced. The needs of the organisation's strategic objectives are assessed and funds are allocated and activity planned to deliver the necessary resources as and when required. Human resources, physical resources, technological resources, funds, systems, should all be in place or planned for. A monitoring and control process should be in place to respond to the need for changes to the plans. If these processed are not followed, then wherever the plans reach a point where the necessary resources are missing, or incomplete, the stress levels of managers and their teams will rise, as they attempt to achieve the set objectives with inadequate resources.

We've talked about many ways in which you could do this for your organisation and also for your neurodivergent employees. There are thousands of other ways, as well! However, there is only so much room in this book for me to discuss some of the options available.

My key focus was raising your awareness and bringing you on board, so that you have the option of becoming a Neurodiversity Works Here pioneer.

This is not just about an awareness, but a complete acceptance of neurodivergent employees and a full accommodation of their needs, so that they can seamlessly work for your organisation and/or any other.

It is the actions of an organisation's leader(s) that have led to the problems or difficulties the organisation is challenged with.

Now, that can be confronting to hear. I know that.

However, if you are truly honest, it is the truth.

In any organisation one of the most common sources of conflict, dispute, and ensuing personal distress, are the related issues of equality of opportunity, diversity, and discrimination (HLRC, 2020). The leader(s) of the organisation must ensure that the culture of the organisation and the actions of individuals supports equality of opportunity and diversity and prevents discrimination of any kind. This is your role. We've touched on this several times, and looked at the ways in which the UK HSE, the U.S. OSHA, the Australian Human Rights Council, the United Nations, the Australian Office of Fair Work Ombudsman, and the various Disability Discrimination Acts across the world have all played a part in ensuring that the needs of individuals who are part of the neurodiverse communities are protected, under various government Policies, Acts and Declarations, of national and international relevance.

All of these are aimed at reducing the stress levels of employees and minimising workplace stressors that may impact on those who find themselves in a situation where they need to ask for a workplace adjustment or accommodation, especially due to a neurodivergent variance or 'condition'.

What Does it Take to Lead Your NeuroDivergent Employees?

Effective leaders do this by: making equality, diversity, and prevention of discrimination an essential, high profile element of the organisation's strategies and objectives; ensuring that all staff are familiar with the organisation's policies in this area and that they understand their personal responsibilities in complying with the policy; ensuring that the organisational structure and processes are receptive to the different needs and abilities of a diverse workforce; implementing a rigorous monitoring and control process to identify and deal with any breaches of the policies; dealing ruthlessly with any employee, of any status, should they act in an unfair of discriminatory manner.

Leaders who do not give strong, visible, leadership in these areas will be risking considerable damage being done. Without strong leadership there is a grave danger of discrimination and unfairness happening, not just at operational levels but also at the executive level. Managers behaving unfairly or in a discriminatory way, or not dealing with such behaviour in others, are the cause of considerable negative stress. The repercussions of these unacceptable actions can include personal distress, employees who leave under duress (often believing that they have done something wrong, when in fact, they have been neurodivergent and unable to convey their needs to an employer who is not able to comprehend what they are saying).

In addition, these stresses and stressors can lead to the break-up of teams, the collapse of projects, internal disciplinary action, industrial tribunals/action or civil court action, and leave a climate of hostility, blame, uncertainty, shame, conflict, and deep unhappiness. The impact in terms of negative stress being generated is enormous.

Effective leaders prevent such disastrous repercussions, by ensuring that promote, support, and insist on fairness and equality towards all.

One of the key responsibilities of the leaders of organisations, indeed in some cases a legal requirement in itself, is to ensure that the organisation complies with relevant legislation and regulations. I have listed some of these in the bibliography, for a few countries I believe this book will receive some readership. Please do your research more fully into what your legal requirements are, especially in relation to the Disability Act in your country and your obligations to your employees, in relation to the provision of workplace adjustments and accommodations.

I want to go a little further and state that, as business owners, it is not only the legalities of business that can present issues for us and challenge us. Oftentimes, it is our moral stance and our ethical approach, or lack of it, to situations and circumstances that may place us outside of our usual comfort zone.

Whilst this is hazy ground, and not covered by "the Law", it is very important to note that you cannot call yourself a leader, if you do not come from an ethical place.

We have already looked at some ethical approaches to business management, so I won't go over them again.

Now that we are closer to the end of the book, I want you to reflect on your own ethical management and leadership practices and ask yourself what you would want someone else to do, if someone you loved and cared about was in that same position as your employee, in their own workplace. Maybe it was your son, or your mother, or your best friend.

In order to show empowered, proactive leadership and truly model it, we have to embrace it and embody it fully.

Is that you?

If it is, that is amazing! Well done!

If it is not you, do you want it to be you?

If so, how could you shift it up and make even just one change to your management or leadership work practices, so that you are more ethically meeting the needs of your neurodivergent employees?

You don't have to answer now.

I have given you a lot of ideas to mull over.

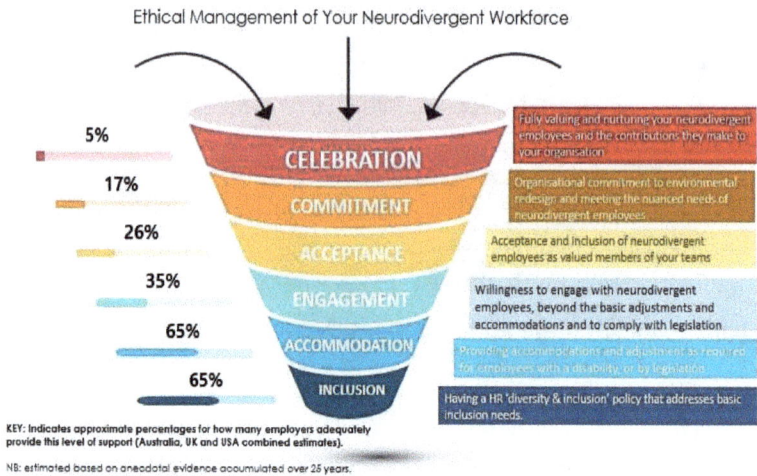

Ethical Management of Your Neurodivergent Workforce

5%	**CELEBRATION** — Fully valuing and nurturing your neurodivergent employees and the contributions they make to your organisation
17%	**COMMITMENT** — Organisational commitment to environmental redesign and meeting the nuanced needs of neurodivergent employees
26%	**ACCEPTANCE** — Acceptance and inclusion of neurodivergent employees as valued members of your teams
35%	**ENGAGEMENT** — Willingness to engage with neurodivergent employees, beyond the basic adjustments and accommodations and to comply with legislation
65%	**ACCOMMODATION** — Providing accommodations and adjustment as required for employees with a disability, or by legislation
65%	**INCLUSION** — Having a HR 'diversity & inclusion' policy that addresses basic inclusion needs.

KEY: Indicates approximate percentages for how many employers adequately
provide this level of support (Australia, UK and USA combined estimates).

NB: estimated based on anecdotal evidence accumulated over 25 years.

The Scaled Cup of Ethical Management of Neurodivergent Employees:

Integrated Management and Leadership

The most visible role of the leader(s) is, by default, to lead the organisation into the future. This means planning and managing desired changes, whilst also responding to external forces of change. The manner in which the leader approaches this can influence the response to the changes by the organisation's managers and employees, which in turn affects the levels of stress caused by the changes. Ways in which to lead change successfully are well documented in this book and in other forms of research.

To lead change in a manner that will lead to negative stress being generated would need the leader(s) to: not communicate their vision of the future (or worse, not to have a vision); to actively of passively discourage consultation and participation in the change planning process; not give individuals clear information on their roles and responsibilities in implementing changes; denying individuals the influence and authority they need to successfully implement and manage change in their area; set objectives which are unachievable; make no effort to provide resources and support for the removal of barriers to change; not provide information on the progress of change activity; not to reward successful change implementation.

The result of such negative behaviour would be to create delays, misunderstanding, tension, uncertainty, and conflicts, and would seriously damage the chances of the any new ideas, innovation, new productivity systems, procedures and processes, and/or change being implemented successfully. The change process raises the negative stress levels of those implementing, or directly affected by the change. Unsuccessful change would inevitably have other negative impacts on the organisation, which in turn would potentially cause more stress.

What Does Ethical Leadership Look Like in Your Organisation?

Effective leaders provide ethical and moral leadership by:

- monitoring the legal and regulatory environment to identify where the organisation must comply;
- developing, implementing and maintaining effective policies and procedures to ensure that the organisation meets all legal and regulatory requirements;
- making certain that relevant people are aware of the policies and procedures and their responsibilities in maintaining them;
- implementing a monitoring, control, and corrective action system to maintain compliance;
- providing appropriate resources for operational managers to carry out the policies effectively.

Effective leaders cultivate and develop a culture that is positive, ethical, and value driven, in order to support the organisation's strategies. The personal actions and behaviour of the leader(s) and the management of the organisation should reinforce this. Agreed values are communicated across the organisation and people are encouraged to pursue these cultural objectives as rigorously as the operational objectives. The condition of the organisation's culture is monitored and corrected as required to maintain the set values. Poor leaders do not view developing a positive culture as important, pursuing instead only the profit-related objectives. Under such leadership the organisation will deteriorate, and managers and staff will have no guidance as to how to behave professionally and ethically.

The role of the leader is, of course, to lead, but to lead in a way which represents the values and mission of the organisation. In areas such as ethics, equality of opportunity, non-discrimination, fairness and openness, the leader(s) must also take on the mantle of acting as a role model for others in the organisation. Positive leaders will ensure that managers throughout the organisation are properly trained in management skills and undertake continuous development, that innovation and creativity is encouraged. This includes, training and development around inclusion of neurodivergent employees and how to integrate these employees more effectively into the workplace, without discriminating against them.

Strong leaders will ensure that managers or staff who behave inappropriately in contradiction of the values of the organisation will be removed or retrained, so that they are able to reframe what they were thinking and start to see the workplace from a different standpoint or perspective.

SELF MANAGEMENT
Emotional self-control
Adaptability
Positive outlook
Achievement orientation
Self-awareness

RELATIONSHIP MANAGEMENT
Influence
Coach & mentor
Inspirational leadership
Conflict management
Teamwork
Empathy

POSITIVE LEADERSHIP
Influence
Positive leadership
Ethical practice
Empowering processes
Mentoring
Modelling

ETHICAL MANAGEMENT
Ethical practices
Creates conducive workplace environment
Looks for methods to optimise performance

SOCIAL AWARENESS
Social competence
Confidence
Emotional intelligence
Emotional Self intimacy

PRODUCTIVITY AND PERFORMANCE MANAGEMENT
Encourages innovation
Promotes autonomous working
Promotes self-managed task delivery
Actively listens and takes action
Creates open-source environment

CULTURAL COMPETENCE
Cultural sensitivity
Self-awareness
Understanding of perspective of the 'other'
Ethical practice

STRATEGIC MANAGEMENT
Growth mindset
Adaptable and flexible thinking
Resolution-oriented
Visionary
Models excellence

Ethical Management & Leadership of Your Neurodivergent Workforce

It is clear that the leader(s) of organisations have enormous influence on the culture, the values, the behaviour, of individuals, teams, managers, and the corporate body itself. It is also the case that poor or inappropriate leadership behaviour will damage the organisation. Until now this has not been linked to the amount of negative stress that is generated within an organisation. But it is equally clear that poor, unfocused, unethical, or weak leadership will cause serious damage to the organisation, both directly in terms of the consequences of poor decision making, or indirectly due to the repercussions of increases in negative stress levels in individuals within the organisation. It is no longer sufficient to assess the success of a leader by evaluating visible success factors only.

In scientific terms, stress for any part of the whole will create stress for the larger organism. This is why illness occurs for people, there is stress' of some kind, on the overall system. This is also true in a business model.

The effect on stress levels on an organisation, caused by the style of leadership and the actions of the leader, should also be taken into consideration. The behaviour and actions of an effective leader will reduce stress levels and generate a positive, productive, healthy workplace. The behaviour and actions of a poor leader will do the opposite and increase negative stress levels and create an unhealthy and unproductive workplace. Those with responsibility for the success of the organisation must ensure that the leader is one that produces a positive, healthy, productive organisation. Without such a leader the organisation will fail to achieve its objectives, decline, and die.

Phase Three: How Can We Make This Work?

Using Emotional Intelligence to Our Advantage

"Far from interfering with rationality...the absence of emotion and feeling can break down rationality and make wise decision-making almost impossible."

(Damasio, 1994)

What is 'emotional intelligence'?

"The capacity to be aware of, control, and express one's emotions, and to handle interpersonal relationships judiciously and empathetically. Emotional Intelligence (EI) is the key to both personal and professional success"

(*Oxford English Dictionary*, 2020)

It is the use of emotions to make decisions, to think about the world around us and to comprehend and interpret what is occurring in our minds and in the minds of others.

Evidence from the field of EI states that rational thinking and decision-making depend on input from emotions. Decisions are never made 'unemotionally', and actions are never fully 'rational', as everyone responds to everything purely from a place of subjectivity.

During organisational change, growth, downsizing, or developing other new ways of thinking, work practice or the implementation of a new way of doing, our workplace managers and leaders need emotional intelligence in order to effectively manage themselves, their teams and the whole workplace dynamic. This is so that they can ensure workplace wellbeing, support employees in navigating the day-to-day terrain of the workplace, and also lead them along their journey towards the future.

EMOTIONAL INTELLIGENCE DOMAINS AND CORE COMPETENCIES

SELF-AWARENESS	SELF-MANAGEMENT	SOCIAL AWARENESS	RELATIONSHIP MANAGEMENT
Emotional self-awareness	Adaptability	Organisational awareness	Influence
	Flexibility		Conflict management
		Compassion	Teamworking
	Positive outlook		
Emotional intimacy with self	Emotional self-control		Inspirational leadership
	Achievement oriented	Empathy	Empowering others
	Resolution focussed		Coaching & mentoring

Adapted by: Leigh O'Regan

- from Daniel Goleman's Emotional Intelligence Domains and Competencies

Growing Team/Workforce Wellness with NeuroDiversity

Einstein said that: "It is madness to keep on doing the same thing, time after time, expecting to get a different result or for something different to happen". For our businesses, our organisational growth and productivity, the development of our organisational culture and the enhancement of our human capital to optimise productivity, it is vital that we grow our teams in ways that are different than we may have done before. Many people, especially those in the personal development and wellness fields of varying natures, would describe it as intelligent to have a goal and be wonderfully flexible about how you go about achieving it.

It is this intelligent idea of enhancing overall workplace wellness and wellbeing that I want to highlight today.

If what you're doing isn't working or increasing your wellness, do something else.

I was working with a corporate client recently and had been working with one of their senior managers various techniques. He had wanted his team to carry out a piece of project work in a certain way. He said to me that he had told them again and again (12 times in total), but they still weren't doing what he wanted. I pointed out that if he wanted them to change what they were doing, then he might have to change what he was doing; too. I also suggested that he be more flexible. Together, we explored some alternative approaches and things started to change.

If you are not happy with the results you are getting, you need to disrupt the system you are using! Continuing to use the same system over and over will only produce the same results. By disrupting your existing pattern, be that your own mindset, the way your team operates, the systems in place to 'manage work processes, or the dynamic of your team, you will be able to shift the dynamic and begin to make some headway again. However, if you continue to follow the same idea through in some way, you'll end up with the same outcome. By placing a different idea/concept or mindset in that arena, by definition you are perceiving it differently and doing yourself lots of favours. You'll be increasing your overall mental health, leading to an increase in physical health, and this will lead to an increase in overall wellness, wellbeing and 'performance' on both a personal and professional level.

How Can You Achieve This?

Firstly, identify an area where you've been doing the same thing over and over hoping to get a different result. Or an area that you want to increase your wellness. It may relate to a behaviour, habit, circumstance or situation; just choose something that you want to change the outcome of.

Then secondly, clarify your goal, that is, clarify what you want to achieve. Do this by asking yourself what you want and how you will know when you have got it.

Thirdly, construct or create a list of the different approaches and behaviours you have tried already in order to achieve this goal or increased wellness. Or note down what it is that you are doing currently.

Finally, and most simply, put together a nice list of some alternative behaviours you will use to achieve the goal and increase wellness. Enlist some help if you feel it would help. When you have compiled a good list (put stuff down on that list that may well not seem right for you, it is good to explore avenues that in the past made you feel uncomfortable from time to time). Then, of course, look at starting to do the things that are on your list; do them.

What I am wanting to get across here is the idea of being more bendy.

Your mind and your body really are a single system, so it follows that physical flexibility can often lead to greater mental flexibility. There are certain activities which can greatly increase physical flexibility, including things like yoga, martial arts, dancing, swimming and lots of other general forms of exercise.

Practicing any of these will increase your overall behavioural and mental flexibility and level of wellness. In addition, find opportunities to break habitual patterns. For instance, most mornings when I shave, I do it in a different way. This requires me to stay aware and vary my patterns. The more flexibility you have, the more flexibility you can bring to situations involving others. Often, when people are seeing me for reducing their weight, I might suggest that they look at the doing things like swapping their knife and fork hands around for a week.

So, go ahead and identify a habitual pattern and change it to enhance your wellness. Especially if it is something you are not entirely happy about.

Here is a list of some things that you can do to interrupt your existing patterns and increase your wellness, you can be as creative as you want with these things.

-Eat a food that you never usually eat

-Go for a walk at an early hour in the morning

-Watch a TV show you would never usually watch

-Take a different journey home from work

-Take a cold shower

-Answer your phone with the opposite hand to usual

-Laugh and smile for no reason

The sooner you start doing this, the more fun you'll have with it. Then often, the higher your increase in wellness. So many people I encounter, know all this stuff or read it and still don't do these things and wonder why they are not getting what they want. Do something different today and you'll be amazed how your wellness rockets.

Why is This Important When Managing My Employees?

The main reason? Because the more optimum condition you are in, the more primed you will be to be able to support, empower, nurture and provide optimum leadership to them.

As well, you will be modelling excellence, which is always important for all of your staff. Our employees can only do what they see. It is the same for all of us. When we are at work, if we see our managers slacking off, not turning up for meetings, being complacent about the promises they made and the commitments they had, they may start to do the same.

It is very important that as managers and leaders, we model excellence in everything we do. If you are planning on facilitating a *Talent Development Program* or leading a 'Wisdom Pod', then it is even more important that you find ways to disrupt your old, out-dated and invalid ways of doing and being and create a new model for yourself, so that you can fully optimise and maximise your own potential in the workplace!

Phase Four: The Needs of the People

Connection, Collaboration, Sustainability & Productivity

The Neurodivergent population, on the other hand, is more broadly defined as those who have diverse and divergent ways of brain functioning, which differ from "standard" brain functionality. These include those who are neurodiverse and others. After some preliminary research conducted in this area, we can safely say that up to 80% of your workforce may be neurodivergent.

There are many different ways in which the way a person's brain may function, and the multitude of ways their brain may diverge from standard functionality, can impact on a person who is neurodivergent. It can also affect, influence and also account for fluctuations in capacity/capability in their work performance levels, which are out of their personal control (from a medical perspective, if diagnosed), and therefore require additional measures, adjustments and controls, to ensure that:

a) The person is effectively supported to optimise their capacity to achieve results
b) The business is able to utilise the skills, experience and knowledge of the individual to maximise productivity for the organisation

How Can the Neurodivergent Workforce Enhance Business?

According to Sue Flohr, from the British Dyslexia Association (BDA, 2020), around 20 per cent of the UK's entrepreneurs are dyslexic. This includes people you may know and admire, such as Virgin CEO, Richard Branson, AMSTRAD founder and creator, Lord Sugar and amiable TV chef, Jamie Oliver.

She states that one of the key advantages of having someone who has dyslexia on your team is that they can often see the whole picture all at once, when many people have to work through the details before they can assess the big picture.

Another knowledgeable CEO who has a neurodivergent team that is flourishing, Viola Sommer, CEO at *Auticon*, an IT consultancy where all the consultants are on the autistic spectrum, states that "neurodiverse teams are more effective than heterogenous teams". This is because neurodiverse teams all tend to think in a similar way, in a similar pattern, and therefore are already on the same page with their thinking. In addition, neurodiverse teams also tend to think of unusual and unique alternatives to problems-solving and decision-making, creating new potential solutions and resolutions for long-standing issues and problems that the organisation may have been challenged by for a long time.

In her interview with Virgin about the benefits of workplace neurodiversity, she stated that the main reason people choose to work with her organisation is because "they have problems that their own staff can't solve. They need someone who looks at their problems with a completely different perspective... Our staff can do that." (Virgin, 2020).

Implementing 'The Framework'

The Framework has been established to ensure that you get the best out of the people who work for you as much as they get the best out of working for your organisation! It is a two-way street, with reciprocal benefit and mutual rewards in place.

For convenience, it is not specific to neurodiversity, however, of you are wanting to make improvements to your systems and processes, organisational culture, leadership and management, or internal human capital development, these areas will be applicable to you.

In addition, this two-way flow of resourcing your internal assets as well as providing optimum service provision will only serve to enhance your overall internal and external stakeholder reputation.

Let's look at *The Framework* a little more closely.

Being mindful of your employees, other colleagues who are in a managerial or supervisory role, taking care of your customers who may be neurodivergent and also thinking more broadly about the broader marketplace, your reputation in the local, regional, national and global marketplace, will all help ensure that you are focussed on supporting and optimising your relationships with the people you work with the closest.

Although we have been predominantly focussed on neurodivergent employees in this book, it is wise to take a moment and have a think about how our management and leadership approach influences and impacts on those in our realm.

This next section relates to how we address the core management and leadership issues for our 360-network of neurodivergent people in our realm, including our neurodivergent employees.

Effective On-boarding and Employee Sustainability

- Creating inclusive and diversity-friendly recruitment processes
- Developing sustainable induction programs
- Engaging neurodivergent employees to guide HR policy and practice
- Enabling Effective Employee Self-Determination in the Workplace

Leading and Nurturing People

-Leading and Inspiring People

-Mentoring and Coaching Staff

-Living Organisational Values

-Empowering and Involving People

-Following Organisational and Ethical Values

-Applying Ethical Principles in Practice

Supporting and Guiding People

-Supporting the Workforce to Thrive at Work

-Providing Leadership Through Performance

-Recognising and Rewarding Outstanding Performance-

-Creating Strategies within the Workplace

-Promoting Life-enriching Structures within the Workplace

-Promoting Creative Innovation

Improving & Developing People

-Providing ongoing development opportunities for people

-Improving systems, processes, policies, procedures and practices

-Accommodating and including diversity in staff members and also external stakeholders, including customers/clients, including neurodiversity

-Enhancing Structures (including the environment) to incorporate fully inclusive practices for internal and external stakeholders

-Branding/rebranding with our neurodivergent stakeholders in mind

-QA/QSM/QM with neurodiversity in focus

Building Capacity & Growing Leadership

-Providing Ongoing Opportunities for Growth and Development

-Delivering Continuous Improvements

-Creating Sustainable Success in Business

-Working with a Progressive Mindset

-Influencing Our Communities

-Having NeuroDiversity Works Here! At the forefront of our business model

-Investing in meeting the needs of the people we work with and for

If you are interested exploring this further, our consultants would love to have a chat with you about the range of ways we could work with your organisation.

The Interdependence Business Model

In talking about the Interdependence Model for inclusion of neurodiversity in business, here. I am aligning with a new business approach to inclusion. Many diversity and inclusion models express a need for inclusion based on not excluding people. This is similar to inviting the whole school class to your child's birthday party, so you don't leave anyone out. It does not, however, address the fact that the children who are not 'included' in play, in the playground, will still not be included in 'play' at the birthday party.

Including everyone is not inclusion.

Just the same as having representation of people from every group, community and identity does not mean that you have nailed it with diversity.

I know it's not what some of you wanted to hear. However, the inclusion of all children in the class at the birthday party is not 'inclusion' not matter how it is framed. 'inclusion' in an ethical sense, is about a standard of behaviours towards others, attitudes that promote acceptance and encourage, celebrate and nurture the many different ways in which human beings present themselves in the world and in our workplaces.

There is no one size fits all.

And, in relation to inclusion, there is no singular representation that will fit the bill for inclusion. So, for instance, if your organisation has a diversity and inclusion policy and practice that means that you will employee 10% of your workplace (at a minimum, who) are multi-lingual, for instance, that is great! However, their multi-lingual skills are only going to be beneficial to your organisation if they are given a role in which they can apply those skills and use them to benefit your organisation.

Otherwise, the benefits of their multilingual background and skill-base are null and void and really irrelevant to why they are working for you. It also then becomes tokenistic as to why you may have employed them in the first place.

Using this same scenario, The Interdependence Business Model would take your multi-lingual employees, utilise their skills, not only in a day-to-day fashion, potentially answering calls from multi-lingual customers or international clients. I would also create and develop team specific projects that enabled these multi-lingual employees to generate even more income for your organisation by thinking up creative ideas, new R&D products, Innovation Projects and leads, that allow the organisation to diversify.

'Strategy' and leadership has never been so important!

But, what do I mean by 'strategy'? More often than not, even though we talk about it a lot in business, it actually means different things to different people.

At a Board of Trustees level, it is usually about overall financial management, governance and risk. From a Senior management perspective, it usually entails ensuring policies are in place and strategies have been developed to ensure long-term business security, sustainability, contingency planning and diversification, if required. On a corporate management level, strategy is more about forward planning, ensuring business mile-stones are met, so that longer term business objectives are not missed, and encompasses business operations, systems management, processes and application of procedures and business protocols. Of course, there are service delivery and production channels to consider, as well as customer service experience, which all have to be accommodated.

The most effective and streamlined business will be able to do this in an interdependent manner, in which all cogs in the wheel are reliant on each other, but can also function independently.

So, what does this have to do with neurodiversity, you may be asking? We have an assumption that, individually, our employees are autonomous, in being able to complete their specific work tasks and individual workloads. As managers, we also make assumptions about the dependence of 'teams' on each other, in relying on each other to 'get the job done'.

In today's business world, this independent team model is not enough to sustain businesses throughout, let's say, a crisis. Such as the COVID-19 Crisis. Or a recession. Or the GFC. Or any major downturn in the external marketplace.

As businesses, and in order to sustain our productivity levels, we have to think more creatively.

Creating systems, processes, procedures and future/contingency planning and business models where our neurodivergent employees are an integral part of our business model is a clear way forward, the only way to approach 'inclusion and diversity from an ethical framework, and a more humane and celebratory model for all of our employees to work within!

Imagine a workplace where people were itching to get to work each day... Where they actively wanted to come and share their ideas with each other, their teams and with their Managers... Where the office environment looked and 'felt' open, inclusive, and well-designed to meet the needs of all staff....

Imagine a workplace where people could gather in spaces that were about open collaboration...Where they were rewarded and applauded for doing this on a regular basis...

Imagine a workplace where your cognitive nuances and uniqueness was celebrated and utilised for the benefit of the organisation... And, where you were rewarded for showing initiative and innovative practice...

Imagine a workplace where Managers sought you out to ask you to solve complex problems, think through issues and challenges that others couldn't solve...

Imagine a workplace where your ability to deeply focus on tasks and projects was applauded! ...Where your specialism in a particular was exactly what gave your company a competitive edge...

THIS is where neurodiversity and our neurodivergent employees can be our greatest assets!

THIS is the kind of workplace that neurodivergent people want to work for. If you want them to work for you, maybe it's time to think about how you can start creating an interdependent Business Model that is fully inclusive, so that they can feel like this, above.

ORGANISATION'S ADAPTIVE PRACTICE	TYPE OF INTERDEPENDENT MODEL PRACTICED	BENEFITS TO NEURODIVERGENT EMPLOYEE
1. Standardised procedures and processes	Separate departmental functions but collaborative overall input that serves to contribute to the sum of the whole	Clarity and concise directions; ability to engage collaboratively
2. Adaptive planning and scheduling	Product/idea or task is produced and then passed on to the next person or department.	This requires some level of time management and limited fluidity of meeting deadlines. However, it does engender teamworking and bonded collaboration.
3. Information sharing	The output of one department is dependent on the input of another to create a wonderful product or service delivery. For example, marketing team is required to develop a great	Collaboration amongst peers and colleagues. The sum is greater than the whole; new ideas and concepts can develop new R&D; innovative practice & 'wisdom pods' can flourish!

4. Mutual adjustment	marketing strategy so that the sales team can sell the product to the marketplace. The training development team is needed to develop an amazing training program so that the facilitators can take that out into the marketplace and run the training	Interdependence becomes a way of living, and this becomes embedded in the organisation's culture and practices; non-neurodivergent employees appreciate and celebrate their neurodivergent colleagues for their contributions.

FLEXIBLE & ADAPTIVE BUSINESS MODEL

This table has been adapted from "Organizations in Action," by sociologist James D. Thompson and combined with the ecology model that establishes eco-support systems for neurodivergent employees.

Damien Mellifont, from the *Centre for Disability Research and Policy* at *The University of Sydney* has recently completed a research paper on the effects of anxiety on neurodivergent employees (Mellifont, 2019). As he stated, this is an often an under-researched and under-supported area within the workplace. Bearing in mind the fact that anxiety plays a key role in influencing neurodivergent employees and their levels of productivity it would seem a natural step forward to assume that this is an area that managers of neurodivergent employees could provide further support mechanisms.

As Damien clearly stated "anxiety-related work performance strengths, challenges and support measures as identified … of the high functioning anxiety concept have at least some basis" in providing support for neurodivergent employees who require accommodations. He goes on to state that: "organizations who invest in supporting employees who identify with high functioning dimensions of their anxiety disorders are the ones who are ultimately rewarded with work performance advantages." This perfectly highlights what I have been emphasising throughout this book- the more we are able to provide accommodations that both support our neurodivergent employees and enhance the workplace environment to the benefit of all who work there, the higher the levels of productivity and therefore performance will be. This will ultimately flow on to higher levels of productivity for the organisation and into profitability and long-term sustainability.

As a final word, the following image provides some examples of how an organisation can integrate its strategies, models and processes to develop and create a multi-disciplinary approach to neurodivergent management and leadership of their workforce, in an ethical and inclusive manner, that also enhances business productivity and profitability.

SYSTEMS, PROCESSES AND PROCEDURES
Re-design for optimization for neurodivergent employees and innovation processes
1

INNOVATIONS
Leadership, management, Wisdom Pods, Competence Loops, Environmental design
2

EMPLOYEE INCLUSION & ENGAGEMENT
Integrated diversity and inclusion of neurodivergent employees; Talent Development programs
3

4 LEADERSHIP
Positive and empowering processes and practices

5 PRODUCTIVITY
Utilising neurodivergent employees to boost R&D, productivity and proficability

Optimising Organisational Productivity by Embracing Innovation and Inclusion in the Workplace

This model the influences that have an impact on neurodivergent individuals in the workplace, as well as recognising the value of an interdependent workplace.

Factors such as:

- Human variables
- Environmental variables
- Internal resources (interdependencies)
- External Sources (generalised and contingency sources and resources)

... can all engender self-efficacy, self-determination and embed a culture of collaboration within your organisation that leads to successful innovation and organisational growth and diversification.

This type of model can benefit not only the organisation, but also your neurodivergent employees, as it allows flexibility in the system and also enables your employees to contribute to the organisation at multiple levels, dependent on their choice of collaborative preference.

As we are coming to the end of this book, I want to say that there is so much more I could have added! However, I will leave the remainder for a follow-up book.

In hindsight, I realise that this book could easily have become three separate books. I did contemplate separating the sections into different books, on several occasions. However, I really wanted you to gain the full awareness of not only how your neurodivergent employees experience the workplace, but also the impacts of a not-so-pleasant working environment on them. And, in addition, how this ultimately affects YOU, the business owner. As it is not just the individual employee who is challenged by   a non-workable workplace environment. Finally, I also wanted to show you that having neurodivergent employees can be a very positive, beneficial and rewarding journey for organisations; one in which your business can grow, develop and flourish through the contributions of your neurodivergent workforce. I hope this has been emphasised enough throughout these pages!

Ultimately, I also hope that your implementation of some, or all of these strategies and neurodivergent-friendly responses will enable your organisational productivity to be significantly impacted and that will lead to a reduction in your ROI and profitability as a business.

I hope you've found the book enlightening.

Come and visit our business to see how we support other organisations:

If you are interested in finding out more about developing your leadership and management team, the NeuroDiversity Works Here! business compliance campaign, working within the guidelines of *The Framework*, or enhancing your neurodiversity policies and practice, talk to us, today.

www.neurodiversityworkshere.com

SECTION SEVEN:

APPENDICES

APPENDIX ONE: GLOSSARY

Acquired Brain Injury (ABI) is an injury to the brain that someone isn't born with, but is acquired. It can involve changes to physical structure and brain function, physical and sensory abilities, processing, memory retention, cognition, planning and executive functioning, and communication (Brain Injury Australia, 2014).

Alexithymia is a condition that has generally been thought to affect someone's ability to identify and process their own emotions and emotional state. Research is not determining that this state of being can also have an impact on other forms of interoception, which can impact on someone's ability to recognise and regulate temperature control, heat/cold, levels of tiredness and exhaustion, heart rate, arousal of all kinds, and so on (Brewer, Cook & Bird, 2016).

Auditory processing disorder is a type of learning disability that may affect the acquisition, organization, retention, understanding, or use of verbal or nonverbal information. It could also create issues with the storage and retrieval of information.

Autoimmune diseases occur when the body's immune system is chronically unwell and starts to attacks healthy cells. Some you may have heard of include Lupus, Hashimoto's Disease (or Thyroiditis/ goitre), some heart diseases and other auto-immune conditions, such as coeliac disease, rheumatic arthritis, Multiple Sclerosis, vasculitis, inflammatory bowel disease, psoriasis, Type 1 Diabetes (ASCIA, 2020).

Attention Deficit Disorder (ADD)

ADHD often results in impacts on focus, attention, planning, problem solving, and controlling emotions.

Attention Deficit Hyperactivity Disorder (ADHD)

As with the above, ADHD often results in impacts on focus, attention, planning, problem solving, and controlling emotions, as well as 'unspent' energy levels.

Auditory Processing Disorder (APD)

This condition presents challenges with the processing of sound, which make it difficult to understand interpret the world. Undetected symptoms of APD could explain a person's difficulties comprehending language and communicating, especially if nothing has shown up on a standard hearing test (Rodden, 2020).

Autism (ASD)

Autism is a neurodevelopmental disorder characterised by abnormal social interaction, communication ability, specialised interest patterns, and behaviour patterns. Autism is found to occur due to the vulnerability to environmental triggers displayed by the human genes. In the USA, one child in every thousand is autistic.

Autism results from the differentiation of the biological and neurochemical development of the brain.

Coeliac Disease

This is an auto-immune disease that affects the bowels. It causes the bowel lining to become unable to properly absorb nutrients and often causes symptoms such as stomach pain and discomfort and diarrhoea.

'Competency Loops'

These are scaffolded building blocks of learned competence that neurodivergent (and others) can utilise to develop larger task and project competency. It is a more favourable way of developing nuanced skill and knowledge capacity than the current 'deficit' model that our society promotes. This is a concept adapted from an educational model by Leigh O'Regan and brought into the training and development realm.

Dyslexia

Dyslexia is known for presenting with challenges with acquiring and using written language. New perspectives on this condition, include those that see dyslexia as "*a difference in language and cognition*" -*Singleton*.

SOURCE: Australian Dyslexia Association

Dyspraxia

This is a condition which refers to challenges with coordinated movement. Messages from the brain are not effectively transmitted to the body and can cause issues with planning, gross motor skills, co-ordination etc.

Ehlers Danlos Syndrome (EDS)

This is a connective tissue disorder that is linked with auto-immune conditions. It causes pain in the tendons, connective tissues and often in the joints. It can also be known as 'hyper-mobility'.

Endocrine System

Makes hormones that control your moods, metabolism, organs, and reproduction and it also helps your body control and manage how your hormones are released. Probably the most well-known endocrine disorder is Diabetes. However, there are many others.

Executive Functioning

The ability to maintain an appropriate problem-solving set for the attainment of a pre-set goal or future goal (Welsh & Pennington, 1988, pp. 201-202.)

Generalized Anxiety Disorder.

This condition is indicative of long periods of constant and uncontrollable worry about everyday issues or events. It is noticeably accompanied by fatigue, difficulty concentrating and feelings of uncertainty and restlessness.

Hormones

Hormones can play havoc with our bodies. We are not in control of our hormones, for the most part. If one of our major internal 'players' is disrupted in its production of hormones, then our body can be out of kilter. If this is a chronic, or ongoing, element of our day-to-day life, due to illness, health or injury, then this will ultimately affect out working life. It is important to remember that hormones are not just related to women's problems.' Don't just occur "once a month". And, are not always only about out sex hormones. High levels of cortisol and adrenaline can significantly impact on someone's capacity to sit in one place for a long time, like sitting in a meeting, presenting a half day workshop or delivering a presentation to a conference. Serotonin, Dopamine and Melatonin can all play havoc with our energy levels, motivation, drive and also our sleep patterns. If any of these are not working well, for whatever reason, then we will not be working at our optimum performance levels, regardless of whether we have a neurodivergent mind or not. It's important to check it your with your GP, if you find that any of the above is ongoing, especially if these are not connected to your ongoing condition or neurodiverse working patterns.

The Interdependence Model of NeuroDiversity

This is another concept developed by Leigh O'Regan ©2020. In line with other 'interdependence models', Leigh has established that this book is written from the perspective that all people who are currently in the workplace have the necessary skills to be there. The workplace environment is generally established to conform to a narrow set of standards that rarely provide for a fluid or free-flow approach to engagement with it. We must all use the seating in a certain way, the desks in a particular manner, sit next to our colleagues facing them or away from them, depending on our workplace's environmental sway. In an interdependent model of neurodiversity, all employees flow in and out of a dependent/independent relationship with both their colleagues and their environment. In this way, they are reliant on the environment to provide them with a sense of safety, security and nurturing/nourishment, and they are still separate to it. It is not "theirs".

Irritable Bowel Syndrome (IBS)
This relates to our gut health and our nutrition. The symptoms of IBS cause the bowel lining to become unable to properly absorb nutrients and often causes symptoms such as stomach pain and discomfort and diarrhoea. It can have an impact on: mental health, including anxiety, depression, stress, and sleep. Research has shown that there is a critical relationship between our diet and our mental health.

Identity First Language

Identity First Language (IFL) is language that is used to identify an individual using 'the condition, illness or injury first. For example, John is Dyslexic. Joanne is Autistic. She is disabled.

Many neurodiverse people prefer to be referred to in this way. It is a personal choice. Please ask if you are not sure. Most people would rather you call them by their first name.

Interoception

This is the body's ability to interpret internal signals from their body, via neural pathways. This includes the body's ability to predict internal states and also to allow for sensory processing. People with a condition that impacts on their interoception may have challenges, for example, with recognising when they need to use the toilet, being hungry, feeling the temperature, knowing what they are feeling (straight away), etc.

Lupus

Lupus is an auto-immune condition that can affect many parts of the body. It is an inflammatory disease that is present when the immune system attacks its self and organs are affected. There are many variations of lupus.

Lupus (SLE) can affect the joints, skin, kidneys, blood cells, brain, heart and lungs.

Monotropism

The ability to deeply focus on a task or activity. A monotropic mind is one that focuses its attention on a highly focussed number of interests at any time. It has been closely associated with Autism and also ADHD.

M.E. (Myalgic Encephalomyelitis) or Chronic Fatigue Syndrome (CFS)

A condition where the person experiences deep exhaustion, tiredness and fatigue that is not alleviated by sleep or rest. There are often associated symptoms, some of which include: muscle pain and aches; joint pain without swelling or redness; headaches or migraines.

Neurodivergent

The word 'neurodivergent', sometimes abbreviated as ND, means having a brain that functions in ways that diverge significantly from the dominant societal standards of "normal." Neurodivergent is quite a broad term and in this book has been used to mean someone who has a neurological variance, someone whose brain functionality, structure or biochemical balance may have been altered due to injury, illness or health conditions, which affects their overall responses to the world.

NeuroDiversity

This is a viewpoint that asserts that brain differences are normal. For the most part they are created by neurological variances in the brain. Some of these can be acquired, via illnesses, injury and health conditions, although many are states of being that individuals are born with. This book is based on a premise that neurological differences should be recognized and respected as a social category on a par with gender, ethnicity, sexual orientation, or disability status.

Neuro-Kin

These are other people who are neurodivergent and form a part of the neurodiversity community. Many individuals who form a kinship with each other in these communities call each other "neuro-kin".

Neuro-plasticity

This is the brain's ability to form and re-form connections, either via the learning process or post-injury or illness.

Neurotransmitters, bio-chemicals, hormones and general health

The brain is made up of millions of cells (neurons). All that we do, our thoughts, feelings and actions, are reliant on the interactions of the cells, which is made possible by chemicals called neurotransmitters These neurotransmitters are the body's chemical messengers (The University Of Qld, 2017), and constantly work to keep our brains functioning, managing everything from our breathing and heartbeat to our learning and concentration levels (Cherry, 2018). Neurotransmitters are directly affected by the quality of our nutrition, the food that we do or do not consume (Altomare et al., 2017).

Pathological Demand Avoidance (PDA)

This is often associated recognised as being associated with children with ASD and potentially an ADHD profile. However, there are adults who still have this condition. It is connected to an anxiety-driven need to be 'in control' of your environment and what goes on around you, including, if at all being able to 'avoid' other people's demands and expectations.

Persistent Depressive Disorder (PDD)

A depressive illness, usually diagnosed, which has lasted more than 6 months.

Person First Language (PFL)

Person First Language is language that is used to identify and individual using 'this person has __' or 'a person with __'. For example, John has Dyslexia. Joanne has Autism. She is a person with a disability. He is a person with diabetes.

Many neurodiverse people do not like to be referred to in this way. It is a personal choice. Please ask if you are not sure. Most people would rather you call them by their first name.

Post-traumatic Stress Disorder (PTSD). PTSD is often associated with trauma that occurs repeatedly or in a recurrent manner. It is linked to damaging and intrusive memories, feelings of emotional trauma, numbing and detachment, and increases in heightened emotional arousal, irritability, frustration and disturbed sleep.

Proprioception

This is a continuous loop of feedback between sensory receptors throughout our bodies and our brain. It is mediated by mechanosensory neurons located within muscles, tendons, and joints.

Rheumatoid Arthritis

This is an auto-immune condition that affects joints, bones skin and other parts of the body.

Sensory Processing Disorders

These are a wide variety of conditions that affect an individual's in relation to their senses. An example of an SPD is someone who may be adversely affected by overhead lighting. This lighting can have adverse effects such as producing migraines, ongoing tension headaches, sight issues, 'auras' in vision, challenges with concentration and focus and so on. These are valid and debilitating issues that can severely impact on the everyday working capacity of an individual in the workplace.

Social Anxiety Disorder or Social Phobia.

This is a 'disorder' or state of being where someone is averse to actively taking part in social situations. Sometimes, this may only occur when they do not know the other people, and at other times, or for different individuals, this social response may happen whenever someone is challenged by a social event or environment where they are asked to participate in a group.

Spatial Awareness

Spatial awareness is an interesting element to throw into the mix, as many people do not believe it has any impact on the workplace. However, it directly correlates to our proprioception, which allows us to interpret our inner and outer world space. With our proprioception, we can gauge, with our body awareness, where furniture is in the room, how far away something is from us when we are walking, how close a person is standing from us, and also it allows us a kind of 'social safety net' or awareness of where other people are in the room. For individuals who have some neurodiverse conditions, illnesses and injuries, their proprioception is completely thrown out of kilter. This means, for instance that their balance may be 'off' on some days. It may also mean that they are very uncomfortable with having people walk behind them, as this is a 'surprise zone' for them, and can be very unnerving for them to have someone come into their personal space from behind, or when they are concentrating on something. This may be a particular issue in an open plan office or a situation where someone is positioned in a thoroughfare.

Stress:

Stress is internal or externalised pressure placed on the body's system. It can be caused by bio-chemical imbalances, micro-nutrient deficiencies, neurotransmitter imbalances, and/or blood sugar imbalances. Any or all of these could be involved when stress is present.

Traumatic Brain Injury (TBI)

This is a complex injury with a broad range of symptoms and potential function issues that may result in a disability. It is defined as an alteration in brain function, or other evidence of brain pathology, caused by an external force.

Thyroiditis (Hashimoto's Disease)

Thyroiditis is an exacerbated thyroid condition that can lead to serious associated health conditions.

Thyroid Conditions

Employees with thyroid conditions can be adversely affected by hormone imbalances. The effect on their work pace, concentration levels, ability to focus for long-periods of time, how they structure, prioritise and pace their day are all impacted on by the hormonal influence of the thyroid. However, dysfunction with the thyroid can adversely affect many cognitive functions and levels of hormonal balance, social interactivity and also levels of fatigue and tiredness, throughout the day.

'Wisdom Pods"

This concept was developed by Leigh O'Regan © 2019. A 'Wisdom Pod' is a specialised group formed to mould and generate high-order concepts that are above the ordinary level of ideas and concepts that may be generated in a day-to-day innovation pod.

APPENDIX TWO: BIBLIOGRAPHY

Australian Bureau of Statistics [ABS]. (2006). *4228.0 - Adult Literacy and Life Skills Survey [ALLS]- Summary Results*. Australia, 2006 (Reissue). https://www.abs.gov.au/ausstats/abs@.nsf/Previousproducts/4228.0Main%20Features22006%20(Reissue).

ADHD Foundation – UK. (2020). *ADHD awareness*. www.adhdfoundation.org.uk.

Advisory Conciliation and Arbitration Service [ACAS} – UK. (2020). *Reasonable Adjustments*. www.acas.org.uk.

Altomare, R., Damiano, G., Palumbo, V. D., Buscemi, S., Spinelli, G., Cacciabaudo, F., Monte, L (2017). The Starved Brain- Can what we eat determine what we think? In the National Eating Disorder Collaboration *NEDC e-Bulletin*, Issue 59. Originally published as: Feeding the brain: the importance of nutrients for brain functions and health. In the *Journal of Nutritional and Internal medicine*. Volume 19(15). pp.243–247. https://doi.org/10.23751/pn.v19i3.4821. https://www.nedc.com.au/research-and-resources/show/issue-59-i-the-starved-brain-can-what-we-eat-determine-how-we-think.

Amabile, T. M. (1993). Motivational Synergy: Toward new conceptualisation of intrinsic and extrinsic motivation in the workplace. *HR Management Review*. 3(3), 185-201. DOI: 10.1016/1053-4822(93)90012-S.

ADHD Australia. (2020). Statistics-Attention Deficit and Hyper-Activity Disorder. [ADHD]. www.adhdaustralia.org.au.

American Psychiatric Association. (2015). *Neurodevelopmental Disorders: DSM-5® Selections*. Diagnostic Statistical Manual- Version 5 [DSM-V]. American Psychiatric Publications.

Australian Government. (1992). *Disability Discrimination Act*. Federal Register of Legislation. https://www.legislation.gov.au/Details/C2018C00125.

Australian Government- Federal Register of Legislation. (2020). *Disability Discrimination Act 1992*. Accessed at: https://www.legislation.gov.au/Details/C2018C00125.

Australian Government, *National Disability Strategy 2010–2020*. https://www.dss.gov.au/our-responsibilities/disability-and-carers/publications-articles/policy-research/national-disability-strategy-2010-2020.

Australian Government- Federal Register of Legislation. (2020). *Disability Discrimination Act 1992*. Accessed at: https://www.legislation.gov.au/Details/C2016C00763.

Australian Human Rights Commission [AHRC]. (2020). *Adjustments in the Workplace for People with a Disability*. Accessed at: https://humanrights.gov.au/quick-guide/11931.

Australian Institute of Health & Welfare, (1999). *The definition, incidence and prevalence of acquired brain injury in Australia*. Accessed at: https://www.aihw.gov.au/reports/disability/definition-incidence-prevalence-of-brain-injury-au/contents/table-of-contents.

Australian Institute of Health and Welfare [AIHW]. (2007) *Disability in Australia: Acquired Brain Injury*. Bulletin 55, December 2007. Canberra. AIHW.

Australian Institute of Health and Welfare [AIHW]. (2020). Diabetes statistics. www.aihw.gov.au.

Australian Institute of Management. (2020). *Leadership and Management*. https://www.aim.com.au/leadership-strategy

Australian Network on Disability. (2020). *Workplace Adjustments*. Accessed at:
https://www.and.org.au/pages/workplace-adjustments.html

Australian and New Zealand Academy of Management [ANZAM]. (2020). Accessed at: https://www.anzam.org/.

Australian Society for Clinical Immunology and Allergy [ASCIA]. (2020). *Auto-immune Diseases*. Accessed at:
https://www.allergy.org.au/patients/autoimmunity/autoimmune-diseases.

Austin, R.D. & Pisano, G.P. (2017). Neurodiversity as Competitive Advantage. Harvard Business Review. 95(3),
96-103.

Autism Spectrum Australia. (2020). Statistics. www.autismspectrum.org.au.

Barkley, R.A (2012). *Executive Functions: What They Are, How They Work, and Why They Evolved.* The
Guildford Press. New York.

BDA. (2017). *Dyslexia-friendly style guide.* Available at: www.bdadyslexia.org.uk/advice/employers/crating-a-
dyslexia-friendly-workplace/duslexia-friendly-style-guide.

Beardwell, J. & Thompson, A. (2014) *Human Resources management: A Contemporary Approach.* 7th Edn.
Pearson Education. Limited. Harlow.

Benton, C & Barkley, R.A. (2010). *Taking Charge of Adult ADHD.* The Guildford Press.

Bewley, H. & George, A. (2016). *NeuroDiversity at Work.* National Institute of Economics and Social Research-
UK [NIESR] and ACAS. Research paper: 09/16. Accessed at: www.acas.org.uk/researchpapers.

Beyond Blue, (2020). *Social Phobias.* Accessed at: https://www.beyondblue.org.au/the-facts/anxiety/types-of-
anxiety/social-phobia.

Brain Injury Australia (2014), *About Acquired Brain Injury.* Brain Injury Australia. Accessed at: www.bia.net.au.

Brewer R, Cook R, Bird G. 2016 *Alexithymia: a general deficit of interoception.* Royal Society of Open Science.
Volume 3. Accessed at: http://dx.doi.org/10.1098/rsos.150664.

Burton, L. J., Westen, D. & Kowalski, R. (2019). *Psychology: Australian and New Zealand* (5th edition). John
Wiley & Sons Australia, Ltd.

Cassidy, M.K. (2018). *Neurodiversity in the Workplace: Architecture for Autism.* University of Cincinnati.

Chartered Institute of Personnel and Development [CIPD]. (2018). *Neurodiversity at Work.* CIPD. London.
Accessed at: www.cipd.co.uk/Images/neurodiversity-at-work_2018)tcm18_37852.pdf.

Chowdhury, S., Schulz, E., Milner, M., & Van De Voort, D. (2014). Core employee based human capital and
revenue productivity in small firms: An empirical investigation. *Journal of Business Research, 67*(11),
2473-2479.

Comcare. (2010). *Effective Health and Wellbeing Programs.*

Covey, S. (1989). *The 7 Habits of Highly Effective People.* Free Press.

Damasio, A. R. (1994). *Descartes' error: Emotion, rationality and the human brain.*

Daugherty, M. W. (2013). *Redefining normal: The path to self-attainment for people with neurodiversities: How do people from the neurodiverse spectrum define self-fulfilment?* (Doctoral dissertation).

Department for Work and Pension [DWP] – UK. (2020). *Access to Work Program.* Accessed at: www.gov.uk/access-to-work.

Elder Robison, J. (2013). What is Neurodiversity? *In Psychology Today.* 7th October, 2013. Accessed at: https://www.psychologytoday.com/au/blog/my-life-aspergers/201310/what-is-neurodiversity.

Employease, (2018). *GDPR for Employers.* 29th March, 2018. Accessed at: www.employease.co.uk/gdpr-for-employers.

Equality Advisory Support Service – UK (2020). *Discrimination Helpline.* Accessed at: www.equalityadvisoryservice.com.

Equality and Human Rights Commission – UK. (2020). *Equality Act (UK) 2010.* Accessed at: www.equalityhumanrights.com.

Exceptional Individuals. (2016). *Dyslexia- Hemel Hempstead.* Exceptional Individuals. Ltd. Accessed at: www.exceptionalindividuals.com/dyslexia.

FairWork Ombudsman (Australia). (2020). Guidance. www.fairwork.gov.au/.

Feinstein, A. (2019). *Autism Works: A Guide to Successful Employment Across the Whole Spectrum.* Routledge. London.

Garvan Institute, Australia, (2020). *Auto-immune Conditions Explained.* Accessed at: https://www.garvan.org.au/research/collaborative-programs/hope/autoimmune-disease.

Goering, S. (2010). Revisiting the relevance of the social model of disability. In *American Journal of Bioethics.* Volume 10(1). pp. 54-55.

Goleman, D. (1995). *Emotional Intelligence.* Bantam Books.

Goleman, D., Boyatzis & McKee, A. (2001). *Primal Leadership: Realising the Power of Emotional Intelligence.* Harvard Business School.

Grant, D. (2017). *That's the Way I Think: Dyslexia, Dyspraxia, ADHD and Dyscalculia Explained.* David Fulton. Abingdon.

Griffiths, C. (2020). HR professionals must nurture NeuroDivergent Talent. HR Future. April 2020, 28-29. www.journals.co.za

Grinder, M. (1997). *The Science of Non-Verbal Communication.* Grinder & Associates.

Hacque, L and Gilroy, S. (2016). *Neurodiversity in the Workplace.* Network Autism. Accessed at: https://network.autism.org.uk/knowledge/insight-opinion/neurodiversity-workplace.

Health and Safety Executive [HSE]- UK. (2020). *Guidance for employers.* https://www.hse.gov.uk/disability/employers.htm

Herring, C., & Henderson, L. (2014). *Diversity in organizations: A critical examination.* Routledge.

HOK, (2019). *Design a NeuroDiverse Workplace.* Accessed at: www.hok. com/ideas/publication/hok-design-a-neurodiverse-workplace.

Holliday Willey, L. (1999). *Pretending to Be Normal.* Jessica Kingsley Publishers. London.

Honeybourne, V. (2019). *The Neurodiverse Workplace: An Employer's Guide to Managing and Working with Neurodivergent Employees, Clients and Customers.* Jessica Kingsley Publishers.

International Labour Organisation {ILO]. (2018). *Asia-Pacific Employment and Social Outlook.* ILO.

Hurley, E. (2014). *Ultraviolet Voices: Stories of Women on the Autism Spectrum.* Autism West Midlands. Birmingham.

IBS- Mind Over Gut, (2020). *What is IBS?* Accessed at: https://www.ibs.mindovergut.com/what-is-ibs/

Information Commissioner's Office [ICO] – UK. (2020). *Guide to the General Data Protection Regulations (GDPR).* Accessed at: https://ico.org.uk/for-organisations/guide-to-data-protection/guide-to-the-general-data-protection-regulation-gdpr/.

John Hopkins medicine, (2020). *Overview of nervous system disorders.* (n.d.). *Johns Hopkins Medicine.* Retrieved on 29th July 2020, from hopkinsmedicine.org/healthlibrary/conditions/nervous_system_disorders/overview_of_nervous_system_di sorders_85,P00799/.

Maximo, J.O. & Kana. R.K. (2019). Aberrant "deep connectivity" in autism: A cortico-subcortical functional connectivity magnetic resonance imaging study. *Autism Research,* 2019; DOI: 10.1002/aur.2058.

Krzeminska1, A., Austin, R. D., Bruyère, S. M. & Hedley D. (2019). The advantages and challenges of neurodiversity employment in organizations. *Journal of Management & Organization.* Vol. 25, pp. 453–463. DOI: 10.1017/jmo.2019.58.

Language and Culture Worldwide (LLC) [LCW]. (2015). The Culture Iceberg. www.languageandculture.com.

Liu, J. (2020). From Privacy Booths to Smart Parking Garages: These photos show what offices of the future will look like. In *Work: CNBC- Business News and Finance.* www.cnbc.com.

Martin, N. (2009). Asperger syndrome: Empathy is a two-way street. *Neurodiversity in higher education: Positive responses to specific learning differences,* 149-168.

Megrew, L. E. (2019). *Neurodiversity and the Organizational Interview Process: A Phenomenological Study of Adult High-functioning Autists* (Doctoral dissertation, Grand Canyon University).

Mellifont, D. (2019). Neuro magnifico! An exploratory study critically reviewing news text reporting of anxiety-related work performance strengths, challenges and support measures. *Work, 63*(3), 435-446.

Menon DK, Schwab K, Wright DW, Maas AI. (2010). *Position statement: definition of traumatic brain injury.* Archived Physical Medical Rehabilitation. Volume 91. pp. 1637–1640.

Moody, R.C. & Pesut, D.J. (2006). The motivation to care. *Journal of Health, Organisation and Management.*

National Autistic Society - UK. (2017). *Autism facts and history.* Available at: www.autism.org.uk/about/what-is/myths-facts-stats.aspx.

NutriPATH, (2020). *Extensive NeuroTransmitter Practitioner Manual V2.* Accessed at: http://nutripath.com.au/wp-content/ uploads/2015/11/NPATH-Extensive-NEUROTRANSMITTER-Practitioner-Manual-v2.0.pdf.

Occupational Safety and Health Administration-USA [OSHA]. (2020). Occupational Health & Safety Guidelines. www.osha.gov/laws-regs.

OECD-UNESCO- Institute for Statistics. (2003). *Literacy Skills for the World of Tomorrow- Results from PISA 2000.* UNESCO. DOI: 10.1787/9789264102873-en.

Office for Disability Issues [ODI]. (2011). *Equality Act 2010 Guidance: Guidance on Matters to Be Taken into Account in Determining Questions Relating to Definitions of Disability.* ODI. London.

Office of Fair Work. (2020). *General Protections.* www.fwc.gov.au/general-protections-unlawful-actions.

Office of the High Commissioner for Human Rights, *10th Session of the Committee on the Rights of Persons with Disabilities* (12 November 2013), Retrieved from: http://www.ohchr.org/EN/HRBodies/CRPD/Pages/Session10Old.aspx on 19th September 2020.

Oliver, M. (1996) *Understanding Disability: from Theory to Practice*. Chatham: Mackays of Chatham.

O'Regan, F.J. (2007). *ADHD*. 2nd edn. Continuum. London.

O'Regan, L. (2003). Reflections on the Power of Context: Engaging Authenticity and Active Participation in Workplace Mentoring. *Innovative Learning in Action. [ILIA]*. Issue 3. University of Salford. UK. http://usir.salford.ac.uk/id/eprint/1831/1/ilia_issue3.pdf.

O'Regan, L. (2006). *Mentoring Online in Europe (MOLIE): Final Evaluation Report*. University of Salford, UK.

O'Regan, L. (2020). *Square Peg, Round Hole: Moving from Workplace Dilemma to Workplace Freedom- A guide for neurodivergent employees*. RISE Publications. Melbourne.

O'Regan, L. (2021a). In publication. *Salmon Swimming Upstream: Life and Times of a Neurodivergent Woman*. RISE Publications. Melbourne.

O'Regan, L. (2021b). In publication. *Tiny Little Houses*. RISE Publications. Melbourne.

Oxford English Dictionary [OED]. (2020). Dictionary (online version). www.oed.com.

Pacific Employment and Social Outlook Report (2018). *Asia-Pacific Employment and Social Outlook 2018 Advancing decent work for sustainable development*. Regional Economic and Social Analysis Unit- International Labour Organisation [ILO]. Bankok.

Park, S., et al. (2017). One-step optogenetics with multifunctional flexible polymer fibers. *Nature, 20(4). Doi: 10.1038.4510*. Retrieved on 20th June, 2020, from nature.com/neuro/journal/v20/n4/full/nn.4510.html.

Pedler, M. Burgoyne, J. & Boydell, T. (2013*). A Manager's guide to Self-Development*. McGrawHill Professional. Maidenhead.

Risquez, A. (2008). *E-Mentoring: An Extended Practice, an Emerging Discipline*. Chapter XLVII. University of Limerick. (Abstract). IG Global.

Rodden, J. (2020*). What Does Auditory Processing Disorder Look Like in Adults?* Accessed at: https://www.additudemag.com/auditory-processing-disorder-in-adults/.

Russo, F. (2018). The Cost of Camouflaging Autism. In *SpectrumNews*. www.spectrumnews.org.

Safe Work Australia. (2020). WH&S Guidelines. www.safeworkaustralia.gov.au.

SANE, (2020). *Obsessive Compulsive Disorder (OCD) Facts*. Accessed at: https://www.sane.org/information-stories/facts-and-guides/obsessive-compulsive-disorder.

Siegel, L.S. & Smyth. I.S. (2005). 'Reflections on research on reading disability with special attention to gender issues. In *Journal of Learning Disability*. Volume 38 (5). Pp. 473-477.

Silberman, S. (2016). *Neuro-Tribes: The Legacy of Autism and the Future of Neurodiversity*. Avery.

Siegel, L., & Valtierra, K. (2017). *Expanding Dispositions for Literacy: General Educators as Literacy Gatekeepers*. The Clearing House: A journal of educational strategies, issues and ideas. doi.org/10.1080/00098655.2017.1289720.

Slorach, R. (2016). *A Very Capitalist Condition: A History of The Politics of Disability*. Bookmarks Publications. London.

SPD Australia. (2020). Statistics-Sensory Processing Disorder. www.spdaustralia.com.au.

STAR Institute, (2020). *Treatment for Adults with Sensory Challenges.* Accessed at: https://www.spdstar.org/basic/treatment-for-adults-sensory-challenges.

Stewart, H. (2013). *The Happy Manifesto: Make Your Organisation a Great Workplace.* Kogan page. London.

Swain, J. & French, S. (2000). Towards and Affirmation Model of Disability. In *Disability and Society.* Volume 15 (4). pp. 569-582.

Swain, J. & French, S., Barnes, C. & Thomas, C. (2004*). Disabling Barriers- Enabling Environments.* Sage Publications. London.

Swinburne University. (2020). *Australian Leadership Index [ALI].* https://www.australianleadershipindex.org.

Synapse (2013). *Acquired Brain Injury: The Facts. The Practical Guide to understanding and responding to Acquired Brain Injury and Challenging Behaviours.* 4th Edition. Synapse: The Brain Injury Association of Queensland.

Taylor, J. (2020). *Why Women are blamed for everything: Exploring victim blaming of women subjected to violence and trauma.* Victim Focus, UK.

The British Dyslexia Association. (2020). *Dyslexia.* Accessed at: www.bdadyslexia.org.au/employer.

Thompson, J. D. (2010). *Organizations in Action: Social Science of Administrative Theory.* Transaction Publishers.

UK Government. (2018). *Reasonable adjustments for workers with disabilities or health conditions.* Accessed at: www.gov.uk/reasonable-adjustments-for-disabled-workers.

UK Government. (2020). *Definition of disability under the Equality Act 2010.* https://www.gov.uk/definition-of-disability-under-equality-act-2010.

United Nations- Department of Economic and Social Affairs (Disability) [DESA]. (2020). *Convention on the Rights of Persons with Disabilities (CRPD).* https://www.un.org/development/desa/disabilities/convention-on-the-rights-of-persons-with-disabilities.html.

United States Department of Labor. (2020). *Occupational Health and Safety Administration.* Accessed at: https://www.osha.gov/.

US Equal Employment Opportunity Commission [EEOC]. (2020). *Fact Sheet: Disability Discrimination.* Retrieved from: https://www.eeoc.gov/laws/guidance/fact-sheet-disability-discrimination.

VCASP, United Brains (2012). *The Social Inclusion of People with Acquired Brain Injury: A Consumer Perspective.* Presentation for the Strengthening Disability Advocacy Conference. Melbourne, March 2012.

VCASP (2014). *Consultations with persons with ABI, regarding the FCDC Inquiry into Social Inclusion.* Conducted in Melbourne on 10th February 2014.

Vibert, S. (2018). *Your Attention Please: The Societal and Economic Impact of AHDH.* DEMOS. London.

Virgin, (2020). *How the Workplace Benefits from Neurodiversity.* Accessed at: https://www.virgin.com/entrepreneur/how-workplace-benefits-neurodiversity.

Walker, C.N. (2020). *Neuroqueering Leadership: Thinking differently about different thinking.* University of Technology, Sydney. (SCOS Abstract).

Watagodakumbura, C. (2014). The need to address psychological and neurological characteristics of learners in the mainstream education system. *Journal of Studies in Education, 4*(1), 94-108.

Winkler, D. (2009). *The Social Inclusion of People with Disabilities.* Australian Philanthropy, Issue 74, September 2009. pp 20-21.

Workplace Fairness- U.S. (2020). *Disability Discrimination.* Accessed at: https://www.workplacefairness.org/disability-discrimination.

World Health Organisation [WHO]. (2018). *International Classification of Diseases* [ICD-11]. https://www.who.int/classifications/icd/en/.

University of Alabama, (2019*). Difference in brain connectivity may explain autism spectrum disorder: Researchers work toward finding the biomarkers of autism for earlier diagnosis and treatment.* Science News. https://www.sciencedaily.com/releases/2019/01/190130161640.htm.

APPENDIX THREE: OFFICE-BASED INDUSTRIES (COVERED BY INDUSTRIES)

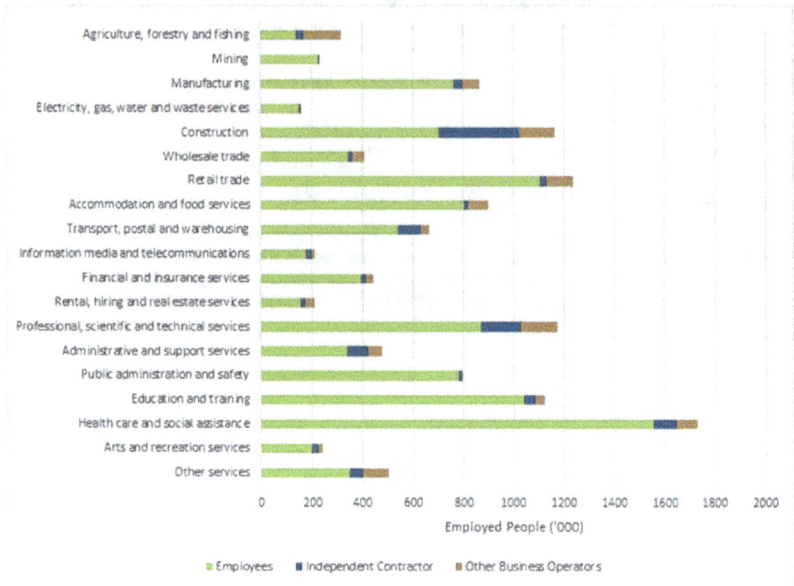

Chart: Employed People ('000) by industry, showing Employees, Independent Contractor, and Other Business Operators.

Industries listed (top to bottom): Agriculture, forestry and fishing; Mining; Manufacturing; Electricity, gas, water and waste services; Construction; Wholesale trade; Retail trade; Accommodation and food services; Transport, postal and warehousing; Information media and telecommunications; Financial and insurance services; Rental, hiring and real estate services; Professional, scientific and technical services; Administrative and support services; Public administration and safety; Education and training; Health care and social assistance; Arts and recreation services; Other services.

X-axis: 0 to 2000, labelled "Employed People ('000)".

Legend: ■ Employees ■ Independent Contractor ■ Other Business Operators

CHOSEN INDUSTRIES

→ Arts & Recreation

→ Education and Training

→ Public Administration and Safety

→ Administration and Support Services

→ Professional, Scientific and Technical Services

→ Rental, Hiring and Real Estate

→ Financial and Insurance

→ Information Media and Telecommunications

** The other industries were not chosen, as they are mixed office-based and non-office-based service provision

APPENDIX FOUR:
Square Hole, Round Peg: How to Move from Workplace Dilemma to Workplace Freedom
A Guide for Neurodivergent Employees

RISE Publications. Melbourne.

This book is aimed at employees who identify as being neurodivergent or are part of the many neurodiverse communities in our workplaces, universities, schools and world.

If you know someone who could use a book like this, one that will provide them with a positive vibe, and inspire them to take steps towards their goals, this is the book for them!

This book provides the background to, and is the companion book of, *NeuroDiversity Works Here!* It is specifically for neurodivergent employees and those wanting to enter into the workforce.

My previous book addressed the needs of our global neurodivergent workforce, and provided insight to managers, team leaders and business owners on how the talents and strengths of neurodivergent employees could enhance and creative higher levels of profitability for their business.

In this book, I am exploring the more personal side of this experience, from a lived perspective. Many people have focussed on the downside of being neurodivergent. Although I will touch on some of these areas, the core aim of this book is one of hope and empowerment for you, the reader.

Ultimately, this is an uplifting and positively focussed book that will guide you through the often-heady maze of workplace minimisation, denial and dismissiveness into a world where your contributions and your skills are more highly valued and sought after than ever before!

Pre-order now:

ISBN:	978-0-6489357-1-1 (Paperback)
	978-0-6489357-3-5 (eBook)

APPENDIX FIVE:
101 Ways to Identify if You Are NeuroDivergent

A Guide for People Who Think a Little Differently

RISE Publications. Melbourne.

This book is aimed at anyone who thinks a little differently. Whether you just don't know, have started thinking you may be, have had someone else, tell you definitely are, or were just curious about the title, this book is probably going to give you a great head-start on trying to figure it all out!

If you identify as being neurodivergent or are part of the many neurodiverse communities in our society, workplaces, universities, schools and world, or feel like you don't fit in but don't quite know why. This book may be for you.

If you know someone who could use a book like this, one that will provide them with a positive vibe, and inspire them to take steps towards their goals, this is the book for them!

This book provides some examples of how it feels to be neurodivergent, what neurodivergence may "look like", and how it may appear as characteristics in your work practices, what you do, how you think and the way you live your life. At a grass-roots levels, I have written this book for all of those people out there who may be questioning whether or not they are, in fact, neurodivergent. It is possible that you are.

In this book, I am exploring the more personal side of this experience, from a lived perspective. Many people have focussed on the downside of being neurodivergent. Although I will touch on some of these areas, the core aim of this book is one of hope and empowerment for you, the reader.

Ultimately, this is an uplifting and positively focussed book that will guide you through the often-heady maze of figuring out what's going on, what you can do about it, what it might all be 'called' and how you can manage it more effectively (or at least find some support from others who also have your condition).

Pre-order now, in bookstores:

ISBN: 978-0-6489357-7-3 (Paperback)

APPENDIX SIX:
Salmon Swimming Upstream

RISE Publications. Melbourne.

This is a real-life story of a little girl who experienced a life-threatening brain injury at 5 years of age. She was the first person in the world to survive the surgery without fatality or severe cognitive deficit. During her time in hospital in the early 1970s, Sydney was changing. Sociologically, it was shifting from a world where the social landscape was predominantly filled with white, men and women were only just stepping out into the workforce in a more empowered way. This new society was to become her greatest gift and her biggest challenge, as she strove to be the invincible being her mother wanted her to be, whilst struggling against the internal conflicts of her neurodivergent mind.

This powerful and emotive psychological journey will have you laughing, crying and wishing with all your might that the little girl comes through okay. The book is structured in Houses'. They signify the differing landscapes that the little girl and then the young woman, and then finally the middle-aged women find themselves traversing through, as they journey.

Travel with her as she explores the many Houses she visits along the way. The House of Friendship, the House of Sadness, the House of Grief and the House of Connection, and many others, as she tries to figure out her own pathway.

Read how she creates a space for herself as she weaves through a life where she is more often than not the unique one, the different one, the eccentric one. When she finally embraces her specialist skills and unique abilities, she is able to forge her way forward and develop new skills that enable her to adapt to any situation.

Pre-order today: In print January, 2021

ISBN: 978-0-6489357-4-2 (Paperback)

               978-0-6489357-6-6 (eBook)